It's All About Showing Up

THE POWER IS IN THE ASKING

Robbie Motter

HAVANA BOOK GROUP LLC
HAVANABOOKGROUP.COM

Preface

Dear Reader,

Thank you for purchasing our book. My fantastic co-authors and I hope that you will enjoy each story as they were written from the heart.

Since 1975, I have been telling women about the power of SHOWING UP and that the POWER is in the ASKING. I have kept instilling this mantra to every woman I have met along the way and today, I am happy to say that women are truly seeing in their lives the great power in both sayings.

This book was designed and created to share the impact these philosophies have had on so many and can have in your life once you implement them. I would love to connect with you and hear your thoughts.

ROBBIE MOTTER
Founder/CEO, Global Society for Female Entrepreneurs (G.S.F.E)
Globalsocietyforfemaleentrepreneurs.org
CERTIFIED NATIONAL SPEAKER, MENTOR, COACH, AUTHOR
AND RADIO HOST

HAVANA BOOK GROUP LLC
43537 RIDGE PARK DRIVE
TEMECULA, CA. 92590

ISBN: 978-1-73531-170-8

Foreword

"This must-read book combines 45 stories of inspiration and motivation. The tools and insights that Robbie Motter shares in this book have been instrumental in elevating my leadership and the results in my business. This is a required reading for any female entrepreneurs ready to move out of their own fears while preparing for success. Robbie eliminates excuses for the next generation of leaders as this legacy work echoes her style of coaching to inspire the world to Show Up and Ask for what you need so that you can be prepared for greatness that is coming "Next". I would encourage every professional looking to get to the next level to read Robbie's book."

AnGele Cade
Speaker, Author & Coach
President and CEO, Executive On The Go;
A division of QueCom Services, Inc.

Testimonials

"Take good notes as you read through all the stories and ideas in this book! The wealth of experiences and insight are invaluable!"

Michelle Bergquist
CEO & Co-Founder| Connected Women of Influence
Co-Founder| SUE Talks

"This book is so inspiring to me, so much heart and brilliant energy and a true value to life. Love you Robbie Motter, you are one in a million, Congratulations."

Chebra Dorsey "OCHEA" Celebrity designer

"For decades, Robbie Motter has been committed to "showing up" and to "asking for what you want". As a mentor, coach, executive and leader she has been an inspiration and example to so many women. Her latest book chronicles dozens of exciting and heartfelt stories from women in all walks of life who have been transformed by Robbie's tireless example of courage and commitment. This book will fuel your faith in yourself and your dreams."

Ardice Farrow
Founder, Director Net Effects Traders

"Who is Robbie Motter and why is her book "It's all about Showing Up and the Power is in the asking" vital reading and your guide to accomplishment? It is because Robbie is the quintessential ambassador to Success: she walks the walk and asks us to join her as you travel the road to greatness. Most of all, if you avail yourself into the network she has developed, and ask each other for help, you will learn the "how to's" and share your accomplishments with those who are following us on what can easily be the greatest path to achievement that you may not have ever dreamed of reaching.

Who is Robbie Motter? Your personal guide and friend who only asks you to be the very best you can be. Buy the book."

Bon Voyage!

Pink Lady Jackie Goldberg
Founder, Senior Star Power Productions
Founder, PinkLadyPresents.com

"For many years Robbie Motter has been talking about and living her Truth, "Show Up" and Ask"! For me, I have learned that when I have shown up and asked, I have met the Most Amazing Women. Some have become clients, while others have become leaders! Most of all they have become friends! Inside this book you will find story after story about women who were willing to Show Up and Ask and how it changed their lives! Prepare to be inspired!"

Tammra Graves
Sales Vice President, Park Lane Jewelry

"Robbie, Great! So proud of you and all you do. You have shaped so many lives, including mine. This book will be a testimony to many more people. Cheers for Angela, for her love and dedication to this publication. The cover is unique and will inspire interest. Thank you, Robbie and Angela."

Mary Greenre
GWWN/ N.A.F.E Director of 50 years

"Amazing things can happen by just SHOWING UP, there is power in asking for what you want, and the happiness you can find when you don't give up on your dreams-no matter how far-fetched they may seem...These are some of the key themes in "It's All About Showing Up-The Power is in the Asking". These inspiring tales come from 45 stories written by women whose lives have been forever positively changed by showing up and asking for what they need and want out of life. These relatable stories are uplifting and so important in these uncertain times-you can achieve your dreams, and these moving personal stories will inspire your own journey to success."

Lisa Gritzner- Founder & CEO, LG Strategies

"It pays to show up as amazing things happen. In 2005 I was nominated for a Women of Excellence Award. For the Outstanding Entrepreneur award, I decided to "Show Up" and allow myself to be celebrated. This was my first award. Many have followed, but this was the most special. I remember there were several lovely ladies who were wearing pink boas! They were lively, fun and fabulous x100! I was mesmerized! Robbie appeared to be the leader! I was quiet and observed from a distance. During the luncheon, I nervously sat at a table with ladies that I did not know. When the awards were being announced my name was called to come up and give a small speech. After my speech, I went back to the table and all the ladies were shocked because I never shared that I was an award recipient. Robbie and another lady came over to congratulate me! I was thrilled that they came over. I thanked Robbie for the congrats and said, "Now who are all these ladies all dressed up? I love your boas!" Clear as a bell Robbie said, "We're the registered divas! You can't be a diva unless you're registered with us!" We all laughed, and I said, "I want to be a diva!" Robbie said, "Well you're not just a diva, you're an entrepreneur diva!" because my award was for Outstanding Entrepreneur it made sense. My eyes lit up and so it began! They even had a website to join! I can honestly say that meeting Robbie on that day, 15 years ago had set me on my Entrepreneur journey as Felisha The Diva. My Colorado license plate even reads; THEDIVA. I have always admired Robbie and always will. She has been a blessing and made such a positive impact for me. Keeping in line with the theme of Showing Up and Asking, I can honestly say that Showing Up that day was one of the best things that I ever did. Asking Robbie and the other ladies who they were, has impacted my life in ways I would have never imagined. Thank you so much."

Felisha Kay
CEO / FeliKay LLC

"Every now and then, I need a little encouragement. IT'S ALL ABOUT SHOWING UP, THE POWER IS IN THE ASKING was written and created by the dearly loved Robbie Motter. She has inspired me as a successful photographer with all these stories, to encourage me to keep moving forward. If you are struggling in life, go to your favorite place and read this heartwarming book."

William Kidston: 3-time Emmy Award Winning Photographer

"Robbie and I met 18 years ago in Newport Beach on a $14,000,000 Yacht. I was producing an event for about 200 of Newport's most beautiful businesspeople when she walked in with a bunch of ladies in Boas. They were loud and colorful, and I thought, here we go, with more crazy ladies. They turned out to be some of the most delightful people I had ever met. In fact, they told me, you must be our first man diva and so it was. Since that time, my love for Robbie Motter has grown exponentially as we go from event to event. In the last 18 years I cannot even count the number of Spectacular Events we have produced together for hundreds and hundreds of people. I have watched Robbie teach her mantra of Just Show Up and Ask for what you want to thousands of people who have come to our events over the last 18 years. She has taught them to implement this philosophy and literally change their lives. I am one of these people and I can tell you it works! Whatever Robbie is doing, you can be sure that it comes from love and it will be uplifting,

inspirational and massively informative. Do yourself a favor and read this book."
This recommendation made with love from Robert "Hollywood" Moreno

Robert "Hollywood" Moreno
Real Estate Wealth Advisor
Master Event Producer/Singer/Emcee

"I have always stated that Robbie puts the extra in extraordinary and kind in mankind. I have known her for several years and her infamous words of "ASK" and "SHOW UP" explode like fireworks. I highly recommend this book without reservation. The authors in this book verify the impact. Go out and buy many, gift it to your friends. IT IS A MUST read. You will be making a difference in their lives through the impact of Robbie Motter's inspirational words of ASK and SHOW UP and you gifting them. She is truly a golden treasure."

Jean Olexa
Miss "O" The Organizer

"Robbie Motter creates golden opportunities for herself and others by both "showing up" and seeking to serve! We had not seen each other in 17 years and Robbie happened to "show up" at a local restaurant where I was singing. Since that day we have enjoyed many golden opportunities together, and I have increased my frequency of showing up, serving and asking due to her inspiration. Robbie is a dynamic, professional person who tirelessly assists other people from San Diego and beyond! Her book is a must read for business and personal interest. The stories contained here will surely inspire and take your life to the next level."

Joel Reese
Sales Manager/ Entertainer

"The multitude of stories under the phrase "Show up and Ask" has been an enjoyable read as well as an inspiring one. Based on the phrase, I tried to think of my own time that I have "showed up and asked" and nothing came to mind, however, after reading the various stories from each individual woman I have realized the complexity of such a simple statement. How four words can change an individual's life and each person can have a completely different experience, whether it involves business and professional growth, personal growth, or the growth of a relationship. This one phrase can be described in so many ways to show perseverance, tenacity, and the strength of each individual person. The individual stories also show that one is not alone. The qualities listed above can take time and each woman can struggle with self-doubt, nervousness, the feeling of wanting to quit, but they push forward despite being uncomfortable. They explore the opportunities that arise when you try. Moving forward does not mean you are fearless; it just means that you want to pursue the opportunities and rewards even if that means getting pushed out of your comfort zone. As one author stated, "everything you want is on the other side of your comfort zone". It inspires hope that one day, you the reader, can also achieve your goals and dreams. Showing up is a huge first step and you are in control of your future. If you want it go after it! I have written down many quotes from each author with their own understanding and truth that they embrace in their life. The phrase "showing up and asking" can take different forms and interpretations, leading to many positive and uplifting quotes that I have taken to heart and would like to embrace in my own life. This has led to the discovery that I myself have had a few "show up and ask" moments that I didn't even realize until reading the many forms this simple phrase can be applied to a person's life. I can't wait to see what my future holds and can hope that I can embrace this statement to all parts of my life and have the tenacity and hope that these amazing women authors have contributed to their own lives."

Heather Schneider
Bachelor of Arts with major in English
Literary agent intern, Havana Book Group LLC

"Robbie Motter is a legend in the field of women's empowerment especially in the small and emerging business sector. With her powerful philosophy of encouraging women to show up, step up and make the ask she has successfully mentored hundreds of women business owners to successfully grow their companies beyond what they thought was possible.

This collection represents a small but mighty assortment of those women leaders and their journey on the road to greatness. This book is the kind of book that you will not only enjoy yourself but can contribute to the success of those you care about by giving it as a gift for any occasion. Robbie Motter herself is the gift that keeps giving!"

Rayona Sharpnack
Founder & CEO, Institute for Women's Leadership
Founder & CEO, Institute for Gender Partnership

"I learned & practiced SHOWING UP and ASKING my whole life, as Robbie Motter's middle daughter. We all learned at a young age about SHOWING UP and ASKING. My life started in Hawaii, the next thing as a baby I SHOWED UP in Bellevue, Nebraska and then to Virginia. From Virginia to Houston and then New Jersey. Then back to Virginia, where I now live...So when one moves a lot you are always SHOWING UP and meeting new people and ASKING, so for me it comes naturally. Using the ASK and SHOWING UP strategy my whole business career, I was able to climb the corporate ladder to having top jobs and I trained my two children Joe and Jessica Soltas on also using this strategy. They too today have successful careers and are living in California. I had been SHOWING UP for several years at the GSFE Conferences my mother runs in CA., and because I SHOWED UP, I always got to meet so many great members of my mom's GSFE networks. I was also chosen to be a GSFE board member when she formed the GSFE nonprofit in 2017. At the 2018 event, one of the women I met was Dawn Schultz, who was running Operation Prom Girl now called the Dresses and Dream Project. When I heard the great work she was doing of providing gowns to teens for the prom, I was inspired and felt I wanted to do something like that in Virginia but wanted to make my group for special needs women. So, when I returned to Virginia, I embarked on putting this project together. In 2020, I contacted a school where there were special needs young ladies and found an interesting group. Because I am also a member of the VFW Auxiliary, I was able to work through one of the retired officers and found a military army escort for each of these special needs young ladies who would escort them to the prom in their military uniform. "Our Special Prom" was beginning to come together. Now, it was time to put the word out that I needed gowns, shoes and jewelry. I want to send a big thank you to Dawn Schultz, CEO/Founder of the Dresses and Dreams Project in California who donated thirteen gowns from her array of gowns in Ca. and mailed them to me, which was the start of my collection. Before I knew it, donations were coming in from numerous other sources and I found my spare bedroom closet filled with over 75 gowns. Jewelry, shirts, ties, and dress slacks for the boys were all donated for this very special event. But then the Covid-19 Crisis set in and all proms were cancelled. It was a big disappointment but in 2021, I will again embark on putting this event together to make a fantastic evening for a new group of beautiful special needs young ladies. If I would not have SHOWED UP or ASKED, this project could have never been put together. I have met many of the women who have shared their stories in this book and they are all heartfelt women who everyday touch a life and make a difference who have learned the POWER of ASKING and SHOWING UP. This book is a must read as everyone will walk away with something they can add to their lives."

Lori Soltas
Account Manager/ First Heritage Mortgage

"YOU HAVE NOT BECAUSE YOU ASK NOT!"

Richard E. Steel Sr.

"I have always believed in SHOWING UP and SHOUTING OUT because I know If I SHOW UP, I will learn a lot, make new friends and collaborate on future endeavors. When I SHOUT OUT it means I am being heard, people will listen, and I am happy. Having a successful event, like a Robbie Motter event or an "All Women Rock" event, when people talk about the events in later days, it is the best word of mouth to others and creates greater success of future events. This book is filled with amazing stories of powerful women "SHOWING UP" and "ASKING". Many of the co-authors have received All Women Rock awards at one of my "All Women Rock" events because of how dynamic they are."

Carl Wilson
Founder & CEO, CD Wilson Events
All Women Rock Creator

Chapter Overview

It's All about Showing Up

MY FIRST TRIP TO HOLLYWOOD

Mirjana Anastasijevic

The woman sitting in front of me told me that our university's music department had an important message in Santa Cruz de Tenerife, Spain. We had received an urgent email from the from Oscars, requesting more information because we were nominated for the Oscars.

I heard, "Oscar Awards and Hollywood". I didn't respond at first. I was too busy practicing and finishing projects.

"So, will you show up?" I heard the woman ask. She had a beautiful smile and she laughed as she waved her hands pointing at me, seeing that I wasn't listening.

"What do you mean?" I asked, feeling uncomfortable, because I wasn't listening.

"I'm asking if you'll go?" I could see that this was serious.

"Where will I go?" I asked, with more curiosity. She called out to me, very loudly. "To Hollywood! You've been invited to the Oscars in Hollywood!"

I looked at this woman with a beautiful smile and I finally heard what she was trying to tell me.

I was shocked, surprised and joyous, all at the same time and at the time, I really didn't appreciate what it would mean for me. How was it even possible that Hollywood and Music Award Oscar had come into my life? I had worked on the soundtrack of a Spanish film, "El Alma de Tacande" translated, "The Ghost of Tecande" and decided at that moment to go and find my colleagues and team members to see if they had heard this incredible news.

The Invitation to Hollywood

Yes, they knew about it, although, I was still not sure if it was true. It was only when I saw the email invitation that it started to sink in. We were, in fact, nominated for the Oscar and invited to go to Hollywood. And so, it began.

At first, I was so happy just to be recognized for our work in a foreign country. Not just any country, but America. I always wanted to visit this country but I'm also very comfortable at home in my beautiful country. I didn't really need the stress of travelling there. Was I ready to go? There's so much bureaucracy and so many restrictions. I didn't know how to apply for a visa.

I had so many obligations at home. I also had a job in the Canary Islands, I had my university, my studies, and my family. How do I juggle all that?

The trip itself was long. I would be flying over the ocean to the other side of the globe and couldn't just leave one day and come home the next.

I also heard that America can be a dangerous place for a woman alone. I would be going to a place I didn't know anything about. This was a big deal. A once in a lifetime opportunity. So, I had to go with my intuition and follow my heart. I had to go. I always wanted to see America. It was my long-time dream. I gathered up my courage and made the decision to GO to America!

A few days later I was holding my boarding pass. My family and friends surrounded me. Their eyes mirrored worry, happiness, excitement and pride. No one could have imagined just a few weeks ago that this could be happening for me. It happened so fast…the nomination, the invitation and now, I was on my way to the Oscars.

It's been a long and gratifying journey. I work hard and I love what I do. Until this day I had a quiet and ordinary life of a musician and composer. I quit my job and packed my suitcase.

I tried to put on a good front and not look as scared as I felt. I was also happy and proud to be the first from my country to achieve such an honor. I knew that by *showing up* my life would change.

It's All About Showing Up!

As I waited for my plane to take off, I was thinking about what it means to 'show up,' and what my life would be like when I got to this foreign country. I said yes to something that I couldn't even imagine. Showing up means being brave; listening to my intuition. It means following my dream and feeling free.

I was on the plane and couldn't turn back. I was travelling with a lot of strangers to a new destination. A destination that included a new country…a place that was probably much bigger than anything I had ever seen. A destination that was going to be life-altering.

I took a deep breath and tried to relax. The trip took 18 hours and finally I arrived at LAX in Los Angeles. The city of possibilities, a tremendous culture, a dynamic film industry and unlimited entertainment. Wow! I was thrilled and suddenly I felt tears trickling down my cheeks. I tried to hide it, I certainly didn't want people to see me cry…they wouldn't understand that I was crying from happiness and gratitude. I had made an important decision when I decided to show up.

I focused on myself and had to get to my hotel as fast as possible.

A Police Officer

My first surprising experience in America occurred when I arrived at LAX. I was waiting in line at border control and noticed how nervous people in line were. More bureaucracy, lots of police maintaining order. It was all so serious. I wondered if I could be denied entry and I had to go home. What would I do? Who would I call? I was definitely worried, but then I said to myself, what will be will be. When it came to my turn, I was fingerprinted and waited to be questioned by the police. I was asked about the big holster on the side of my suitcase. Suddenly I seemed to forget my reason for being in the country. I got my bearings back and said, "Oh, it's a film commercial. Do you want to see it?"

"No, that's not necessary. Are you an actress?" He asked,

"No, I'm a composer and pianist. I composed the music for a Spanish movie, "El Alma de Tacande" and I was nominated for the Women's Oscar Award at the International Film Festival in Hollywood. In English, the film is called "The Ghost of Tacande". We're also on the nominations shortlist for an Academy Award. Here is the form that we had to fill out." I showed him the papers.

"May I take your name and go to one of your performances?" He asked me. I was so surprised by this kind police officer.

"Of course, I would be glad." I replied. I was now able to relax. I knew I had been approved entry into America. And then, I heard him say, "You are very welcome to America. Enjoy discovering our country."

I was very surprised. I didn't expect that. I had been warned that the police in America were ruthless. But instead, my arrival was made special by a very kind police officer. Now, I was really looking forward to getting to my hotel.

The City and the Girl

I went out of the airport and couldn't believe how busy it was with cars and people. I did manage to find the shuttle to the hotel, but it wasn't easy. It was a long ride and even though it was five o'clock in the afternoon, it was starting to get dark in Los Angeles. The palm trees and warm weather were similar to Tenerife and to the Canary Islands, but everything was so different. There was so much life here. The streets were lined with shops and the lights seemed to flow with the traffic. I was happy and knew that this trip was worthwhile.

When I got off the shuttle bus, I couldn't see a hotel, and was very worried. I noticed a girl from the shuttle who looked like she was waiting for someone, so I asked if she knew where the hotel was. Unfortunately, she was a tourist and couldn't help me, but said that she was waiting for her friend, who lived in Los Angeles and she might be able to help me. So, I waited. When her friend arrived, they started to speak in Spanish. I told them I spoke Spanish too. They told me that a lot of people here speak Spanish. So that felt good, like home. The friend told me that there was a hotel nearby, I couldn't see one. The street was crowded, and it was quite dark. They saw that I was afraid and offered to take me to the hotel and they did. I was so pleased that in this busy city, she took the time to help me. Quite amazing!

My first illness

When I checked into the hotel, I was already feeling sick. I thought it might be the time change, all the excitement and the long flight. I was tired and tried to sleep, but I couldn't. I felt like I was going to collapse. A Russian girl, Alexandra, gave me some pills she takes when she travels. I worried about taking pills offered by a stranger in a strange country, but I went with my intuition. I trusted her. A couple of hours later, I was feeling better and started to get ready for the big event…the Film Festival and of course, the red carpet.

The Event and the Red Carpet

Hollywood Boulevard! Walk of Fame! I've arrived! Everywhere was glamour, elegance and celebrities in gorgeous gowns and suits. I was alone. I didn't know anyone. I decided to ask a nice young man who was standing in the hall to help me find my place. I found trust at first sight. He didn't just help that night but continued to help me throughout my stay in Los Angeles. His name was Daniel and he was a minister. I recalled how my friends in Tenerife prayed that I would be safe and in good hands during my stay in America.

I wondered if this was a coincidence or a sign of a miracle. Everything was so fantastic. I started to love this country, and its people. After the award ceremony and receiving the award for the Best Composer in 2018, I went to a party where I met Shelly.

I really wanted to come back to California again so I asked her if she knew anyone who would be interested in my music. She told me about Robbie.

Showing Up!

So, miracles happen when you decide to show up.

I learned that when I invest in an activity and participate to the fullest, I can do a lot for myself and much more for my loved ones. No one can take an experience away from me. I made a choice that changed my life. It became clear to me that we are responsible for ourselves. We have to love ourselves. No one else can make decisions for you, but you.

This is Showing Up.

I met Robbie Motter, who is one of the most amazing and inspiring women I have ever known.

Her faith and belief in women and her ability to help them succeed is an extraordinary gift that enriches everyone who comes in contact with her.

She looks for your skills and talents and inspires you to never give up on your dreams.

I visited Robbie a few months ago and was on the receiving end of her supportive, unconditional love. She gives without expectations and shares her big heart with everyone she meets.

God bless you Robbie Motter! You are an angel on earth and my beautiful friend.

Get Out of Your Comfort Zone

Kimberly Anderson

I t takes a lot to get out of your comfort zone and do something that stretches you, no matter what that is. To do something uncomfortably and with fear because you believe in what you need to share. Showing up and asking for what you want are the only ways of taking you to that next level, and I am here today doing what I do simply because I showed up. My dear friend Robbie Motter's motto is, "Showing up is like a treasure map; you never know what you will find". Well, it is because of her motto that I show up, and even when I don't feel like going to a meeting, for example, these seem to be the times I find the most treasure and am glad I did go. I have met the most amazing people, and have created incredible connections because of simply showing up, and I have gained wonderful opportunities because I have asked for something, or made it known that I want to do something. I wanted to start public speaking more and getting out in front of a variety of audiences… and because I put that 'out there' and made that known, opportunities kept coming my way and still do. Now, different audiences are hearing me speak, and I am being asked to speak more.

It is a ripple effect; you do one little thing, and that leads to more things and so on… Many years ago, I went to a women's meeting, showing up in a marketing capacity for a company with the intention of meeting people. This meeting was where I first met Robbie Motter. I didn't know anyone there and I don't even remember how I heard about the meeting, but at that same meeting I also met two other women with whom I became very good friends, and who helped me step into more of what I really wanted to do in my life. We are still very good friends today, and by meeting these ladies, it gave me the courage to really step into what I am passionate about: helping women tap into their intuition, empowering them to step into their power, and live their best life. It was also through one of them that I got back into real estate. I am still a realtor today as well as an Intuitive Transformational Coach and Business Creative. By maintaining my connection to Robbie, keeping in mind her insisting always that we must show up, I kept showing up at events where she was participating. At one point I told her I would love to speak at her group meetings, and she booked me for quite a few of them. The result was that I was asked to speak at many other venues.

At the very least it's about networking. You get out and meet people, make connections, and build relationships. This is how you grow your business; it is how you foster lasting relationships, and it is how you build your community and your 'tribe'.

I created my 'Unleash Your Inner Goddess' series and had to ASK people to be part of it. It started out as an online virtual summit, and now it is a 3-part series: The Virtual Summit, a book, and a Goddess Retreat. I am able to highlight and give massive visibility to the ladies who participate, and they also get marketing tools for their businesses. It offers great value in general for the people in the audience, and even greater value for the ladies. I started out asking for people to become part of this series, and now people are asking me to allow them to be part of it because of the value and visibility… And it's fun! I am able to make a difference in many lives because I created this platform. As a result of this, I have created a community of amazing people. One of the things I love most about this, is being able to make a difference in so many lives. There are twenty-one women who share their life experiences through sharing the real and raw truth about what they have overcome, and this shows people that they are not alone; that they can also get through their own situations. What a beautiful thing!

Creating this platform has also allowed me to find a publisher and start a TV show. Funny thing about that is, I was asked if I wanted to do a show, not me seeking to do it. And now, the perfect opportunity presented itself to host my own TV show. This allows me to help people even more, not only with reaching huge audiences, but also with getting the message out there... And that we all have an inner strength, an inner knowing, that we can tap into at any time. It's within us. So, by showing up and asking, we are putting ourselves in a position to use that insight, gain the knowledge of our inner strength, and make things happen in our lives. If you need something, 'ask'. If you want to get out there and have more exposure, 'show up'.

Because I now have a publisher and a TV show, *Unleashed with Kimberly*, I am also able to add extra value to my coaching programs. This creates another space for people not only for people to be able to simply show up, but to give people the chance to show up *for themselves*. There is so much power in showing up and asking; there is so much power in tapping into your inner strength and inner knowing and in following that inner voice. You are powerful and you have the power to do whatever you want.

Another thing that I believe that is important to bring up, is asking when you don't want to, or are scared to. I am an advocate against Domestic Violence and am affiliated with three non-profit organizations that reach out to help women and children in need. Services will eventually be available for men too, in one of them, as of now, they are all women- and children-focused since right now this is the largest group affected by abuse.

1. The **I am Enough Movement** and **Freedom Haven** shelter:

The I AM ENOUGH Movement is a 501(c)(3) non-profit organization that provides visual coping cards free to people all over the world. The foundation for this movement is to give joy and help others live a life filled with more hope and happiness. Freedom Haven is at its beginning stages of development: The MISSION of Freedom Haven is to empower domestic violence survivors to gain freedom in life through housing, education and placement programs in the San Diego area, with a vision to expand nationally.

2. **Dresses and Dreams** Project:

The Dresses and Dreams Project is much more than dressing up for special occasions. It is an opportunity for any girl to discover her passion in life and find her purpose. Because of the great need for mentorship and guidance in the lives of challenged teen girls and young women, the founder's vision includes a physical showroom for gowns; office locations for holding workshops and counseling services; restoration and recovery opportunities; career counseling; resources to victims of human trafficking, domestic violence, and other crisis matters; pregnancy support; art for healing through music, painting, and poetry.

3. **Leave No Woman Behind Domestic Violence Advocacy**: called DV **Warrior Sisters**

Mission: Empowering women in their communities by providing access to resources that promote healthy habits and lifestyles. Vision: Leave No Woman Behind is committed to uniting all women through self-love, self-confidence, empowerment, friendship, strength, courage, unconditional love, and acceptance.

As a survivor of Domestic Violence on and off for over 20+ years, it is crippling to have to search for the courage to reach out and ask for help when you need it most and are at your most vulnerable. I empower you to reach out and ask for what you need; ask for help. It becomes easier if you take one step at a time... Then you find yourself moving from survivor to thriver. At this point you get to ask yourself, "What next? What do I need now to upgrade my life then my business?" I have discovered that it is not only about following your intuition and inner knowing but also about having integrity toward yourself. Believing in yourself so that you can 'ask' and 'show up' for yourself. Do it for you, and you alone. We can only pour from a full cup, so fill yours first and trust yourself. You have permission to step into your best self; step into the powerful person you that you fundamentally are. Trust yourself, you've got all this.

So just 'show up' and 'ask'. These will take you to wherever you want to go! You've got this, and we've got you!

Generations of Showing up

Angeline Benjamin

Have you ever considered what it would be like to change your name? Would changing your name change your identity? I was born in Jakarta, Indonesia, and named Bong Mei Lie. You know me as Angeline. Why was my name changed?

I was the firstborn of six children. Both my parents are of Chinese descent; however, many generations of my family were born in Indonesia. In America, this is a foreign concept as babies born in the United States are natural citizens whatever their parents' heritage. No matter how many generations were born in Indonesia, those of Chinese heritage are always considered Chinese. This is still true in Indonesia.

My mother was adamant that all her children were to be treated the same unlike typical Indonesian and Chinese families, who only invest in their sons. It was important that my siblings had the same educational opportunities. My dad supported my mom's beliefs. Each of us were given the same opportunities and we all came to the United States for our college education. Eventually, my entire family came to live in the U.S. My parents, in their later years, lived with my youngest brother. He was unmarried, until they passed away.

When I was a young child, my father knew he needed to protect our family. The political climate in Indonesia was such that people of Chinese heritage were discriminated against. One of the ways to ensure our safety was to write a declaration to the government that we were born in Indonesia and we choose to give up our Chinese citizenship. My father submitted this document officially to the courts on December 28th, 1960, and my dad made sure that I continue to keep these documents in a safe place.

My father was a successful self-made entrepreneur, so I was fortunate to have attended private schools. In fifth grade my parents sent us to one of the best Catholic schools in Jakarta, called Tarakanita. This was both to get a good education, and to protect us from discrimination. Also, this school did not offer students to learn Chinese language.

To protect us even further, my dad, who was much respected in the community ran for a school board position and was even voted in as president. He did this to further ensure our family's safety. This was important because there was a lot of political unrest in Indonesia and the Chinese population were believed to be communists and the government of Indonesia feared communism. On September 30, 1965, a group of Indonesian military personnel captured and murdered six powerful generals and the coup led to the fall of President Sukarno, Indonesia's first president. It also began a year of the great rebellion, referred to as The Indonesian Communist Purge. From what I remember, it involved a group that supported the Indonesian Communist Party. The army leadership at that time insisted it was a plot to seize the power from the Indonesian government, which was not communist. In the months that followed, the military slaughtered hundreds of thousands of people, who were communists or alleged communists. According to Wikipedia, there are up to three million people that may have been killed. My father had the foresight to protect us during these difficult times.

During the year of rebellion, there were months we could not attend school, because the hatred against the Chinese people in Indonesia put us at risk. Even years afterward there were many demonstrations throughout Indonesia.

This is the background to why my name was changed. To further protect us from being accused of supporting the communist party, Dad decided we should change our name to remove our Chinese identify further. On August 1, 1967, we formally adopted Christian - Indonesian names. I became Angeline Liestyawati Benjamin instead of and Bong Mei Lie. My dad chose his baptismal name, Benjamin as our last name. Angeline was my baptismal name, and Liestyawati is my legal Indonesian name. Typically, Indonesian's have only one name with no first or last name, so my Indonesian name is Liestyawati. I now use my Indonesian name as a middle name.

Our new names were accepted during the unrest and showed Indonesian officials that we weren't communists. But the discriminations continued, and my parents feared that we would not be able to go to the university of our choice. My parents decided to send my sister and I to study in America, earlier then they had planned. Our priest, whom my parents respected and trusted, found an all-girl Catholic college preparatory school, Marywood High School, in the city of Orange in California. This is how I came to America. We showed up in a new country not speaking its language or an understanding of its customs.

I arrived in the United States on January 6th, 1970 with my sister, Indria. We had just finished our junior year of high school. I was already 18 and Indria was about to turn 17. My parents gave us the greatest gift…a chance for a better education and a better future. I am incredibly grateful for this gift and for their sacrifice.

Because we didn't speak or write English, we both started school as juniors and graduated in 1971. My sister and I learned the value of showing up not only in a new country but also in our classes. Every afternoon, after our regular classes we attended an accelerated English class for foreign students. While other students were enjoying the dormitory life watching TV, we went to classes to learn to speak English. We were dedicated to learning fast and our grades improved. We joined high school clubs and on weekends volunteered at the hospital. We both received foreign student academic scholarships to the college of our choice…another amazing gift.

I chose to go to the College of Notre Dame in Belmont, California and my sister attended St. Martin College in Olympia, Washington.

After college, I attended graduate school with a fellowship at the University of Alberta in Edmonton, Alberta, Canada. I had planned to go to medical school back in the U.S. Then in graduate school, I decided against it for two reasons. One was financial but more importantly, I developed a passion for microbiology. I give credit for this to my science professor and mentor. I decided that I loved science more than taking care of patients, so I transferred to the Food Science Master's Program.

Back in Indonesia the political situation continued. So, I decided to help my parents bring my two brothers to the U.S. We rented a condominium in Tustin and moved in together. They were sponsored by my American family and attended Foothills High School.

In 1980 I applied for a job as a microbiologist technologist at Hunt-Wesson Foods, Inc. in Fullerton, California. It was my first job in my chosen profession. I realized how important it was to show up and ask. Although I was unsure of getting this job, I thought, *what do I have to lose*? That was how I felt when I applied for a college scholarship in high school. I prepared by practicing my answers to possible questions in front of the mirror. I also practiced questions I wanted to ask them. I showed up with confidence and asked the questions I had been practicing. I got the job! I was excited and surprised.

My goal was to get promoted to supervisor, and I asked for more and more responsibilities and did more than they asked for. I knew that I would learn more and prove myself. I showed up to work early every day, which was difficult for me, since I'm not a morning person!

Three months later, during my first performance review, I asked my manager how I could qualify for a supervisor position. A strategy I learned when preparing for interviews to indicate I was willing to go further with the company. He was very helpful and gave me guidance. He told me later he appreciated my confidence and commitment. Three months later I was promoted and began my career in quality assurance.

Eventually I landed a job at the Taco Bell Corporation and spent over 18 years there. During the last five years, I led a crisis management program and was a Food Safety Officer, with responsibility for all of the United States. At Taco Bell, I learned the importance of having a mentor and a coach to help me accomplish my goals. I also discovered my passion as a coach and trainer for restaurant franchisees' management.

My husband, Michael, started a packaging business, in 2007. I retired from Taco Bell to support him. We moved to Albuquerque, New Mexico. I used my experience and education and became a food safety consultant while Michael started his packaging business. I marketed and promoted our packaging business and did consulting work.

As an entrepreneur, I saw the importance of showing up and asking about other businesses. I learned to network with business associates. I became a member of the Albuquerque Hispano Chamber of Commerce and joined their ambassador group. I showed up at almost every event and asked the members what the Chamber could do to support them. I was voted by my peers to be the Vice President of the Chamber Ambassadors. My efforts paid off and our packaging business improved even during the economic downturn of 2008, which was a remarkable accomplishment.

One of our customers in the packaging company introduced me to Nerium's anti-aging night cream in 2013. At first, I was skeptical, but I got amazing results. People noticed how nice my skin looked so I joined the business. I loved the company's philosophy, the products, and the enthusiasm of the people.

Michael was offered an attractive position to run a packaging company in Orange County, California. So, in 2014, we closed our packaging business and moved back to Orange County. I now had the opportunity to put into practice all that I learned in New Mexico. I was then working with Nerium and made an effort to network and make friends in my new community and joined The Heart Link Network in Laguna Niguel and also other networking groups.

Through ongoing personal development and appreciating the value of showing up and asking for what I needed, my business grew. But I knew that I needed to do more. I had to take the right actions and always follow up. Working with Nerium, which is now called Neora, and attending the networking groups, I met a lot of wonderful and helpful people whose positive outlook helped me learn valuable lessons, like when you value people they want to be part of your life and business.

Menifee became our new home in September of 2017. It shortened Michael's commuting time to his job. Shortly after our move, I found and then joined the National Association of Female Executives and met Robbie Motter, a Global NAFE Coordinator. If you know her, you know she is a dynamic woman who wants the best for women. She also founded a non-profit organization, the Global Society for Female Entrepreneurs. Robbie appreciated my qualities of being organized and sharing my knowledge. And I showed up to everything. I loved her motto, *Show Up and ASK!* I knew then she would be an important person in my life and a mentor. So, I asked her to help me advance in the organization, and with her help and because I worked hard, I became Co-Director for the NAFE network in Menifee, and later the Director of South Orange County NAFE. I have been honored with many awards for my commitment and hard work: the Appreciation Award at the First Annual Lady in Blue Sapphire Awards and Fashion Show; a Call to Service Award with a certificate and medal from the President of the United States; Certificates of Recognition from California senators and members of the California State Assembly; and the All Women Rock Award. I strive to inspire and help others and appreciate the recognition and the difference I'm able to make in women's lives. I'm grateful to the people who have believed in me.

As I have traveled through my 68-year life's journey, I've appreciated the time people took to mentor me and I have, in turn, mentored others. I'm especially grateful to my parents. They were my first role models, and I learned many life lessons from them. They taught me to value people, to sacrifice for what you believe in, and to find people whom you admire and learn from them. I learned the importance of showing up, asking, taking action, and following up. I am grateful for the gifts they gave me, and the sacrifices they made to give me an education and a better life. My Dad taught me to take action and build a better future for ourselves. Today, I live to honor my parent's legacy.

I am also grateful to the many people who have guided me. Robbie Motter mentored, coached me and helped me achieve more than I ever imagined possible. I continue to show up at networking, special events and conferences, and work hard to help others achieve their goals. I know that showing up is like a treasure hunt, you never know what's ahead until you find it. People build bridges to help each other achieve their destination. With Robbie's encouragement and guidance, and my new coach, Lori Raupe, I have the courage to write this story and together with Lori's coaching I am working on my first book to help guide and encourage my readers to take action and get results. "Life Lessons Leading to Success" will be published in October 2020. Please look for it.

Asking for My Plum Position

Barbara Berg

In 1975 at 22 years old, I had just graduated from Douglass College (The Women's College) of Rutgers University with a specialty in Early Childhood Education. One thing I knew for sure: I would NEVER stay in New Jersey! All during my undergrad years, I commiserated daily with my activist boyfriend that I would someday become the director of a newly formed "corporate onsite childcare center" that didn't even exist yet. But most of all, I knew I would be moving OUT WEST.

On October 1st, I headed for Jackson Hole, Wyoming, where my college best friend Dee and I had promised we'd go after graduation. I envisioned I would try my hand at being "a ski bum." I also considered the idea that maybe I could learn to teach young children how to ski. After all, they would most likely be beginners and since I really liked working with young children, this whole idea would be a slam dunk!

Upon arriving in the little town of Jackson, I realized two major aspects of living in this part of the world. Number 1: Winter starts really early. In fact, as I drove my old Buick LeSabre through Yellowstone National Park on October 7, 1975, the ranger closed the gate behind me, saying the main driving roads were now closed for winter. Number 2: The first thing you need to do upon rolling into town, is to get yourself a strong, long, "winter-ized" extension cord. If you don't plug it in every night, the engine block will surely freeze and that will be the end of your transportation. While I still don't know what an engine block really is, I made a point to plug in my car every night from October to at least the end of April.

Upon barely adjusting to living in this amazingly beautiful and cold climate, I was told I would have a better chance of getting a job teaching skiing if I started at the local ski mountain, Snow King, rather than immediately trying out to teach at the world renowned Jackson Hole. I took my best self over to the mountain to see what and whom I could find there and was struck by one particular thing: Snow King Mountain may not be the largest ski area in the world, but there is no doubt it is the steepest. Frankly, after just looking up, I knew I most likely wouldn't last up there as an employee very long. But a little bird in my head kept telling me to give it a try. I was there to meet new people and start a new life.

So, I showed up at one of the first informal trainings, but most of the people there had done this a million times and they already knew the drill. Since the snow was still patchy, and the leaders of the ski school didn't get a good chance to see how I really ski, they just assumed I must be pretty good. I was given the job.

I was scheduled to teach my first "subjects" on the first crisp morning after a major snowstorm. Fueled by pure human guts and naiveté, I showed up early to meet my students. Yes, I was given the youngest individuals there. What I wasn't prepared for was how incredibly adept they were for only being (no kidding) two and three years of age. Yes folks, these future world class Olympians had already been used to toddling in mountainous terrain, and since they were so close to the ground, putting on their short little skis seemed like a no-brainer. They didn't have poles, they certainly didn't need much direction, and I remember they had the rosiest cheeks I had ever seen! Absolutely nothing hindered them in any way. Except me.

We were helped onto to a lift where we all sat together on one long seat. Apparently, this wasn't their first time going up such a steep incline—but it was mine. While I had skied a number of places back east and had even competed in some pretty complex NASTAR races, my small mountains were nothing like this! After exiting the lift, it became obvious that all I needed to do was pick each child up and position them downhill like perfectly agile little penguins.

My students did fine. When they got caught up around a mogul that was bigger than they were, they simply sat down and contemplated their next move. I on the other hand, ran into a tree on the first turn. I had to be fished out by the local ski patrol, and when I got down to the bottom of the hill, I realized my students were met by another teacher and I was promptly relieved of my job.

As I was somewhat politely dismissed for botching up my first and last ski class, I actually heard some incredibly magic words come out of the Head Master's Mouth, that I still appreciate to this day: "We could see how much you wanted the job, and how willing you were to keep showing up with ENTHUSIASM and a smile on your face. Because of that, I'm sending you back down the hill to the newly built Snow King Resort that is just about to open for the coming ski season." They didn't much care for outsiders in this very protective and sought-after little town, so I particularly felt grateful that I had another chance to possibly work this wonderful valley.

So, I marched back down the hill, and was thrilled to be introduced to the acting manager of the almost built Snow King Resort. He asked me what I thought I had to offer, and I told him "I really like working and I want to find a way to make a good life for myself here in this beautiful town." He said, "Go on."

And then, from somewhere in the deep recesses of my soul, my heart, and mouth, I delivered this forthcoming soliloquy: "I just graduated from Douglass College of Rutgers University, where I interned in teaching pre-school and kindergarten, I have been a camp counselor for many years at girl scout camps, took care of boy scout leaders' children at Philmont Scout Ranch in New Mexico, and would someday like to own my own preschool or childcare center. I have just recently begun subbing at daycare centers here in town, and I have an idea about having a childcare center for tourists right here at your hotel. We could even start it by licensing it for up to twelve children like a Family Daycare Home right in one of your larger ground floor rooms. One or two assistants and I would be enough to start. And then next summer, while everyone is crossing the country to celebrate our 200-year anniversary of the United States, parents will want to raft on the Snake river, and they won't always be able to take their young children along."

The acting manager looked at me as if I had two heads. On the one hand he said the tourist childcare center really wasn't such a bad idea, especially as they had other hotels to compete with in this valley. And besides, Snow King Resort is now the closest hotel to the local ski area. On the other hand, as this meeting was taking place, we were both standing in sawdust with yellow hard hats on, and tape still on the windows. This brought us back to reality, as the manager said to me, "While that's all nice and everything, what can you do for me right now?"

Recognizing I'd certainly have to pay my dues and perform a whole lot better than I did at the top of the mountain, I said, "I am very personable with people, what do you need?" Somehow, seeing that I was willing to rise to almost any occasion as long as I wasn't on skis, he said, "How about you take down some of this construction tape from the lower windows, and report tomorrow at 6am for breakfast waitress training?"

Well, I did. Exactly two weeks later, while I was holding a carafe of coffee during my breakfast shift, the acting manager was sitting at a table with the head foreman discussing final building details. The manager asked me over and as I poured them both coffees, he asked me to explain my tourist childcare center idea to both of them together. After a 45-minute discussion, during which I was finally asked to sit down, a deal was struck. I was given a trial chance to run my own little tourist childcare program over this coming ski season, to see how it would fly. Barely trying to curb my own enthusiasm, and trying not to spill coffee on anyone, "The Punkin' Patch" was born.

Now this would have been enough on its own as a good "Show Up and Ask" story, but this is not the punch line. After the Punkin' Patch did quite well the first ski season, it really became a hit during the summer of 1976 during the US Bicentennial, when the number of families more than doubled coming into town. The Punkin' Patch was in high demand.

However, the next winter was about to come. In terms of weather predictions, all of the Jackson area was warned that the winter of 1976-1977 would be so cold, that the numbers would fall well below 0 degrees! This would mean it was too cold to snow. That's right folks! It didn't snow in Jackson Hole all winter. The Snow King Resort even offered me free rent to try to stay open, but by January of 1977, it was obvious Mother Nature had no intention of cooperating with the ski trade that year.

As I literally watched the tourists, many inhabitants, and my clientele march right out of town, it occurred to me that I truly needed to rethink my plans for the future. I decided to move back East, (not New Jersey), and after a number of many "Show up and Ask" situations, I was admitted to the Graduate School of Social Work at Virginia Commonwealth University in Richmond, VA.

I loved it! My major was in group work in mental health, and during that time, one of my internships involved teaching human development at a nearby University. In May of 1980, just about 5 weeks before graduation, I met and fell in love my then husband and father of my child, who was graduating from med school at the same university. I moved with him to Dallas, Texas, right after we both graduated, where he would begin his internship program to be a doctor. At that time, I had no job, but was truly looking for one, and hoped with everything I had done, Dallas would have the right job for me.

Now here comes the miracle I was referring to earlier. I was in Dallas Texas for approximately 1 week, and every day was hotter than the next. While I was so thrilled to be with my amazing new love, I was wondering how to go about getting a job that I would love reporting to everyday in 100-degree heat.

One week after arriving in town, I opened the main Dallas newspaper to the available jobs section, and there it was, right on the page as if it was screaming at me: "Needed. Onsite Child Care Center Director for the newly formed Zale Diamond onsite childcare center at their international corporate headquarters." I started to scream to my newly beloved, "Ronnie, here is my job!!!!!"

Looking at me with a sweet smile, not yet fully knowing what a "go-getter" he had on his hands, he said, "Give them a call!" (Remember back in the first paragraph of this essay?) This was the job I had dreamed about in undergrad long before I started out West. That was back in 1975. It was now 1980. And the weirdest part was, I honestly don't remember even consciously thinking about it while in grad school. (I see now that dreams fashioned there would manifest later.)

However, in this very moment, there was no doubt in my mind, THAT JOB WAS MINE! NO ONE ELSE CAN HAVE IT!!!!

Dialing the phone with the primal intensity of a 4-year-old pushing other children out the life-size dollhouse at FAO Schwartz, I called the number listed in the paper for Zales. The lady on the other end was very nice. When I let her know I was inquiring about the childcare director job, she informed me that it was filled.

I asked again as if that couldn't be so, but she let me know one more time that the job truly was filled. I just couldn't see it that way, so I said (no kidding), "But that's *my* job." The lady on the other end, apparently hearing all kinds of things from people, went on to say, "Alright, I'll put you on the phone with the project creator. He's a psychologist and the Vice President in charge of this program."

Somehow thinking that's how this conversation should go, as if I had been in this situation in some other life, when I heard his voice on the other end, I replied with, "It's so good to speak with you Dr., is the job still open?" He replied, "Yes, as a matter of fact it is. The person we originally were going to hire wanted more money than we were willing to give."

Now, although money was definitely an issue, being single minded on the matter of wanting this position led me to the next statement and question. "Great, when may I come in for an interview?"

Well, I went in for the interview, got the job, and loved (almost) every second of it. It was perfect for my skillset. I loved working with children and groups of people in general. I started a parent involvement group including bake sales and newsletters, initiated training for the staff, got interviewed by myriads of press interested on how almost 150 parents working next door in the main building could come visit and participate as much as they did, went on field trips, spoke for the New Mexico Governor's corporate child care task force in Santa Fe, New Mexico, and did the Bunny Hop on the Today Show.

And part of the miracle was, I hadn't realized that directing corporate childcare was actually the plum position I had been wanting since undergrad, but it came back alive when the timing was right. Showing up and asking works best when the other party involved has a dream that incorporates with yours, so you both are willing to help make it come to fruition—all at the same time! I wasn't the only one showing up and asking- my potential new boss showed up and asked too!

Three years later, my husband and I decided to move to California after my husband completed his internship and residency. I look back at this center with fond memories, and I heard Zale went on to build a bigger and even better childcare center at their new world headquarters. Much thanks to ROBBIE MOTTER, our powerful role model and Co-Founder of GSFE, I smile to know now that wonderful things happen when you show up and ask—and if something is meant to be yours, it will be.

Today, Barbara A. Berg, is a Licensed Clinical Social Worker who has been conducting psychotherapy and critical incident stress debriefings for almost 30 years in the State of California. She writes self-help books, has conducted over 550 workshops and keynote speeches, also has guested on over 550 radio and tv interviews.

It's All about Showing Up

My dear friend, Robbie Motter

Kelly Breaux

The Power of Showing Up

Robbie Motter...My Fabulous Diva Goddess Friend, True Earth Star, and The Queen of "Show Up and Ask." This planet has many types of stars like movie stars, rock stars, television stars and also Earth Stars. An Earth Star is a person whose soul is so bright that it shines love, light, and inspiration on all those lucky enough to cross their path.

A wise woman once told me, "the measure of a great life is not about how rich or famous you become; it's about how many lives you touch in a positive way while you are here." If that's true, then my good buddy Robbie Motter is a billionaire on the inside. I can only imagine how many lives she has uplifted, nurtured, and inspired by her infectious personality, warm heart, and ability to communicate from the soul. One of Robbie's greatest teachings that she has shared with thousands is her discovery of what happens when we "Show Up."

Life is like a mystery unfolding and when we have the courage to face our fear and "Show Up" into the unknown, that's when the real magic happens. Synchronicities and coincidences become our road maps guiding us to those divine appointments when souls are destined to meet. It seems to happen most on those days when we are exhausted and want to cancel plans and then something deep inside says go. It is in those sacred moments when doors open, and your dreams begin to manifest right before your eyes.

My "Show Up" story is about the day I met Robbie. It was on a beautiful Sunday about 10 years ago. I had plans to go with a friend to Malibu Beach for the day and at the last minute, she had to cancel. I was really looking forward to that relaxing beach getaway and was feeling a bit disappointed. Two minutes later I got a call from my good friend Peggy DiCaprio. She said, "Hey Kelly, I have an extra ticket for a benefit lunch today and thought of you. It's to raise money for the 20th Anniversary of Women's Day at the Hollywood Bowl. Can you meet me in the Hancock Park area in about 30 minutes?" My initial thought was I am in beach attire, have nothing to wear and how much will this cost? My fear was trying to talk me into saying no, but my spirit kicked in and I found myself saying, "Yes!"

I hung up the phone, shifted my attitude, and with excitement dashed down the hallway to my closet. I picked out one of my favorite outfits and off I went. I arrived in the neighborhood, turned down the street, and to my surprise there was a long line of cars waiting to be valeted in front of a huge estate. I was not expecting anything like this in my vision of what the day would bring. The valet greeted me with a big smile as I pulled up. I walked up the steps and rang the doorbell. A huge door opened, and I was greeted by Melanie Griffith. She was very sweet, introduced herself, and welcomed me into her home. I didn't see any of my friends. My heart was racing, but I tried to stay cool.

Behind the front door was a big courtyard and a few people were standing in line waiting to sign the register. Just past the check-in, there was a red carpet with lots of photographers. As I stood waiting, I inhaled a wonderful and familiar scent from the man standing in front of me. He slowly turned around, smiled, and introduced himself as Deepak Chopra. I was straight-up 'trippin' inside but remained calm. I introduced myself and smiled back. Thoughts of all of the books that I had read of his were flashing in my mind. He was one of my top three New Age Spiritual authors at the time, along with Shirley MacLaine and Louise Hay. Right when I had that very thought, the door opened behind me and guess who arrived? Shirley MacLaine walked in. Oh! My Goddess! I'm freaking out now! I felt like I was in a spiritual twilight zone!

At the same time all of this is happening, Robbie is driving in by herself for the same event from Menifee, 98 miles away. She thought the event was at a park called Hancock and was also surprised by the house and the valet parking. She rang the doorbell and guess who answered? Shirley MacLaine opened the door for her. Robbie was so stunned and had no idea what she had just shown up to.

By now I was enjoying the delicious food. The walls were covered by beautiful, sexy photographs of Antonio Banderas. I had been chatting with my friends in the dining room for about an hour when I decided to go into the living room. As I walked down a few steps, I saw Robbie sitting by herself on the sofa looking stylish and wearing an elegant hat with a bling pin that said, DIVA. I went over as if I had always known her, and I told her that she looked fabulous and asked who she was. She introduced herself and said she was alone and invited me to sit with her. I sat with her all evening and never left her side. There were a lot of celebrities there that evening, but it was Robbie Motter whose light was shining the brightest. We became instant friends and have enjoyed so many fun times together since, working to connect powerful women friends from all over the world.

It seems there was a divine plan that day for Robbie and I to meet. Because we both showed up, our lives are richer and better for it. You never know where life will take you when you have the courage to just say yes. Surrender to the universe and the outcome will surprise you every time. What a gift she has been to me and to so many women around the world. She has taught us all so much and her legacy of "Show Up and Ask" lives on inside each and every one of us. Every time I think about canceling or avoiding going somewhere, I hear Robbie's voice saying to me to just "Show Up" and watch what happens.

The Power of Asking

One of my favorite quotes by the fabulous actress, spiritual trailblazer, and bestselling author,

Shirley MacLaine is, "In order to get to the fruit of life, you must be willing to go out on a limb." Asking for what you want is going out on that limb. Letting go of the tree trunk of life and fearlessly dancing on that tiny branch, manifesting your deepest desires and making your own dreams come true.

The power of asking is also expounded in so many religious and spiritual doctrines. The words may be different but the message, "Ask and you shall receive" is the same. This seems so simple, but it's so hard for many to do. I was also one of those who was afraid to ask for help until I met Robbie Motter. She made it easy and explained it in a way that made so much sense. She said that most people expect others to automatically know what their needs are without expressing them. She suggested that we make it easier for ourselves and others by just being open, honest, and asking for exactly what we want. We call Robbie the "Queen of Show Up and Ask" because that is exactly what she does and teaches others to do as well. Robbie invites thousands of women to "Show Up" at networking events to share their hopes, dreams, and visions with each other. There's no competition, judgment, or fear. The women are there to empower and lift each other up in a way that feels tribal and ancestral. Women are a force to be reckoned with. When they combine their talents and resources, they become catalysts for change.

This is my story about the Power of Asking. I'll give you a brief background about how I came to this journey. I've always loved working with children and have been able to communicate with them quite easily. I didn't have kids of my own, but I was very close to my nieces and nephews. They called me the "cool" aunt and I got to buy them special gifts and always sit with them at holiday dinners. They were an inspiration to me, so I majored in education and got my teaching degree, but my path took a different turn when I watched my first Jane Fonda exercise video. I became obsessed with teaching aerobics. I loved encouraging my students and watching their mind, body, and spiritual transformations.

I became a fitness professional and choreographer and traveled the world teaching and certifying aerobics instructors and fitness trainers. I opened my own gym in Houston and later became a World Champion Houston Rocket Cheerleader. Eventually, I got the courage to move to Los Angeles where I became a fitness specialist, dance teacher, choreographer, numerologist, and life coach to stars and executives. Those were 10 very exciting and super fun years, but I was feeling incomplete and had a deep yearning in my soul to get back to the kids. There was a crisis with childhood obesity and diabetes and many of my client's children were overweight, unhealthy, and living a very sedate life of watching tv and playing video games. Although the excitement of training the rich, famous and powerful was gratifying, I had to answer the call in my heart and take my positive energy and light to the kids.

My best friend William and I decided to take the plunge and start a new business that focused on the health and well-being of our youth. We developed a Kids Health and Fitness Assembly for Elementary Schools which includes the F.U.N. approach to a healthy lifestyle. (F is fitness made fun. U is uplifting and inspirational and N is nourishment and nutrition.) This school assembly embodies the energy of a huge rock concert, 400 kids at a time hula hooping, playing their favorite songs, and learning all of the latest dance moves. We also cover subjects such as anti-bullying, climate crisis, and cleaning up the earth. It took us an entire summer to hand-make every hula hoop and we spent our entire life savings on materials. We knew we had something special, but we ran into financial problems when we had to rent a van, a stage, and storage for our hoops for every assembly. We were running out of money. We just couldn't catch a break. We had pushed ourselves to a point of exhaustion and were about to give up when a voice in my head said, "Last resort before you give up. Just ask your parents for help." I fought that thought and felt that asking for help would indicate failure. Was I going to let my fear and ego stop me from my dreams coming true because I was too afraid to ask for help? Was I scared of being rejected or seen as being a loser? Little did I know that my parents were watching my struggles and wanted to help but didn't want to seem like they were interfering. Finally, I swallowed my pride and called my parents and when I asked, they responded with "we have wanted to help you since you started and be part of your journey to help the kids!" My heart opened up in gratitude to my wonderful parents.

William and I found a good used van for $4000 and named her "Savanna Van-Geaux" and she became our greatest asset and blessing. We loaded her up with 400 hand-made bright-colored hula hoops, stage, sound equipment, and Hoopitup Worldwide was launched.

It's been 10 years and we have gone to thousands of schools and have reached over 2 million children throughout America. We learned how to incorporate the hoops, dance, and exercise to uplift and empower kids and encourage them towards a healthy lifestyle. We also implement powerful messaging about being kind, anti-bullying, and self-esteem. We have been successful in touching the hearts of many kids, teachers, principals, and school workers. We have had the honor of performing at the White House for the Easter Egg Roll with Michelle Obama's "Let's Move" initiative and performed with Disney actors at The Window Between Worlds Benefit for Abused and Battered Women and Children. We received "The Call to Action Award and

Lifelong Achievement Award" from President Barack Obama. We have been voted California's #1 Health and Fitness Assembly for Elementary Kids and have no plans to stop this beautiful journey of empowering America's future population. We average about 5000 high fives a week from the most amazing kids and our hearts are always overflowing with joy.

We've made it a tradition to call my 85-year-old parents on the way to every assembly to hear the excitement in their voices knowing they are a part of helping America's children live a happier and healthy life.

I am forever grateful for my awesome business partner William, my adorable and loving parents, and for Robbie Motter giving me the strength to let go of my pride and just ASK.

Kelly Breaux
Founder of Hoopitup Worldwide

Silent Requests

Angela Covany

A s I pondered the writing of this chapter, a lot of feelings and emotions began to surface. I was reluctant to contribute at first and decided after being ASKED several times to share from my heart,

The INCREDIBLE POWER FOUND IN THE ASKING. I have not been one to "Ask" for much but, I have been blessed with more than I have asked for. My mother once told me that my first complete sentence was "I can do it myself mom."

As life progressed from childhood till the present, I have learned it is okay to ask. I have learned it is also okay to receive. I have learned to not deprive others of the joy found in giving or contributing. I believe that for someone who gives freely from the heart with no expectation, these are important lessons one must learn.

MY FIRST ASK

Early one morning at the age of 9, I was awoken to the sound of loud screaming outside my bedroom door. My Uncle Monte was screaming my mothers name. All I heard was "Deborah come back to me!" repeatedly. I got out of bed and rushed to the door. Upon opening the door, I seen my Uncle standing up hugging my mother who was soaking wet and wrapped in a blanket. She was a bit lethargic but alive.

My Aunt quickly pulled me into another room and consoled me. She told me in many ways that my mother would be alright. My mother was taken to the hospital and stayed for several days. I was an only child, so I was very scared. Prior to this time period, my mother had taught me to take all things to prayer. I prayed my mom would live and be my mom forever.

After a few days she returned home but she was incredibly sad and did not talk much. I kept asking her "What happened?" no response. "Why are you so sad?" no response. She simply refused to speak and cry instead. This made me extremely sad. My mother was always the most optimistic, positive, selfless, and loving woman that smiled in the face of all adversity. When things did not playout as planned, she would step forward in faith. No matter what chaos happened she faced it almost fearlessly.

One morning about a week or so after the "event", she finally decided to ask me to sit with her.

She said, "I need to tell you something and you're not going to like it!" Tears rolled down her beautiful face. She began again crying hysterically, so much so that I could barely understand what she was trying to tell me. Through the muttering and tears she said to me "The doctors told me the day before I went in the hospital that I'm going to die, and I have less than 6 months to live." She told me she never wanted to leave me, and we cried and hugged for what felt like hours. After some time, she wiped her tears and said, "I love you more than life itself and what we are going to do is enjoy everyday together." She made me promise her that day that we would make the most out of life and our time together.

I think we both went through quite a bit of shock for the next few weeks. She began to constantly assure me with the phrase, "I know what the doctors say but my God is in control." My First important "ASK" began. Every night, before I slept, I thanked God for another day with her and asked for at least one more. I am positive that she prayed the same prayer. Due to the fact we both thought we had an extremely limited amount of time together, we truly got to know one another.

Looking back on my childhood, I felt like a "human sponge". She wanted to share everything she knew with me and share all knowledge she could provide me with. We would talk for hours each day about everything and anything. She taught me how to cook at an early age which developed into a passion. Through all the years of counseling, I decided to pursue art rather than talking which is another passion of mine. Words cannot describe the gratitude I have always retained for having such a wonderful mother that guided me in this life. She taught me how to be a good mother, a good woman and a good friend. She was my best friend.

My mother transitioned twenty days after my 21st Birthday. Our "ASKS" were heard each night for over 12 years. I am a firm believer that there is POWER in PRAYER. I also know for certain, that there is incredible POWER IN THE ASKING!

FOREVER FRIENDS

After all the years of pursuing art as therapy for myself, I decided to put together a compilation of 30 abstract pictures others could color. This way it could help others in a therapeutic way. On my Birthday 2016, SILVER LINING ABSTRACTS was published through Bluestar Press. I was so excited to be able to inspire my children as an example of chasing one's dreams until they come into fruition. I decided shortly after the books release that I would self-promote my book, in addition to the marketing that would come from my publisher. I went to many places to sell my books. My children Matthew and Natalia even woke up at 5:00 am to go with me to one event. I love my supportive children. One day in July, my beautiful daughter Madison helped me set up my vendor booth at an event in Temecula. She brought Blue balloons in the shape of stars as a surprise for me. I am so blessed. On that day, a man dropped off a business card for website design. Although I did not need website design, I decided to call to thank him for reaching out and ask him about the other services he offered. The following day I received a phone call from Gary Hawthorne, the man who left me the business card. He said, "I know a lady that I think you should meet." He informed me of a women's networking lunch meeting I should attend. At this point in my life, I had focused more on my family than myself or career. In doing so, I did not make time to extend myself many places to make friends. I had a handful of great friends, that have been my friends for many years and did not feel that I needed any more. My life felt complete. I felt happy with what I had. My mother had told me growing up, "If you make five authentic genuine friendships in your life, consider yourself blessed because a lot of people never do."

Well, I decided to JUST SHOW UP! Walking into a room filled with like minded women was the start of a completely new chapter of my life personally and professionally. I easily made friends with more women, that genuinely cared for other women. No competition, only collaboration. It seemed somewhat surreal. I know that day was a pivotal divine interaction in my life. I have been able to meet the most amazing dynamic women. I have learned so much and made quite a few FOREVER FRIENDS.

The greatest treasure that came out of that meeting was finding THE RARE JEWEL, MS. ROBBIE MOTTER. We have been friends now for over 4 years. She has been an inspiration, a mentor, a forever friend and a beautiful addition to my life. Her love and light extend outward in a magnitude of ways. Every once a while, I believe I have seen a sparkle in her eyes, on more than one occasion. I am truly honored to have her on my journey. Her mantra of "JUST SHOW UP" rings in my head each time I contemplate showing up, where I have been invited. I am always glad when I "SHOW UP" to see the beauty, in what showing up transpires into my life.

It's All about Showing Up

The Benefits of Adding
S.A.L.T. To Your Plate

Caprice Crebar

Robbie Motter's message to "show up and ask" is something I have been doing since I was a young girl. At some point in my life I was taught that if you don't ask, the answer is always no. "Ask away!" I must have told myself. I am quite sure I was a four-year old kid who asked questions at nauseum!

I was truly blessed to grow up in the Chicago area, and in a community where there were no fence lines. Neighbors often gathered for garage sales and block parties, we borrowed eggs and sugar in our pajamas, and huddled in basements together during tornado watch. We later moved to the beautiful Northern California Bay Area.

My parents are positive people. My dad is a former FBI agent, a dedicated family man and gardener. My mom comes from a large Hispanic family, a homemaker whose hobbies include singing in choirs, crafting and spreading joy. They both instilled the love of music in us. My brothers were in garage bands. I played classical and jazz piano in high school and accompanied church choirs. Like a lot of kids in our community, my brothers and I spent most weekends playing a variety of intramural sports.

I was comfortable around a lot of people my entire life. Because of this, I learned that I could be heard and have a better likelihood of getting what

I wanted by being brave enough to use my voice and ask. This philosophy served me well in childhood when I showed up to welcome new neighbors and establish new friendships. I was always a people person and felt that a smile or a wave could brighten someone's day. This is how I began showing up for people at a young age and asking if I could be of help to them. Focusing on serving others first has led to many opportunities for me as well. Sending positive energy always returns like a boomerang.

At every stage of my life, I have stayed curious. This curiosity drives me to show up, to ask, and learn. I continue to show up on educational calls, podcasts, team events, and seminars. Almost every day I show up in some form or fashion. I believe in being a life-long learner, and that if you are not learning, you are not growing. The power of showing up and asking is turning what I learn into action. I applaud anyone who shows up and asks. It is what you do with the answer that makes all the difference in the world. As the saying goes "knowledge is power," though I extend that further by saying "power is action."

Even though I consider myself a people person, I am not always comfortable showing up and asking. It depends on the subject matter and the person, right? There have been times when I thought of someone who could benefit from my products and services and hesitated, wondering what they would think of me when I asked. Maybe they would think I was trying to sell them something for personal gain. Maybe I pre-judged them as someone who wouldn't give me the time of day, was too busy, or couldn't afford it. Maybe I was just afraid of the "NO" that I might get.

The only fears we are born with are fear of falling and fear of loud noises. Fear is a learned behavior. That is why my four-year old self wasn't afraid to ask questions at nauseum! Over time, I learned that fear is in my own head and never to pre-judge anyone. Thanks to the brave acts of showing up to ask people on my "chicken list" if they were open, the health of many who said "YES" has been positively impacted! If you don't ask, the answer is always "NO".

I showed up to an event years ago where a neuroscientist was speaking. I am so glad I did because she taught me something about fear that I carry around in my life toolbox. Often people say "Conquer your fear! Be fearless and just do it!" Some will advise "Get over yourself and have no fear." She taught me that you GET to face your fear, though you do not immediately become fearless. You will "Fear LESS" each time you attempt that action until eventually it is comfortable for you. It literally re-wires your brain as you continue to stretch it out of your comfort zone until your comfort zone is bigger! Once I recognized that I could chip away at the fear, until one day that fear transforms into comfort, it became easier for me to show up and ask.

There have been times in my personal and professional life when I felt shame, guilt and tension that required showing up to ask for clarity and understanding ("rumbling" as Brene Brown would say). Most of the time this process uncovered stories that I made up in my head based on perception, not reality. When I am brave and show up to initiate what usually feels like a scary discussion, it always feels better and improves relationships. Throughout life, one of the most important reasons to "show up and ask" is for our relationships.

I view showing up and asking like stepping through a door of opportunity to better oneself and serve others. We are experiencing this in our communities at a time when understanding, bettering ourselves and serving others is paramount. I believe everyone has many doors of betterment and greatness to step into if they can work on being brave enough to Show up, Ask, Learn and Take action (acronym to remember: S.A.L.T). Adding a good quality S.A.L.T. to whatever is on your plate will usually change what is on it for the better!

I approach differences among people this way. I think our world would be a far better place, and we could become more unified if people made a greater effort to show up and ask for understanding. Everyone has a unique story. There is no life that is exactly the same. Human belief systems are formed based on life experience. We can show up for that person, listen, understand, and have more compassion for one another even if we have different viewpoints. Showing up and respectfully asking WHY someone feels the way they do, and without judgement, can impact people and their beliefs in such a positive way that creates change and brings them closer together.

I see how S.A.L.T. spiced up my life and led me to where I am today. My courage to show up and ask has created leadership opportunities, landed me jobs, allowed me to learn and grow in ways I would never have been able to.

At California State University, Sacramento, studying marketing and communication, I showed up to ask for information about communication clubs and found none. As a result, I founded The Organizational Communications Association. I showed up to serve others by giving students opportunities to build relationships with like-minded students and enhance communication that could help them achieve business success. I showed up and asked business and community leaders to be guest speakers to teach communication and networking skills to OCA members. In the process, I learned so much!

When I showed up to ask about internships, I was fortunate to have been met with an opportunity to work in the marketing department of the earliest wireless phone company, PacTel Cellular, which launched my career in sales and marketing.

When I showed up at events to learn more about health and wellness, I found myself in my dream career which allows me to show up and serve others every day!

When I showed up for my son's music career, I then taught HIM the value of showing up to seize every opportunity. He is rarely without one!

In 2011, when I showed up with him to stand in line with thousands of people auditioning for the X Factor, he had an experience of a lifetime reaching the top 200. The best outcome was the lasting musical friendships he made along the way.

The relationships you build by showing up, initiating a conversation and being interested in what another person has to say, is the greatest gift of all. Someone once taught me to be more interested than interesting. This philosophy has paid huge dividends.

You can probably tell that I love quotes. I would like to take a moment to thank my dad for that. He often encouraged me by posting an inspiring quote on my bulletin board or sending an inspiring quote with my rent check in college. When I landed my first career job, I thanked him for helping me get there by returning a quote he had sent to me. It is the epitome of what happens when you have the vision, the will, and the bravery it takes to S.A.L.T. "To dream anything that you want to dream, that is the beauty of the human mind, to do anything you want to do, that is the strength of the human will, to trust yourself to test your limits, that is the courage to succeed." – Bernard Edmond.

14 years ago, when I showed up to my first Heart Link women's networking meeting, I asked myself "Is this something I could do?" My answer was "I think I can." I called Heart Link Network founder, Dawn Billings to ask how I would do this. I had my own chapter the next day!

As my friend Kerry always says, "JUST JUMP!" That is the "taking action" part of S.A.L.T. Since I responded YES to my own question, and then took action, the course of my life entirely changed as I grew into a community leader supporting female entrepreneurs. Doing so also gave me a larger platform to be able to educate and impact peoples' health. What I did not realize then was how enriched my life would become by having had the opportunity to know and learn from women in the Heart Link Network sisterhood. All of this came from stepping out of my comfort zone, showing up to a meeting where I knew no one, asking myself, and then asking Dawn Billings how to create a Heart Link community of my own. I am grateful to Dawn for giving me the opportunity to show up and ask to become a Heart Link Network leader.

When I started my Heart Link Network group I showed up to events and asked people to come. I showed up on Facebook and Meetup where female entrepreneurs hang out and asked them to attend. When people attended, I asked them to invite friends. When I showed up with a Facebook community, I asked them to join and engage. The benefits of showing up and asking has continued to grow a sisterhood that consistently brings value to thousands of women.

For years I have coached my teams, and my Heart Link community on the importance of creating opportunities to be more visible so they can add more value for more people. When the music industry started to use social media, I showed up and learned primarily to help my son's music career. I asked social media experts how to do it right. When businesses began leveraging Facebook and Instagram, I paid attention, showed up and asked how to make it work for business. When Facebook LIVE became a tool, although I felt uncomfortable, I showed up to ask how to do it, and did. Now I show up on Facebook Live weekly and coach others on Facebook strategy.

More recently, due to coronavirus keeping us from gathering in person, helping entrepreneurial women VIRTUALLY become more visible, vocal and valuable became my goal. Familiar with Zoom, having used it in my business for years, I immediately took Heart Link Network meetings online and created ways to add more value for the women who participate.

I feel fortunate that I had already built a strong Facebook community, where members can plug in, build relationships and be visible between meetings. Now we get to livestream networking meetings into our Facebook community, which generates hundreds more exposures for participants all over North America. The members who have consistently showed up, asked, learned, and taken action, have had tremendous growth both personally and professionally.

Take a few minutes to dig deep into your memory bank and think about a time when you used S.A.L.T. on your plate. Did you show up because you wanted to? Did you show up when you didn't feel like it? Think about your experience because you showed up. Did you learn something? Did you ask someone about themselves? Did you ask for help or did you ask to give? Did you take action on something as a result of being there? Did anything change for you, or for someone else because you were there? I bet my last dollar it did.

Step into your greatness by adding more S.A.L.T. to life's plate. It will spice up your life, make everything on it better, and allow you to make a greater impact for more people!

I specialize in connecting female entrepreneurs with community, relationships, and resources to improve the health of their business and their life and offer coaching on Networking, Marketing, Social Media Strategy and Nutritional Solutions for Personal Well Being.

My Angels On Earth Have Given Me Magical Authentic Connections!

Marcy Decato

I was born and raised in Manizales, Colombia in 1966. I have always been blessed to be surrounded by amazing people, have a family who loves me, and I adore, I have life-time friends from school, college, and childhood. When I came to America in 1987, I met people who now I consider my family, and the list goes on. It seems like God continues to place angels on my path that have given me magical authentic connections.

There have been angels placed on earth to get me to where I am today. Not diminishing the importance of the rest of the people around me, everyone is important and has a place in my heart, but I think these individuals have in one way or another steered my wheel in a specific direction:

1. **My Angels of Love:** My parents, Carlos and Norma, of course, and not for the obvious, but because their influence and unconditional love raised me to be the person I am today. So many of my big decisions in life were made so that I wouldn't disappoint them. One of the most important things I learned from them was responsibility, *"get up, show up and not only to get it done, but to thrive"*!

2. **My Angel of Braveness:** My brother, Andres came to America in 2001 and we decided to start a business together. That was a brave and drastic steering, of the wheel which changed my life overnight. I left a high

position in the company, great relationships with co-workers, and a regular hefty paycheck and benefits. It was scary but at the same time exciting and fun to go on a business venture with a person who I love, trust, and admire. Unfortunately, it only lasted a couple of years because he decided to go back to Colombia. Although I was devastated, I had to continue the business myself. I became stronger and learned the power in the asking. I got involved in the local Chamber of Commerce as part of the board of directors and an ambassador. I learned to network and asking for business became very natural. My cheerful personality, my willingness to help the chamber and the incredible connections I made, helped me get tremendous recognition and the start of a successful business.

3. **My Angel of Generosity:** My friend and coach Matti Ameli was the reason I joined Soroptimist International of Corona. Matti was my coach in 2004 and she invited me to visit this organization, which rapidly became my passion. What a great direction in my path. Here is one example of the power of showing up. I never imagined that attending that lunch in February of 2004, Soroptimist would become a powerful engine in my life that moves my sense of giving to the community. So, I am always grateful to Matti for introducing me to this amazing organization, and to all the Soroptimists in my life, for their generosity, compassion, and love for women in the community.

4. **My Angel of Inspiration:** I met Ursula Mentjes in 2006. She was a young businesswoman full of energy, compassion, and positive vibes. Ursula inspired me to continue my business and to value my skills and knowledge. I showed up to all her conferences, trainings and mixers which inspired me to _NEVER GIVE UP_ despite my terrible financial situation at that time.

5. **My Angel of Connections:** One evening in 2017 I showed up to a Nafe network meeting dragged by my business partner Gigi Banks. That night we met Robbie Motter, what an amazing woman. She has become our friend, our customer, and one of our best business connectors. She

knows that I like public speaking, so she has opened the doors of many networks in Southern California to give me the platform to educate women in marketing.

6. **My Angels of Friendship:** I have so many beautiful friends and it feels unfair not to mention them all. They all play important roles in my life, but three of them have moved the wheel to get me where I am today. Seema Lechner became my sister, almost my mom, an incredible positive influence and has given me unconditional friendship. Paola Ringer, my sweet sister, with her sensibility, and compassion she has always offered the best advice and has always looked for my wellbeing. Finally, my business partner Gigi Banks, she is not only my angel of friendship, but of finances. She makes sure that we will have a secure future with financial freedom. I know I <u>can ask</u> these friends anything and they will do whatever is in their power to help and support me.

7. **My Angels of Solidarity:** I see these angels walking along and around my path. They hold hands with my Angels of Friendship, we have fun, we support each other and most importantly, I know I can count on them and they can count on me during difficult times. I have them classified by groups, my Coronians, my Latinas, and my Soroptimist sisters. In May of 2019, my husband Tom suffered a heart attack and had open-heart surgery with three bypasses. We had recently moved to a small house that he was fixing, so this house was not habitable in his condition. One Saturday before he was released from the hospital, a crew came to my house with tools, paint brushes, food, and booze. They were ready to paint, install appliances and clean. They made sure the house was ready for Tom to come home. What an amazing feeling to know that I was not alone during this difficult time in my life. *"You ask and you shall receive" Matthew 7:7*

8. **My Angel of Resilience:** In 2004 I was invited by Kathleen Moon to speak at the Corona-Norco Realtor's Association. She wanted me to speak on creative marketing strategies for realtors. I prepared a good presentation, I practiced, I had handouts, I even paid a coach to critique

and help me improve my presentation. But that was not enough. When the day came, I was extremely nervous, and even though I was covering a familiar topic, I sounded like an amateur. I didn't sound credible. Afterwards, Kathleen and I signed up for Toastmasters, an international public speaking program. She pushed me to learn from that terrible experience and not to give up on public speaking, but to become a pro at it. Well, I attended Toastmasters for 12 years! I loved it and now, public speaking is one of my great skills rather than a handicap. When you are an effective communicator, you put yourself forward as a master in your field much faster and much louder. So, I consider Kathleen Moon my Angel of Resilience, because she helped me recover from an extremely negative experience into a positive one multiplied by ten.

9. **My Angel of Ambition:** My business partner, Gigi Banks has made me want more out of life. One question she asks me is, "What do you want to accomplish during your lifetime?" I am not a planner. Thank God for Gigi and her excellent planning and administration skills. So, as our three-year-old business flourishes, I am ambitious for happiness, ambitious for peace of mind and most important, ambitious for leaving a legacy. One should not go through life without leaving a positive footprint. Since I do not have kids, I want to spread some good and my knowledge to those around me.

10. **My Angels of Support:** A reliable support system is fundamental to bringing peace of mind, especially when you live 4000 miles from home. The Duque-Gomez family back in Colombia takes excellent care of my parents. My parents, my brother and I call them our angels! Talking about the power in the asking and showing up, this family is always there when my parents need them, they are my extension abroad, and I can count on them to be "me" with mom and dad. What a blessing!

11. **My Angels of Culture:** Once a year I go back home, I spend Christmas and New Year's, and I stay for a festival that my hometown celebrates at the beginning of January. Being around my entire family brings me so much joy, it is hard to describe. Every time I land at the tiny airport in

Manizales, Colombia, I get emotional. My town, my family my friends, the culture, and its idiosyncrasies, all combine to make me who I am today. So, it is important for me to SHOW UP and to BE PRESENT, it recharges me to start a new year with clear thoughts and positivism. As I always say, *"America is in my heart, but Colombia is in my soul"*.

12. **My Angels of Motivation**: What is it that inspires you to be in business for yourself? Is it money, recognition, being able to volunteer, self-satisfaction, interactivity, spirituality, or maybe freedom? My motivation in business is linked to <u>authentic connections</u>, freedom, and self-satisfaction. I am not going to name one or two people or a family in this section. I get motivated when I network with women (yes, more than with men) and we all share experiences, knowledge, and business contacts freely. What's even better is when our authentic conversations include fashion, business, politics, hot flashes and even labor pains. I am in awe when I see a woman fearlessly go up on stage and speak from her heart, sharing her deepest thoughts and feelings. I am inspired and immediately identify that woman as a genuine connector. So, my angels of motivation are fearless, passionate, and authentic women, who <u>show up and are not afraid to ask!</u>

13. **My Angel of Self-Love**: This is me; I am my angel of self-love. This book is all about the power of asking and showing up, and if I believe that God has put all these people on my path to help me through life, the good, the bad and the great, I also believe that He has a plan for me to leave a legacy. I am probably some other people's angel, here to help them through difficult times, or to bring a smile to their faces, or to give some advice. So, I must love and take care of myself inside-out. <u>In this case the asking is within</u>, in my prayers and meditation. One good example is when my cousin Sue's daughter, Debbie, needed a kidney transplant and I offered mine. Debbie was extremely ill, and she needed to get better before they could even operate on her. Long story short, she died before I could donate my kidney to her. The question is why me? I loved her, but we were not that close. The family didn't ask me, but at that time, fifteen years ago, I felt that if I could help save her

live, I would have left a legacy, I would have shared something special which in return would have brought many more years of life to her and beautiful memories to her family.

Showing up, asking, and authentic connections, have been the common denominator for love and success throughout my path. These amazing angels that God has placed on earth, hold my hand to get me to the next step without falling.

I am writing this article on May of 2020, whether you read it a month from now, or ten years from now, you will know that we are living through a horrible pandemic. Coronavirus has ruled the entire world for the last three months. The way we connect, communicate, show up and ask is not the same as it was before. We have learned to network, to work and to socialize remotely. Zoom, GoToMeeting, Amazon Chime, Messenger and WhatsApp have become our vehicles of communication. I am not complaining, in fact, I think this is a wonderful thing among a tragedy. I am doing the best I can. I connect with my networks regularly – I show up. I connect with my friends and family – I am present. Gigi and I ask for business through Facebook and Instagram which is keeping our business alive – well, there goes the power in the asking!

It's All about Showing Up

The Decision to Show Up

Darla Delayne

I made a major lifestyle change a few years ago. I had just started a coaching business then moved to California. I was settling in and was deeply into online marketing, but what I really wanted to do was connect with other women entrepreneurs. I was concerned about reaching out; a Texan from New York City, new to California and just starting my business. Would I fit in?

My mind was in overdrive and I came up with every excuse to stay at home and work on my own, focused on my fear of being embarrassed. Those who know me would say, "No way!" because I'm outgoing and love the company of people. While in New York I was a heavy-hitter networker; never at a loss for words and feeling completely comfortable in crowds. And how could I not be? I'm also an actress!

Relocating to a new place was natural for me, so I asked myself what I was scared about. As a life coach, I knew without a doubt why I was feeling that way.

Our thoughts direct our actions and our thoughts arise from decisions we make every day based on whether we are focused on fear or love. In each situation these mutually opposing feelings are how we process the circumstances of our lives. There are variations on this theme but in the end, you assign your feelings to one or the other.

For example, when you focus on love, you may have many of the following feelings: contentedness, hopefulness, optimism, enthusiasm, eagerness, empowerment, freedom, passion, appreciation, joy, and happiness. When you live in fear, your reaction may be one or more of the following: boredom, pessimism, irritation, impatience, frustration, being overwhelmed, doubt, worry, blame, anger, guilt, shame, embarrassment, revengefulness, hate, rage, jealousy, insecurity, unworthiness, or hopelessness.

When you step into a new situation, your brain scans for prior experiences. If it remembers a similar situation it will bring on the feeling you attached to it. The stronger the emotion you felt at that time, the clearer the memory; the brain had made a clear path to and created the program on how you will react to that situation again. Your brain signals these emotions, your thoughts will match them, and the resulting action will be similar to what happened at that time.

For example, if you were bitten by a dog as a child, you were scared and even terrified. Unless you've had some positive experiences with dogs since then, you may continue to be afraid of dogs or just not care for them. Although you recognize that the dogs you meet as you walk down the street are harmless, your brain will send out signals that you're in danger and if you accept this feeling, then you'll believe that there is in fact a threat and you'll act accordingly. You might cross the street or actually run away.

The same applies to positive experiences. If you've moved several times and each place was nice and comfortable and you had some wonderful experiences, the next time you move, your brain will conjure up strong, happy emotions. Moving and change are difficult and usually hard work, but your emotions will deal with this and you'll do it all with eager anticipation of both the new place and meeting new people. Once again, your brain will have conceptualized the process of moving and defined your expectations.

These programmed emotions arise from our perceptions of our past experiences. They also come from what we've heard from our parents, from other authority figures in our lives or our culture in general. These thoughts and suggestions, whether real or not, when repeated often, become beliefs. Our culture bombards us with ideas every day that builds this picture of our world. When we're young people try to keep us safe and their behaviors can create love or fear. The things our families teach us about money, relationships, the environment, and people in general, become your truth until the day you decide to question their validity and decide for yourself.

So here we are each day, living our lives thinking that we're in control of what we do and say and of how we respond to situations, when, in fact, we have pre-programmed our brains to guide us based on our past experiences and beliefs. We scan the files from the past that relate to what's happening today and we translate them, providing the thoughts that we can apply today. It's often a flight-or-fight response that helps us stabilize ourselves. It might not be the right action, but its purpose is to keep us alive.

So, I'm going through my day reacting to my perceptions of what appears to be happening, not what's really happening, and I'm acting on the basis of beliefs I've experienced or heard about often over time that may or may not be true. No wonder I'm fearful so much of the time for no obvious reason.

The fact is that I can decide to be happy as much as I can decide to be fearful. So, let's go back a little. There was a time in my life when things were going badly, and I knew that in order to survive and take care of my children I had to make some personal changes. I decided that no matter the situation, I choose to be happy. I took note of the times I lived in fear, then decided to put myself into the driver's seat and took control. This worked for me and our situation improved.

When I became aware of the emotion of fear, I knew that at that moment I wasn't feeling love. I reviewed the facts and explored where my brain was leading me. Once I did that, I purposefully decided where I wanted to be and went there. This applied both to daily events and the decision to undertake a bigger leap of faith. Meeting new people in California was one such big leap, but I decided I wasn't going to be afraid and I was strong enough to overcome any obstacles.

I explored the fear, as if it was real. I considered how the women I'd meet would respond. Would they accept me? Would they judge me to be unworthy? Would they be kind or mean? These seemed to be reasonable fears, but I really had no idea and nothing that had happened before should have led me to think about worst-case scenarios. So why was I so concerned about the unknown?

The reality was that while my business was new in California, I already had years of experience helping women grow their businesses, create successful marketing strategies and fine-tune their mindset to successfully define and reach their goals. I knew that once these California women heard me, they would appreciate my skills and services. I acknowledged that I was good at what I did and had the knowledge, experience and skills to help them. I had to clearly define my story and believe in myself.

I got in front of my fears and stopped them in their track. I stopped listening to the fear and realized that I would soon be connecting with other women just like me. I was excited at the prospect of sharing with them my successes and failures, and in the process, we would be helping each other. These relationships would help our businesses grow. We win some and lose some, but that's life, isn't it? Being fearful of new situations and experiences is senseless, but we all feel this sometimes, and I appreciate that my childhood experiences have left behind scars, some physical, but too often emotional. I understand that my brain is locked into humiliations of being ignored or hurt in the past and was trying to protect me. But as an adult I know how to deal with such past hurts and decided that I would not allow them to impact my life today.

So, I attended women's networking groups, met and connected with a few very nice women, then went to a Chamber of Commerce meeting and met others. It was getting easier. I saw a very professional ad on Facebook about a Fempreneur Picnic in Orange County. The woman hosting this event was beautiful and looked like she had it all together. I admired her from afar and wanted to attend the event and meet her.

Oh yes, the fear kicked in again. I was nervous. Worried that I couldn't measure up and she'd reject me. Fear took the reins. I deep dived into these feelings, decided that they were ridiculous, took back the reins and immediately sent an RSVP to attend the picnic. I even invited a new friend from the women's networking group, and we both went.

Little did I know how showing up at that picnic would change my life and business. I learned that the host came from my town and had been following me on Facebook. She wanted to meet me too. She was very happy that I came, and we immediately made plans to meet for coffee. Later, at coffee, I learned that she had the same discomforts about meeting people and especially about meeting me. She didn't think she would measure up and I might reject her. But despite both our fears we both showed up. That meeting launched a wonderful business relationship that is still going strong today and a friendship that will last a lifetime. I met several other women at that picnic who became my clients, collaborators and some, friends. What if I had given in to my fears? I would have missed out on fun, friendships, clients, money and so much more. But instead, I went with my love and my truth.

The only time fear is helpful is when you're in REAL danger and even then, if you follow love and positive thinking, they'll serve you well.

The steps are easy. Be aware of your feelings. If there's fear or negative emotions, investigate them. Check for truth. Be objective. Analyze the data. Is it true? Is it false? Are you sure? Then decide from a place of love. You might decide to be content or hopeful, and after further analysis you'll be encouraged to take positive action.

This is your life and you can be as happy as you decide to be. If you want something and decide to go after it but feel fear creep up, decide to take back control. You deserve to be happy. If I hadn't shown up at that picnic, I and so many others would have been denied more success and happiness. Our actions affect others as much as they do us and when you act out of love you achieve so much more.

So now you know…and you can't unknow. It's up to YOU. No more blaming others or the past for why you don't have what you want. Notice how you feel, and you'll be on your way to living an empowered life and running the business of your dreams.

It's All about about Showing Up

The Magic In Showing Up

Virginia Earl

There are so many stories I can tell you about the magic that happens when you show up. Showing up is a huge factor in the magic but there are other forces that impact the outcome, like what we do and when we do it.

Some of the other forces include listening to our inner voice and intuition. Yes, that little inner voice that's there to guide us. Unfortunately, we don't always pay attention to it. That little voice and that gut feeling, *which is your intuition*, provides the five "W's": "what" you should or should not do, "where" you should or shouldn't go, "why" you should or shouldn't do something, "when" you should do it and, most importantly, "who" you should surround yourself with to achieve the success and the joys of life. These are the elements that give us direction and we might not always understand the reasons until much later when the answers are revealed.

You might also attribute the guidance to a higher power; God, The Universe, Spirit Guides, Guardian Angels or a combination of these. When we listen to our inner voice or follow our intuition, synchronicity occurs. This has happened to me many times and because I listened, my life has changed.

A business card that led to a wedding

In 1995 I was the managing editor for an international bilingual food and beverage magazine at Cahners Publishing in Des Plaines, Illinois. On my last day at the company, a co-worker invited me to lunch. We chose a nearby restaurant. The food was excellent, and we were reflecting on the many happy years we worked together. A man came by our table and very casually handed me a business card for the Tall Club of Chicago. I just smiled and asked him why he chose me, and his answer didn't really surprise me. He said, "You're tall and you might want to meet someone. The Tall Club is for tall people like us." The card was for a nationwide social club whose members were required to be a certain height, and I certainly met the requirements.

I told him that I was moving to California, he shrugged and said, "Well, if you're interested, you can call the number on the card and they'll put you in touch with a local chapter." When I got to California, I moved to Park Newport Apartments in Newport Beach and my life was filled with all the things change brings, a new place and a new job.

So, the card sat in my wallet for several weeks and I almost forgot about it. Making new friends in a new place is never easy, and I was a little lonely. So, I took out the business card, looked at it, and decided that I had nothing to lose by calling the number. The next day I made the call. The person on the phone was very nice and welcoming. She told me about their next meeting and suggested that I join them at a dance club near Huntington Beach.

I was actually excited when the day arrived. I had a good feeling about this. I wasn't alone for long. I saw a nice looking guy with silver grey hair, taller than me and engaged in deep conversation across the room. I watched him and saw that he kept looking at me, and without hesitating I asked my contact who he was. She smiled and asked me if I'd like to meet him. "Of course," I said. He came over and she introduced us. His name was Guy G. Earl, and I learned that his family was one of the oldest families in Southern California. We had a very nice time together and danced all night long.

At the end of the evening he handed me a napkin with his phone number, and, with a wink, he asked me to call him. I liked his style, but the napkin stayed in my wallet for several days until a little voice told me to call. He was very happy to hear from me and immediately suggested that we meet for dinner. Before I knew it, I was meeting his friends and family and to make a long story short, we were married a year and a half later in a small electric family boat called The Sweet Pea in Balboa Island, in Newport Beach. We had 20 amazing years together and a beautiful daughter who is 15 years old today. Sadly, Guy passed away five years ago. My daughter and I still live in the same house in Murrieta, California, with our wonderful dog Chaos, our baby.

So, my magical moment occurred 21 years ago. I showed up at this obscure restaurant where a stranger gave me a little black and white business card. I made a phone call, showed up at a dance, and my life changed. Miracles do happen when you are open to the opportunities that present themselves. You just never know when one of these magical moments will change your life.

The sign that I needed to change direction…

It was late one night as I drove north on Winchester Road in Temecula, California, with my radio tuned to a talk show station that I had never listened to before. I don't even know why I had selected that station. The host was interviewing someone about The Akashic Records, which is an ancient spiritual technique that goes all the way back to the period when the Pharaohs ruled Egypt. The topic was intriguing.

In Egypt, it is believed that people who could read The Akashic Records were highly respected and sought-after by Pharaohs on day-to-day issues.

Basically, The Akashic Records is a library in a different energy field that contains the records of each human being's soul since the beginning of time to the present. This library stores a compilation of every action, feeling and thought that every individual has ever experienced on Earth.

This intriguing topic was just what I needed to hear at that time in my life. A few days later, I told a friend about the radio talk show. He warned me not to think about it again and said, "Don't go there." Anyone who knows me, knows that if you ask me not to do something, I will do the opposite. There was a nagging feeling and my inner voice told me that a miracle was waiting to happen. I knew in my heart that there was a reason why I was guided to listen to that radio talk show. This was one of those moments where I was mysteriously and magically guided to my next journey.

As soon as I got home, I did a Google search and found on YouTube a wonderful interview with Ernesto Ortiz, the owner of Journey to the Heart in Miami, Florida. I was hooked and wanted to know more about their retreats. Deep down I had always searched for something that I knew was missing in my life. I couldn't let this go. I listened to that inner voice again saying that there was so much more than the life I was living. I just had to find out more and what God and the Universe wanted me to do next.

I called Ernesto and we talked for a long time and I liked everything he shared with me about the retreat and The Akashic Records. He encouraged me to sign up for the retreat and said that my life would change. I found myself filling out the application for a seminar and making plane reservations for Antigua, Guatemala. I flew to Guatemala with an open mind, a full heart, and great anticipation. I met with the retreat group and we all took a bus and a boat to Lake Atitlán. When I arrived to Villa Sumaya, I trusted and allowed things to unfold effortlessly, through the magic that was all around us. The magic of Lake Atitlán captured my soul.

I was attracted to the metaphysical world and to The Akashic Records because I discovered that this was not new to me. I'm an old soul and have been on this life journey many times. The trip to Lake Atitlán was exhilarating. Mysteries were revealed, new friendships made, and I was reunited with old souls from past lives. I discovered previous spiritual gifts there and again at a retreat in Bali, Indonesia. I'm ever so glad and grateful for these opportunities.

My destiny was waiting for me and I'm glad I didn't ignore the messages. It was my courage, determination, and strong belief in a high energetic field – a higher spiritual realm – that started out as a way to help myself, but that has gradually evolved into something bigger and greater, a real yearning to serve and to make a difference in people's lives.

There's a reason why they say that change starts within us. Our personal growth has a ripple effect on everything and everyone around us. Whether our own experiences have or not a positive impact on others, it's up to us. "Showing up" and the "power is in the asking" are important, not just for our own personal growth, but to help others. By "showing up," we are able to share the accumulation of our own experiences and feel empowered to help and guide others. By not "showing up," we are not only doing a disservice to our own personal growth but we are also doing a disservice to others as we are not giving them the opportunity to learn from our own experiences. We are all intertwined by our life experiences, and so it is our responsibility to help each other grow by sharing our life stories and the lessons within them.

Had I not listened to my intuition, to my inner voice, I would not have gone to Guatemala or to Bali, met my spiritual teacher, or followed my spiritual path. Seven Mystic Rings was born because I showed up and followed my inner voice and calling. So, listen to that little inner voice and follow it, and when an opportunity presents itself, don't ignore it because it may not show up again. If it feels right, go for it! There are no reruns! Pay attention to the synchronicities, to the signs, and seize the moment! Seize the opportunity!

An afternoon stop

We're pulled in different directions all the time. Sometimes the decisions we make are made on the spot without much thought. We just go with the flow. Always remember the five W's: who, what, when, where and why. That one decision that we make or don't make, what we say or don't say, what we do or don't do, can instantly change the outcome of our day and of someone else's day, as well as the course of our lives and of others forever. We make room for certain events to transpire because we are led by curiosity and a desire for new opportunities. The mystery of the unexpected allows for miracles to happen.

One evening in the summer of 2018, I got sidetracked. I was running errands in between meetings and although I was in a hurry, I decided to take a break and stop by Tonino's Restaurant & Wine Bar in Murrieta, California. The owner, Tony Saad and his family are like family to me. I always enjoy stopping by to say "hello", and have a glass of wine. That's what I did on the day that changed my life.

As I got out of my car, a very energetic and gracious lady, filled with a special spark, walked towards me. I felt the magnetism and realized it was a powerful moment. Tony came over and introduced us. He introduced me as a Clairvoyant and Medium. This amazing woman, Robbie Motter, out of the blue said that she had just mentioned to her friends inside the restaurant that she needed to meet someone with these skills. She put her intention out there; she asked and I showed up.

She was filled with so much energy to the point that it was contagious. At that moment she invited me to join her and her group for dinner, I immediately accepted, and I just went with the flow. Of course, I had other things to do, but my intuition told me to stick around, to listen and to watch the dynamics of this fun group. Thanks to my unexpected stop, I met some very interesting people and some of them are now my close friends.

A few months after I met Robbie, I became a member of the National Association of Female Executives (NAFE) and later on, a member of the Global Society of Female Entreprenurs (GSFE). It's been a life-changing experience, and it all happened because I decided to take a break and do something different. I took a detour and ended up in a new road in my journey that has since changed my life.

A funny fluke

The crowning jewel experience that I haven't shared much is when I was a new member of the Murrieta/Wildomar Chamber of Commerce. I really wanted to experience what they did and how they benefited the community. I decided to attend an Ambassador's meeting. I didn't know what the protocol was and I wasn't quite sure how often I could attend their meetings without joining. I attended a meeting, met the members, and introduced myself.

After the introductions were done, someone asked how many people were attending for the second time. I raised my hand. One of the leaders of the ambassadors' team asked the group, "Who would like to sponsor Virginia?" Someone volunteered and before I knew what had happened, I had a sponsor and I formally became an Ambassador. It was such an honor and I never really imagined it. I left the meeting smiling at the unexpected and surprising turn of events.

The decision to show up that day again changed my life for the better. I've made new friends and business contacts and clients and most importantly expanded my personal and business world. My businesses, Seven Mystic Rings and Translations Unlimited South America are doing great and I am so grateful.

Filled with gratitude

I am grateful for all the people in my life, my daughter, my friends, my clients, for everyone who has touched my heart, who has elevated me, who has supported me, who has believed in me and who has changed my life every day by just showing up. When I hear my clients tell me, "Virginia, you changed my life," it's a magical moment because I know that they are living happier lives with more clarity and purpose. They have learned how to release their emotional blockages and as a result this release has opened paths to other things to come into their lives. They did it by showing up and by allowing me to show up into their lives and become a part of their healing process.

The decisions I made to join these amazing organizations have come at critical moments in my life. I wasn't fully aware of the "whys" when it all happened, but I recognize now that they always happened for a reason. So, be open to change and opportunities and have the courage to step outside of your comfort zone.

As human beings, we can not go through life alone. We need the love of family and friends, a smile, a hug and to feel acknowledged and validated. When life gets tough and we get off-track, aside from the love and support of our family and friends, it makes a huge difference to have the gift of laughter and a childlike spirit. All of these combined, will give us the strength, the determination and perseverance necessary to help us achieve our purpose, fulfill our soul's dreams, and to help others along the way.

When we least expect it, the seeds of kindness and love that we carry in our hearts, can make a huge difference in someone's life. Moreover, what we put out in the form of thoughts, words, actions and feelings are all intertwined with the Universal energy that's all around us, and they will be replicated and come back to us in mysterious ways. So, it's important that we sprinkle compassion, kindness, love and gratitude as God and the Universe will reply in kind. This is when the magic happens. All we have to do is "believe," "trust," "ask" and "show up."

"Ask, and it shall be given to you. Seek, and you shall find. Knock, and it shall be opened unto you." — *Matthew 7:7*

— Believe —

Virginia is a recipient of the 2019 All Women Rock Award, an Ambassador for the Murrieta/Wildomar Chamber of Commerce, a member of the Global Society for Female Entrepreneurs (GSFE), Trusted Business Partners (TBP), VeriDiva and a former member of the National Association of Female Executives (NAFE) in California. She is also listed in Who's Who Among Hispanic Americans and Who's Who in American Women.

Great Things Happened to Me Because
I SHOWED UP and ASKED!

Sandie Fuenty

I first met Robbie Motter at a Menifee Chamber Mixer. I didn't know then what a great ride this lady would take me on. I continued to attend NAFE meetings and local events and our paths crossed often. We were in the process of closing my husband's 30-year-old business due to health issues and I now had to get ready to re-start my Mary Kay career again.

I had already reached Directorship, managed a very successful unit for 10 years and earned four cars. But at the time, my mom was having health problems and I wanted to be there for her and decided to resign the Director position but continued to work with Mary Kay. After my mom passed away, I got involved in my husband's business and helped him re-build it after the recession.

At one of my first NAFE meetings at a restaurant, Robbie talked about the young man who owned the restaurant and his generosity and helpfulness. Thankfully, it was a small group, and, for me, showing up was a bold move. I even put a 'goodie bag' at each seat. I got up to tell my story and what I discovered was a group of women who were of such generous spirit that it took my breath away. They shared their ideas and made suggestions to make me comfortable. They told me to stop thinking small. They told me to be bold and ask for what I wanted and needed.

So, I asked Robbie to introduce me to the owner, and she graciously did. I gave him a sample goodie bag and suggested that if he would like, I would love to come work with him and give one to every woman who came into his restaurant on Valentine's Day. It was very successful, and I was invited back to do the same on Mother's Day. Both days were a great success for the restaurant and a blessing for me. This happened because I showed up that day and asked. Within a few months, I met more than five hundred women and my business was flourishing again.

A short time later, I asked Robbie if I could help her with her annual Success Strategies workshop and she was so grateful for help. It opened more doors for me. I met many members and received Certificates of Appreciation from a Senator, the Riverside Board of Directors and from the President of the United States.

At that same NAFE meeting, Robbie asked me to write an article for the Menifee Buzz newspaper. I accepted the honor and today I'm still a featured writer with my Menifee's Beauty Buzz column. Robbie and I often talk about our dreams for doing good. We have talked about writing a book as a legacy to leave to my adult children and granddaughter – a book that would be a treasure chest of my memories and those of my relatives. Children would enjoy and learn from the past, and the wonderful stories left to me by their grandparents and great-grandparents, so that these stories won't be lost. A world that included outhouses, no indoor plumbing, coal stoves, and mail delivered by a train that rumbled past their homes. I have written that book and am in the process of putting the finishing touches on it.

With each of my dreams Robbie would introduce me to the right person, be it the magazine publisher or the writer who would help me with my book. I see Robbie often and I never fail to listen to her advice. She has an immense circle of influence and infinite energy.

Robbie loves gardening and the first time I was at her home I was amazed at her beautiful garden. She recently gave me some cuttings of an assortment of Geraniums. I love gardening, and flowers that began in a friend's garden are very special and always remind me of that friend. I have spider plants and aloe vera in my backyard that remind me of the NAFE sister who gave them to me. There are jade plants and money trees from an elderly couple that were good family friends in Orange County and are no longer with us.

It's because I showed up and asked and the wonderful people I met said yes, that helped me re-vitalize my business and re-build my life. The greatest honor came when I was asked to take on the role as Director of the Murrieta NAFE, and without hesitation I said yes! I served in this capacity for several years and now, I'm delighted to take on the new role of Director of the Global Society for Female Entrepreneurs, a 501(c)(3) nonprofit, of the Lake Elsinore/Murrieta/Wildomar network.

During the Pandemic of 2020, life continues, but we've had to learn new ways. I've learned to recreate my business and life by showing up virtually and always asking. Our GSFE Meetings are being held via Zoom and it is quite amazing how many people are showing up. We continue to flourish.

I'm delighted to serve, and you can reach out to me.

Success and the Power of Showing Up

Raven Hilden

W hat is success? How do you know when you have reached it? How do you even get there?

As a small business owner and CEO of a successful nonprofit (Valley Resource Center), I don't have all the answers to those questions. However, I can share a few of my insights, challenges, and inspirations I have experienced along the way.

It all started by showing up.

As a single parent for many years, I did not have a great support system in place. I worked part-time in a school district while my children were in school. I did not have the means to pay for a babysitter or have family members to pick them up from school or watch them. My time was very limited and so was my paycheck. I could not seem to find any resources to ease my situation. This also limited my ability to try new things and change my circumstances.

My default answer to new opportunities was always "no" because I did not have a babysitter. I was not out looking for change because it was difficult to find time. But my situation was growing worse and I was having a difficult time providing for my three children.

One day, feeling defeated, I decided that I needed to apply for public assistance. We had very little food and I had a 3-day notice to pay or quit on my door. I walked into a social service office and was denied benefits because I had a part-time job and was not homeless - yet.

That was one of the worst days of my life. I cried and felt so hopeless. I vowed to somehow get through things and when I did, I wanted to be able to help others. This started and fueled my passion for resource assistance.

Soon after, I decided that in order to have a different life with different results, I would need to make some drastic changes. I started reading self-help books, changed my narrative, and started saying, "yes" to new opportunities, even if I wasn't sure how they would turn out.

In my 30's I decided to take a leap of faith and attend college. I didn't have a penny to my name and was still raising 3 kids and working part time. I took out student loans and worked while my children were in school, cared for them after school, and did full-time schoolwork until the wee hours of the morning. I wouldn't allow myself to watch movies or attend parties with neighbors anymore. It was the college courses that taught me to think outside the box and evaluate my responses and role in my current situation. I asked myself how others were so successful and how could I come close to that?

I learned that in order to make meaningful change, we must let go of the things (and people) that are toxic in our life. We can identify those things better by aligning ourselves with those who help bring out the best in ourselves. This is the hardest step because we feel like we must hold on to things that we have invested in. It is important to remember that not all people and things are meant to last forever. Sometimes they show up as a lesson or an experience – just as we might have a fleeting effect on that person that we helped at the grocery store.

First impressions are so important. I noticed that not only did I not feel worthy, I also held on to a victim mentality. Yes, I experienced significant trauma in my past, but I was allowing it to keep me from moving forward. I also learned that in order to change my current situation, I had to do things very differently.

The narrative that I was telling others only showed my traumas, it did not reflect my strengths, nor did it give others a reason to want to develop a relationship with me. How could I expect them to believe in me when I didn't even believe in myself?

The narrative that I was telling myself was even more damaging. You know that internal voice that talks to you when you are alone? Or when you are having doubts or fears? That internal voice needs to be reformatted so you can listen to an even stronger voice. One of adversity. Past circumstances have no influence on our current situation unless we allow them to. Does this mean you are without fear? No way! We ALL have fears. We all make mistakes, and we all fall down. The strongest of people get back up again and again. We learn and we adapt by stepping outside our comfort zone and blazing a new path. This works for businesses and for personal challenges.

This doesn't mean that we become a different person. What it means is that we have learned to move forward. It also means that we choose to align ourselves with the good in the world and allow others to take part in our journey. This can be a gift for others. Wherever you go, whatever you do, you are still the same person you were when you were younger. We have the same fears, the same doubts, the same heart. Our qualities remain the same. The wonderful part of growing older is that you become able to share your voice and express yourself. Your thoughts, ideas, and talents are an asset to the world.

I was working on my bachelor's degree when I decided to apply for an internship at a local Senate Office. I'll admit, I did not know much about politics or the difference between a Senator and Congressman, but I was willing to try and determined to learn. I started at the bottom and showing up to that interview changed everything for me.

During that time, I learned more about how laws were made. I also met Donna Thompson, my first mentor. I learned of the local resources in the community and met some very influential people. I made it a point to learn as much as possible and absorb as much as possible.

I learned so much that I ended up working for City Government and for an Assembly Office. I developed great relationships with community members of all types, walks of life and stature. I also found more mentors. You would be surprised to learn that many people, regardless of their stature, are willing to help you along and teach you new things. If they aren't, they probably do not have your best interest at heart anyway.

In order to grow, we must consistently challenge ourselves. One of the ways to do this is to create a list of people in your community that you admire. Make a list of those people and commit to reaching out to them and having lunch or coffee with them. By doing this I have slowly changed my circle of friends and learned some amazing things! This is where I often draw inspiration.

The best part is that once I had some experience in the field, I was able to mentor others. This is one of life's most gratifying things. After all, the secret to happiness is forming great relationships and giving back.

Since then, I decided to follow my heart and open my online business again. This gave me the flexibility to spend time with my children while they were still kids and to explore my true passions. I had always wanted to give back and start a nonprofit to help others. I spent many years dreaming about it and what it would look like. However, I didn't feel like I had enough time, enough money, enough knowledge. So, what did I do? I kept showing up!

I met Robbie Motter while I was working in the State Assembly. As a Field Representative, I attended various meetings in the community and learned about organizations and community leaders. At the time, Robbie was running local National Association of Female Executives (NAFE) groups. I was in awe of her giving spirit and the way she was able to support so many women in the community. She had more energy than most people I know and a passion to help others succeed. I just knew she was special, and I wanted to learn more about her. I continued to attend the monthly meetings after leaving the State Assembly. This helped me realize that I could make my dreams a reality. The speakers at the meetings were a wealth of information and the networks were a great source of support when I felt lost.

Robbie's membership grew tremendously and since then she has started her own nonprofit organization to support female executives called Global Society for Female Entrepreneurs (GSFE). Not only did she expand her reach from the community, but she was now headed toward going global! What an inspiration! She has led by example and shows the importance of networking, developing relationships, believing in others and finding the hidden gems in any experience.

I worked on my web design business and things were going great. I learned that showing up is so important, but it is just as important to follow up. Following up nurture's relationships, builds trust, and helps to find your tribe. Your tribe are the folks who have your back, support your endeavors, and inspire you to be a better person.

This was the beginning of the Valley Resource Center.

The focus of the Valley Resource Center is to make an impact in the community by assisting people with resource information and providing services that are not otherwise available. On our website www.valleyresourcecenter. org there are hundreds of resources for seniors, veterans, families related to food, utility assistance, employment, housing, events and more. We personally assist and advocate for people to ensure they find what they are looking for. I never forgot how it felt to need help and not know where to find it.

The Valley Resource Center hosts infant/toddler food giveaways throughout the year at no cost to families in need. Every month we teach seniors technology at the senior center to help them learn to access resources online and connect with their loved ones.

We are best known for our work with veterans and active duty military. We support veterans in the community by assisting our local VFW's, donating items monthly to the Veterans Village at a local military base and helping others access needed resources. It can be very difficult to navigate resources and frustrating without an advocate. We even partnered with local organizations to fix a WWII Veterans flooring, paint his house, and obtain hearing aids so he can call his daughters again.

Our number one program is our military care package program. We support hundreds of people and units. We send each one a military care package every month for the duration of their deployment. What makes us unique is that we take special requests and do our best to ship the things they need the most. Boxes are typically filled with snacks, nutrition items, hygiene supplies, and lots of letters from the community. How do I invite prospective volunteers to get involved? I ask them to join us at an event – to show up!

Things seemed to be going well for a little while until I started having breathing problems. I was diagnosed with asthma but still struggled with fatigue, debilitating muscle and joint pain and more. It was scary not knowing what was wrong and feeling like I was so very sick. It was during this time that I decided that I would really regret it if something happened to me and I was not able to fulfill my dream of starting a nonprofit to give back to others. I took my knowledge from college courses, experience in the community working for local government and decided to go for it!

I would find out after many tests and biopsies that in addition to Asthma, I had a number of autoimmune disorders Sjogren syndrome, Hypothyroidism, and Lupus. Five years ago, I had no idea what any of these were and a Google search sure makes them sound pretty scary. Some days are very difficult to get through and others are okay. I have not had a 'normal' day since before the founding of the Valley Resource Center. If I had known of my diagnosis prior to starting the nonprofit, would I have gone forward? I am not sure. I do know that I am pretty stubborn, and I am not one to give in or give up. There are always excuses to not show up but there are also always reasons to continue to show up – this is your WHY.

Your 'why' is the reason you choose to do something. The reason you find ways to make things happen, even when the odds are against you. The reason you press on as an entrepreneur when others cannot envision your ideas. The reason you continue to help others even if you have been hurt in the past. The reason to move forward when staying still is painful.

My 'why' is the desire to be the person that I did not feel I had growing up. My 'why' is to be a positive example for my children. My 'why' is to inspire others to reach their potential to be the best version of themselves. My 'why' is to make a small positive difference in the world while I am in it.

My 'why's' were the reason I started the nonprofit even though I didn't have a lot of money, perfect health or perfect timing. I believe that action is better than inaction. I have helped numerous businesses start and I have also seen people with amazing ideas never start their business because they always find a reason why it isn't the perfect time yet. Don't get me wrong, I do not advocate jumping in without doing your research. However, perfect timing is not something that happens, it is something that is created.

The nonprofit all started with a website filled with resources. It was important to me to find a like-minded group of volunteers to help the nonprofit grow. Our team is the reason the nonprofit is thriving as they have a heart for helping others and a desire to make a difference in the community. They are the wind beneath my wings when things get tough. I also strive to support their goals and dreams in a way that inspires them. As I mentioned earlier, it is all about the relationships we create in life. With that, anything is possible!

So how do you know if you have reached success? Successful people strive to attain more, to do better, learn more, and when they reach a goal, they set more! Success is not a destination – it is a challenging, sometimes painful, beautiful journey that all begins by showing up!

SHOWING UP AND BEING FLEXIBLE

Nanciann Horvath

I've always believed in the need to be accountable, reliable, trustworthy and yes, at times flexible!

I'd like to share with you something that happened to me a few years ago. I was scheduled to speak at a large women's group for a newly formed 501(c)(3) group in Southern California. Everything was planned and all my materials and handouts were ready. The morning of my talk I got a call from a friend from the East Coast who was in town and wanted to visit. I asked him to give me a few minutes to figure out how I can do both.

Sure, I could tell him that I'm committed to speak at a women's event and I won't be able to see him. I could cancel my engagement, which I knew I would never do, or I could ask him to come to the event. I decided to invite him, and everyone was happy to have a man present. He helped set up tables and all kinds of heavy lifting that had to be done when preparing for a large event. He hadn't seen me give a talk and was happy to participate in the discussions that followed. He was so impressed he invited me to Alaska to speak at the PTA Convention. I was thrilled. That was a dream come true.

In April 2019 I was the keynote speaker at the Anchorage PTA Convention! The entire 4-day trip was paid for and I had the opportunity to meet the most amazing people and visit some of the most beautiful tourist areas. The dream came true!

My business is IMPROV FOR HEALTH. I teach and speak on the need for improvisation in our daily lives. I'm a licensed nurse, a SAG/AFTRA actor, a mental health advocate, speaker, comic, mother of two grown sons, wife, and community volunteer. I was born in Bethlehem, Pennsylvania. I Graduated from nursing school in Norristown, Pennsylvania, and then moved to Morristown, New Jersey to work at Morristown Memorial Hospital. While living in New Jersey, I took the train into NYC for acting classes. After a few years, I moved to the Upper West Side of NYC. I worked part time at an oncology doctor's office; part-time at Radio City Music Hall and did commercials and off-Broadway musicals. After living in NYC for a few years, I moved to Los Angeles to continue my journey into acting and nursing. I believe it was while I worked on the cardiac unit at UCLA Medical Center, that I started to see the need to use improvisation in medicine for people with heart problems.

I remember a young man telling me that he holds everything in, and that he often ends up in the hospital. As an actor, we are taught to use flexibility and improvisation. It's a skill that teaches us to think fast on our feet, adapt to changes, and be present for ourselves and others.

When we improvise, we eliminate negative feelings and create space for openness and positivity. One of the examples that I use often is being on a bus where someone accidentally steps on my foot. If I say "ouch" and they say sorry -- it's over. Imagine if we held it in and weeks later, we see that person and the hurt and anger flares up. They probably don't even remember the incident, but it has been eating away in us. This happens all the time in our family and in business.

By speaking the truth, short, direct and to the point, and handling the problem when it occurs, we avoid letting it fester into something bigger that we carry with us into every part of our lives.

Here are some practical tips to incorporate this into your day:

*Speak the truth using fewer words

*Repeat back to the person you're speaking with for clarification and validation

*Use the words YES AND, so the person knows that you have heard his/her point of view.

This takes practice, but like everything worthwhile you have to persist. It's like when you exercise to develop a muscle. Over time it becomes second nature.

Did you know that emotions can harm your body?

Anger - weakens your liver

Grief - weakens your lungs

Worry - weakens your stomach

Stress - weakens your heart and brain

Fear - weakens your kidneys

The good news is:

Love - brings you peace and harmony and strengthens your mind and body

Laughter - reduces stress

Smiles - spread happiness

Remember, Life is 10% what happens to you and 90% how you handle and react to it.

My motto is, "ENJOY YOUR MOMENTS" because that is really all we have. Each and every moment is very important. I have learned in my nursing career that we are here to make a difference and each day is truly a gift.

I'd like to give a big thank you to my fellow GSFE sisters and especially Robbie Motter who continues to encourage us all to show up and go beyond. I would also like to thank Angeline Benjamin who said "You can do this, write the article …just DO IT"

Without hope and encouragement, we are one woman. But, with the encouragement we get from others, we are larger than we ever thought possible.

If you want to try something new today and start enjoying all your moments, contact me for some *Improv for Health* and grow in ways you never thought possible!

Wishing you much happiness and success!

Now go **ENJOY YOUR MOMENTS~**

It's All about Showing Up

Showing Up with Boxes of Love

Lauryn J. Hunter

All my life there have been mentors who have inspired my passions and nurtured my leadership skills. Their guidance was the foundation to my "showing up for things I believed in". Many saw my passions and were eager to help when I Asked!!! The following three stories demonstrate how this has defined who I am today. Each story added to the next and my asks got bigger. I embraced the courage to ask, the bravery to follow through, and the power to act. With intention, I discovered that I could touch thousands of people's hearts with one random act of kindness.

I grew up with a single mom and realized early that I had less than some and more than others. My family demanded that I get an education, be kind, and if someone had less than, be of service. My grandfather encouraged me watch my words because language can build or damage relationships. He encouraged me to think outside the box, to solve problems, and 'ask' who, what, when, where and how something happened, and less about why. This was a powerful focus when working on a solution.

While still in high school, I learned about a local battered women's shelter on our street. I lived in Orange County, by the beaches in Southern California. It bothered me that these women and children had to live in fear and had to leave their homes with nothing and were without their basic hygiene products. I was active in two youth groups: my school's water polo/swimming team and in Girl Scouts. I was working towards my Gold Award and had to choose a leadership project. I thought about these women and children and wanted to help. I hit on an idea to provide them with toiletries. I planned to create boxes with signs asking people to donate new toiletries which I called 'boxes of love' and distributed them at local supermarkets, schools, churches, as well as my family and friends who donated items to fill these boxes.

The number of people who donated touched my heart. We added another dimension by writing notes to each person we gave the gifts to. My girl scout leader Katie Slattery, showed me how to prepare string bags out of donated material and we filled each with women's hygiene products, including toothbrush, toothpaste, lotion, deodorant, shampoo, conditioner, make-up, body wash, and so much more. I spent the year filling dozens of boxes and engaged the girls in my troop to help me make and fill the bags. These little bags were a symbol of hope and made an enormous impact on their emotional wellbeing. It felt especially good when I received the Gold Award for this act of kindness. Because I knew that my intentions were pure, the award might influence my peers to look for ways to help their communities.

Now, as an adult I'm blessed to have an amazing group of women to laugh, sing, drum and cry with. We show up for each other and celebrate birthdays and successes and weep together over losses. Sadly, we had a catastrophic event when two of our members were sickened one night when a man in a bar slipped GHB (a date rape drug) into their drinks. Some of us went home safely, but these two friends had cardiac arrest and ended up in the hospital where one survived but the other died. As news spread throughout the community, the grief and loss were enormous. When her birthday came around several months later, we talked about how we could honor her memory. She was in the middle of making a movie when she died. The movie was about skid row in downtown Los Angeles. She was an environmentalist, filmmaker, and model. After travelling the world, she became very passionate about the homelessness of people everywhere. I recalled the generosity of my community when I 'asked' them to support the gifts to battered women, so I decided to do the same for the women's homeless shelter in Los Angeles. This time I used the social media platforms to reach out to family and friends in my friend's name. I put the following message out, "Hello family and friends, we are collecting women's hygiene products for the downtown women's shelter. Please drop off your donations at my house or I can pick them up."

On the day of our friend's birthday, I invited the ladies over to sit together in the garden, fill bags, and tell stories about our friend. The collection was a huge success and we packaged many boxes of love. We filled dozens of bags and wrote beautiful words of inspiration and kindness on index cards. The next day, we went to the shelter with our boxes and the woman, whose name was Angel, greeted us and was blown away by the colorful boxes. We told her that we did this in the memory of our angel Hanna who left us too soon.

Years later, my 'ask' to the community was bigger. A dear friend of mine is an environmentalist and had just returned home from Standing Rock, North Dakota. She talked about the war like behaviors towards our brothers and sisters of the Sioux Tribe and was concerned about the children. People had come from all over the world because they heard the ask to defend the water supply on the reservation. As well, an oil pipeline was going to be built on their sacred ancestors' burial site.

Three groups of water protectors were formed. One group came to pray but were also filled with hate. Several native nations came together and were unified for the first time in their history. They were unified in their traditions and quality of life.

We chanted *Mni Wiconi* which means *Water is Life* and my friend shared an 'ask' that was made to her from an elder at the schoolhouse and wanted my help. The children were showing signs of trauma and their education had been impacted by the conflict and the harsh winters of below zero temperatures. Supply trucks were being stopped and nothing was getting into the camp. These families had limited supplies for the coming winter. I'm of the Cherokee tribe on my father's side, and I work as an art therapist specializing in children with trauma. When she asked for my help, it really touched my heart and I worried about these children.

During the next week, I would wake up at 4 am, not questioning why, but concerned about the who, what, when, where and how I could help. I came up with a creative solution and what happened next was truly magic. I searched online for hours looking for camping gear for zero-degree weather. I also planned to create an art therapy tent and decided that this time my 'ask' would be for children's winter clothing and art supplies. I collected hats, scarfs, gloves and socks. Once I realized that the cost of the art tent was more than my budget, I stepped out of my comfort zone and asked my community to help me pay for shipping the supplies to the children. I created a Go Fund Me account and posted daily about this community's needs. As the donations started to come in, I was amazed at people's generosity. There was plenty of money to buy and ship supplies. We filled Ziplock bags with a hat, gloves, scarf and a pair of socks per child in various sizes. We created bags of art supplies with everything from paper, markers, color pencils, oil pastels, scissors and glue. The Go Fund Me project was a huge success and now it was time to get on a plane and go to the reservation for two weeks around Thanksgiving 2016. Before we left, I had 'asked' the kids I work with at two elementary schools to write thank you cards to the water protectors. I collected more than 250 cards of drawings and messages of gratitude.

My mom Lorette Hunter, Kelly Breaux, (CEO of Hoop it Up) and I, flew to Standing Rock North Dakota. Nothing had prepared us for the violence we walked into. We had to drive over the local bridge to get to camp, but the bridge was on fire, and we had to drive two hours out of our way just to get to our hotel. We arrived at the casino just after a large attack where we found a group of people who had been on the frontline praying in a circle. When the organization (DAPL) attacked these peaceful protesters with rubber bullets and water hoses in zero-degree temperature, it caused many innocent people to have skin wounds, multiple injuries, camp cough and suffering from mild to severe hyperthermia.

So much hardship. My mom invited people to our hotel room for a warm shower and continued throughout the week. We learned more about the camp and the reasons they were there. People patiently waited to use the bathroom, with as many as twelve people were sitting around at any time sharing their stories as we distributed our packages and the children thank you cards. These cards of kindness affected them more than I anticipated. People laughed and cried as they read the sweet words and drawings made by the young children. They were so well received and so badly needed that we were asked to bring them to the local high school for the community Thanksgiving dinner was to be hosted by Jane Fonda. More than 4,000 people were at the dinner. The school gym was opened up to them all day so they could shower. The dinner was in the auditorium where our cards filled an entire wall. People feasted on dinner and the messages of love from the children. These water protectors were given the appreciation they so deserved.

We discovered that many donations were being stored and not used by the children. This upset us and we decided that rather than giving them to the schools, we would distribute them directly to the children. We drove around the three camps and handed them out to families. They were so grateful. We had been given an extraordinary donation by our sister, Alysia Gaye, (Medicine Flower), who, when she heard about the "ask", donated more than a thousand bottles of healing essential oils. We distributed these oils of lavender, peppermint, sage, eucalyptus, and wild orange. We would ask people what issues they were struggling with; sleep, anxiety, anger, depression, skin wounds, camp cough and we were able to give them the appropriate oil and explain how to use them. There was so much joy on their faces.

We saw how much of a need there was in this community, so we continued our Go Fund Me campaign and the money kept flowing in. We would purchase more art supplies and stuffed animals then drive around to distribute them to the families. We were so blessed to be going back to our safe and comfortable homes and knew that sharing our light and love would forever change us. I was so grateful to be honored with the Distinguished

Service Award from the American Art Therapy Association. This experience changed my perspectives and who I am today.

I wanted to share these three stories for the similar messages they illustrate of giving kindness to those in need and the power of the community "Ask". These stories demonstrate a common thread of struggle, strength, hope, empathy and basic human dignity. When you're 'asked' to be of service and give love to those in need, the experience will leave a permanent impact on the world, one person at a time. This generosity and compassion can grow over time making the next ask bigger and much easier.

It's All about Showing Up

Showing Up & Asking
Opens a World of Opportunity

Deborah Irish

The act of Showing Up and Asking are basic concepts and yet so valuable to anyone who wants to grow their business or grow as an individual. I have lots of stories about the miracles of Showing Up and Asking. I'm going to share 3, but this first story warms my heart because it involves one of my 12-year old art students, Nicole Marie Barnes. She was able to witness firsthand the power of "Showing Up" and "Asking" and she understood that power because we both took action together with amazing results.

One day during Nicole's private art lesson she asked, "Have you ever heard of The Pink Lady?" Nicole had seen the Pink Lady online and told me that everything she has is pink, including her hair, and she thought that it was pretty cool. If she had asked me about a month earlier, I would have said, no. It just so happens that my friend, Robbie Motter, is friends with the Pink Lady and had given me her book, "Get Up, Get Out, & Get A Life". Every year, Robbie hosts a Vision Board Workshop. I showed up to the event to create a vision board with like-minded businesswomen. Robbie had a case of the Pink Lady's books to share with the women at the event. Because I showed up, I was presented with a book that would end up leading to a very special opportunity for Nicole and myself. I learned through her book that The Pink Lady is an actress, producer, and motivational speaker inspiring others to live life to the fullest. She also has a full recording studio where she interviews other inspiring people. Her videos are on her website, pinkladypresents.com. I showed the book to Nicole and she was so impressed that I knew someone that actually knows the Pink Lady!

About a month goes by since Nicole asked me about the Pink Lady and I find out that I am being honored with an All Women Rock Award – Orange County, 2019. The event was in Costa Mesa, CA and would include vendors, live music, fashion show, keynote speakers, luncheon, and awards presentation. The Pink Lady was being honored with a Lifetime Achievement Award at the All Women Rock Conference. I knew I had to bring Nicole with me to meet her in person. However, this is an adult event geared toward women executives and entrepreneurs. Nicole is mature for her age, so I decided that I was going to ask the host and creator of the event, Carl Wilson of CD Wilson Events, for permission to bring Nicole to the conference as my guest. I called him on the phone and asked. He reminded me that there are no kids allowed. I assured him that Nicole is very mature for her age and explained that her Mother, Emma Malik, would also be with us. I also told him that Nicole was a big fan of the Pink Lady and how awesome it would be for her to be there when the Pink Lady receives her Lifetime Achievement Award. I expressed what a great opportunity it was for a mature young girl to experience an event like this. He agreed with that and said if she dresses and behaves appropriately that he would allow it. He gave me permission to bring her! Thank you, Carl Wilson!

I invited Nicole, her mother Emma and my Mom, Sue Padilla-Sampson, as my guests to the All Women Rock Conference. Nicole seemed star struck when I told her about the opportunity to meet the Pink Lady in person. I was excited too! I was excited to be receiving the award and I knew it was going to be a fabulous event. But honestly, I think I felt more excited for Nicole, because I knew that through this experience, she would see firsthand the power of showing up and asking.

It was the day of the event, June 29, 2019. We were dressed up in our fancy clothes, heals, make-up, etc., and I brought the Pink Lady's book, "Get Up, Get Out, & Get A Life". The room was full, but I spotted the Pink Lady right away. She was the only one dressed all in pink with pink hair. She looked fabulous! She was up in front. We were in the back. The luncheon was buffet style, so tables were taking turns helping themselves to the buffet while I monitored the Pink Lady and the crowd. And then it happened…the Pink Lady was by herself, alone at her table of 10. I picked up the book, handed it to Nicole, grabbed her other hand and said, "Let's go meet the Pink Lady," and we zigzagged through the crowd with excitement.

I could tell that Nicole was nervous and excited. How could I tell? I felt the same way. You can't let those nerves get in the way of taking action. We were prepared and determined to meet the Pink Lady and there was nothing stopping us. There was no time to rethink or second-guess ourselves. We took action and politely approached the Pink Lady and introduced ourselves. The Pink Lady was so gracious and kind. So warm and welcoming without any hint of being bothered that we interrupted her meal. She stood up and talked with us. She listened to me brag about Nicole's artistic talents and I got to share with her my passion for art and my Mobile Paint & Sip business. The Pink Lady noticed that we had her book and she signed it addressing it to Nicole and posed for pictures with us. (For your information, the book, "Get Up, Get Out, & Get A Life" is not a children's book. It was written for senior citizens and touches on adult themes. I gave it to her mother to keep until Nicole is old enough.) The Pink Lady was so loving and encouraging. Then she asked me to send her an email with both of our bios along with photographs of our artwork. I don't think we'll ever forget it. What a great experience Showing Up!

I emailed The Pink Lady our bios and photos of both of our artwork right away. A couple of months later, I received an email from the Pink Lady inviting Nicole and myself to be interviewed. Nicole and I were beside ourselves with excitement! Nicole and I had the great opportunity of being professionally interviewed by the very inspiring, one and only Pink Lady! We planned what we were going to wear, we talked about what we were going to say, and we dreamed of what other opportunities may come from this. There's no way of knowing what or where this will lead. We decided that we were going to prepare and then have fun with it. So, that's exactly what we did.

Nicole and I Showed Up to our interview and it was fabulous for both of us! We were happy and excited to see the Pink Lady again and being in her recording studio was, yet again, another great experience. Her studio has a sparkly background with lots of lights, cameras and microphones.

Prior to the day of the interview, I was told that there would be a slideshow of our artwork during the interview and I would not be able to bring any artwork to display, due to the studio set up. I brought one anyway, just in case. My favorite painting to date, is a total solar eclipse oil painting that is part of a triptych I painted depicting three different stages of the total solar eclipse I witnessed in Stapleton, Nebraska during The Great American Total Solar Eclipse, 2017. My painting was positioned slightly behind and centered in between the Pink Lady and I for the entire interview. I was absolutely thrilled that my latest creation got to be in the shot.

The Pink Lady asked each of us questions about our art and what inspires us. Prior to the interview I told Nicole that the Pink Lady would ask why we create art and what inspires us. I let her know that, at her age it's ok not to have a deep answer for these questions and it's ok to simply say, "Because I like art and I like creating". I explained to her that she is building her artistic skills and as she grows and matures, she will know why she is an artist and what inspires her. I told her that it takes a lifetime to be an artist because you are always trying and learning new things. The more that you experience, the more you will know about yourself, which leads to know-ing why you are an artist. She did great and was very articulate. I shared about my passion of creating art and my mission to inspire, encourage and nurture our creative side; spreading the joy of creating art to everyone I meet. Then I got to talk about my experience of witnessing The Great American Solar Eclipse of 2017. I get very excited when I can talk about my experience seeing a total solar eclipse! Being interviewed about it was fantastic! Afterwards, I thought, "when is the next interview" and "how can I improve the next time?" After the interview, the Pink Lady informed us that we could end up on KSCI channel 18, a local TV station in Los Angeles and Orange County.

Nicole had an art lesson with me the following week. She looked me straight in the eye and said, "We made that happen, didn't we?" I said, "Yes, all because you asked me about the Pink Lady." She understood the power of showing up and asking.

My second story is short and sweet, but still powerful. Robbie had created a group of Divas. Each Diva member chooses a title that best describes her or what she does. I am The Eclipse Diva. Artist was taken, so I chose Eclipse Diva, since I create fine art oil paintings of total solar eclipses. Robbie planned a poolside event for the Divas at a really nice hotel, including barbecued hot dogs & hamburgers, side dishes, snacks and drinks. Afterwards, we would have cocktails on the patio on top of the hotel.

It was a hot summer afternoon and us Divas were having a great time in the shade chatting and snacking. The pool was full of boys. Turns out it was a soccer team of 11- and 12-year old's from Simi Valley. They were in the area for a soccer tournament. Counting the kids, the parents and the coaches, there had to have been over 20 people in their party. When the boys were done swimming, they were hungry. One of the coaches asked us where they could pick up some food to put on the grill. Robbie brought plenty of food, more then we needed, so there was plenty of everything left over. We were finishing up, so Robbie generously donated all the untouched food to the team. The parents, kids and coaches were so grateful. As the hungry kids made their plates of food, the moms came over to thank us. We asked them the name of their team. They said, "Eclipse". I couldn't believe it! I introduced myself as the Eclipse Diva. It was such a cool coincidence and the moms were so grateful for the food and drinks, they ended up giving me one of their Eclipse team jerseys. We took a group picture together and I wore my new jersey for the rest of the event. Showing Up and Asking make a great team!

My next story Robbie hosted a fabulous NAFE Christmas Luncheon at a local winery in Temecula, CA. Robbie arranged for entertainment and the food was amazing, paired with really good wine. We were all in red cocktail dress attire and brought a gift for a gift exchange, for those that wanted to participate. I volunteered to help people check in and keep track of the gifts. It was a large event with around 200 women. By the time everyone was checked in, there weren't too many seats available, so I found an open spot, not knowing whom I would be sitting with.

When you have a business and attend a networking event, the point is to meet new people, build relationships and share about what you do. Being at a table where you don't know anyone is more of an opportunity than sitting with only people you know. We all introduced ourselves and talked about our businesses. I shared about my mobile paint & sip business. Afterwards, I went into my story about seeing the solar eclipse and how it became my passion to recreate what a solar eclipse looks and feels like through my art.

After seeing the Great American Solar Eclipse, I began creating solar eclipse oil paintings. I get very excited when I talk about the eclipse and I like describing my experience with others. I can describe in great detail what I saw because I relive it and see it in my mind's eye. At the time of this event, only 5 months had passed since the eclipse. I was working on developing a new technique to get the rich colors I had witnessed during the eclipse and had four or five oil painting studies I was working on. The colors of a total solar eclipse are so beautiful, and the corona is like nothing I've ever seen. I explained that any photograph they have ever seen doesn't really depict what it looks like in real life and that you can't really photograph a total solar eclipse. One of the ladies at our table, Aggie Kobrin, responded that she had lots of photographs submitted to her of a total solar eclipse. I correct myself and said, "You *can* photograph a solar eclipse; however, the photographs don't accurately capture what it looks like in real life." The next thing I asked was, "What do you do to have solar eclipse photographs submitted to you?" Aggie explained to me that she is the Managing Editor of the space magazine adAstra. Her quarterly magazine goes out to the all National Space Society members. Then she said, "If you want me to put your solar eclipse painting in my magazine I will." My jaw dropped. What are the odds that we would be sitting at the same table? You just never know until you start a conversation.

It was Springtime when I see Aggie again. A Reciprocity Tea in honor of all the members of the GFWC Woman's Clubs in the area hosted by Robbie. I was so happy to see her. I bee-lined it to her to say "Hi". She had flyers promoting the International Space Development Conference 2018. As it turns out, Aggie is the event coordinator of this international five-day conference put on by the National Space Society and it just so happens that it is being held in Los Angeles! This conference is held at different locations all around the country annually. And here it was, practically right here in my own backyard. When I told her, I was interested in attending she asked me what day I wanted to go. I didn't know what to say so I said anything that you offer me I will happily take.

Thanks to Aggie, I was able to attend a full day at the International Space Development Conference 2018 as a volunteer. I went with no expectations, but to be of as much help as possible, meet new people and enjoy the opportunity. I met some amazing people and saw some amazing space art as well as cutting edge space technology. It was a great day working the silent auction, but it was coming to an end. Vendors were tearing down and the lights dimmed. It's not over…. it's cocktail hour! My work was done, and I was able to mingle a bit. Then, Aggie asked us volunteers if we would like to join in the Grand Ballroom for the Governor's Dinner post meal awards ceremony with speakers. The keynote speaker happened to be the richest man in the world, Jeff Bezos, CEO & Founder, Amazon and Founder of Blue Origin. I had the opportunity to listen to Jeff Bezos speak about his dreams of space travel and colonizing of the moon and Mars. It was so unexpected, but there I was, listening to the richest man in the world share his passion for space travel. All because I asked and showed up!

This story has not come to fruition as of yet. I would spend another year working on my new technique and another year on my first triptych. I am confident that me and my art will be in adAstra magazine, the same way I knew that Nicole and I would meet the Pink Lady in person, by Showing Up and Asking.

New experiences lead to more experiences and more experiences makes you experienced. So, be prepared, then over prepare so you can soar when you Show Up and Ask!

It's All about Showing Up

Step Out and Speak Up

Rosalyn Kahn

From a very young age, showing up and speaking out was something I did naturally. People may say that they don't have time, but we make time for what's important to us. Experts say that personal growth occurs when we come up against a wall. We have two choices; to stay safe or to push through to the other side to the incredible opportunities that await us.

If we listen carefully, our intuition will guide us and block out the distractions that surround us. Let's explore some of the gifts received when we show up and speak out.

Messages on Life

I remember the times when I showed up. I showed up for my Bat Mitzvah when I was 12 years old. I was called up to bema (the synagogue podium) to lead the prayer service surrounded by my family and friends…all the people in my life who loved and cared about me. I thought about my grandmother who was likely beaming from the other side (too sick to travel). I remember thinking that in every celebration there's often moments of sadness. The lesson in that is 'be humble, don't get cocky.'

Today, a life filled with a bushel of roses is an exception, not the norm. That might explain my love of roses and everyone who does, are intricately connected. My dear friend, Robbie Motter, dedicates a day each week to tend to her rose garden. Every Sunday I share my garden's bounty with my neighbors. Every day and every moment that we open ourselves to nature's glory we are blessed with calmness. When there is so much beauty just outside your door, on the other side, what are you waiting for? Go see for yourself.

Appreciating what is present

I was married thirty-one years ago today. My dress was covered with a lace of intricate rose pattern. My grandmother was absent, and so was my younger brother, who couldn't make it to the wedding. Life teaches us to appreciate what you have and feel blessed. I was blessed by the two people I loved so much, my college girlfriend and my favorite cousin. They adorned the stage and surrounded me with their love and made the day even more special.

We are given lessons on how to live better. A job in advertising had brought me to Los Angeles. One of our clients was Drexel Burnham Lambert who was affected by the economic meltdown of the 90's. A co-worker spoke up about it and told me that I would be fired for working with them. In fact, she was fired.

Educational Battles

If tomorrow was the last day of my life, I would want people to remember me for the following: Rosalyn studied hard, but due to the job market for teachers, she spent one year as emergency credential teaching bilingual 3rd graders. She entered the field to devote herself to her love of children and to help shape their lives. She also enjoyed working with diverse cultures and speaking Spanish. She was later hired under the emergency credentials program who had a mentor from CSUN and another teacher.

Your success as a teacher depends on your ability to control your students. I struggled with this, but my understanding of children's needs brought much success. I was able to help a student who came to school with, what looked like bed sores, but turned out to be cockroach bites. He was saved from future pain when I met with his parents and by talking to them about my own experience with cockroaches convinced them to get him a new bed. Another young student's mother came to talk to me about her nightmares. By asking the mother a few pertinent questions I was able to learn that her husband had abandoned them. I explained to her that her seven-year-old daughter was feeling the loss and it resulted in nightmares. The next day the child brought me three miniature coca cola bottles from her Barbie Doll play kit. Then there was little Jesus who was one of the smartest children in my class. He was definitely a gifted child and he was encouraged to do more. These are some of the rewards of teaching young children, but these are just some of the stories.

One day, life changed. There are strict guidelines about inappropriate behaviors between teachers and students. One day, as the children were lining up to go outside, one child wouldn't get into the line and I nudged her gently to move her into her position. Word got out, and like the telephone game, the story was that I had grabbed the child and left bruise marks on her arms. I was removed from the classroom and was sent to the district office, where I spent days straightening out paper clips.

It was time to reach out to my network and change the trajectory of my life. Thirty people supported me and explained that I was not capable of doing such a thing. Letters were sent by the 5th grade religious teacher, my rabbi, colleagues from Toastmasters, the Salvation Army, family friend and so many more. Six months later I came in front of the Los Angeles Board of Education and was able to state my case. I explained that a child became angry with me because I didn't let her participate in the cheerleading program. They cleared my record and left me with a gift that I treasure to this day. It's a baking tool I use all the time. I learned a great deal from this experience that has helped me in my 20-year teaching career in both high schools and colleges. I'm writing a book entitled, "Flowers, Food and my Fury Friends".

Educational Success

I'm proud to say that because of my love of teaching, I got involved in politics to protect the rights of part-time faculty. There was a ballot that ignored the disparities between part-time and full-time staff. I became a fierce advocate and gathered well over 1,000 signatures to get this measure on the ballot. It failed, but in response to my fierce advocacy, I was awarded the Part- Time Advocate of the Year in 2007. It was such a special moment for me. My family, and all my siblings came out to hear me address over 500 people and tell them why this honor was important to me.

One of the greatest joys of teaching is empowering others to believe in themselves. A good example of this was when I went on vacation to Ensenada. I watched the majestic beauty of the blowhole, not the whale's but nature's own theatrics, as the ocean brought its mighty waves to create the force of volcano erupting and forcing the water to soar hundreds of feet into the air. I must have had mental myopia, as I wondered up the hill to catch my bus back to the cruise ship. As the green cape of the forest stole my attention I fell and fractured my wrist. What followed were two sleepless nights and long days on massive doses of ibuprofen. My husband wouldn't let me sleep it off. He came in to tell me that he entered the cruise honeymoon competition. Just like the "magical mystery tour" we became the instant celebrities and our achievement was broadcasted throughout the Carnival Cruise line. There was no time to recuperate. I just smiled and enjoyed the celebrity status.

Setting the Mark

After this accident, I needed six weeks to recover. The physical pain was nothing compared to the psychological abuse of my employer. One of the institutions had conveniently lost the voice message I left them about the accident and refused to accept my medical leave request to switch to a six-week late start. They denied my leave and because I didn't return to work in time, chose to terminate my employment. It's interesting how life works. Just a few days ago, I received a LinkedIn friend request from that same department chair. Did he know that I was now in a more powerful position?

Another school mistook my physical injury, my arm in a cast, for mental deficiency and cut my class load. Determined to return to teaching I mastered the art of writing with my non-dominant hand. At my first lecture, I told my students at two different campuses that if I could teach with this monstrosity on my arm, nothing could stop them from winning the school's intramural speech competition. I set the bar high and they did just that. Other schools and students followed, and today, though I'm not a forensic coach, two of my students are in the final round of competition.

Uncovering the TEDx

I get a lot of inquiries about my books, but I'm also asked how I got on the TEDx stage. This is a platform for people to share their unique messages with the world. It all began when I became friends with Thom Lenzo at the American Society of Training and Development. Thom invited me to a special event and suggested that I just come out. Little did I know that **showing up** would be like falling in love. This event left an indelible mark on my brain. I still remember most of the seven performances. I determined that day that I would get on that stage one day.

A colleague shared my road to the TEDx stage. We both learned that volunteering is one of life's joys. One line stands above the rest, **giving and helping others is the key to success.** As soon as I became the Operations Manager, for TEDX 2.0 Pasadena, I took steps to accelerate the process. I just kept showing up. I attended a number of meetings held by TEDx organizers. At one of these, I was introduced to John Bates who later became my mentor. He was a TEDx organizer and a speaker. I promoted myself to TEDx coach by inviting John to meet our speakers and to coach them. Once again, speaking up moved me from the background to the foreground.

After he coached the others, I said, "It is my turn". Indeed, it was, and two weeks later I was given my first opportunity to speak on the TEDx stage. It was short-term notice and I practiced more than any time in my life. I must have delivered it 23 times and modified it 18 times. I was told the week before that it was all wrong, and on the day of the event, I nailed the coffin shut and sealed the deal. In my talk, "Language comes to life" I describe how I prepare my students for the theatre and it's now one of the most popular videos on TEDx. Since then, I've given the two additional TEDx talks.

Speaking at my high school

I returned to my high school alma mater and showed up to give a speech, which turned out to be even better. My niece and nephew attend the school today. I shared with them that I was just like them and I wasn't the most popular and didn't have a lot of friends, but I made it. If I can do well, so can you.

Small acts on the way

I was humbled by the students who told me that they had nothing to live for and were considering suicide. I was there to help them. One student even threatened me so that the police had to watch the campus at every school I worked at. Another was when a lady came to tell me that her husband had left her and I looked for ways to help her, like finding local food banks. I'll never forget the note she sent me: "you will never know the impact you made on my life and helping me in ways that I could never imagine." And there was a student who wrote to say, "I want to tell you how grateful I was for your lessons in speaking that helps me in my job today. I work for the military and it is my job to bring the flags to those who passed on. Thanks for all that you have done."

The stories I tell here just barely scratch the surface. All of us are gifted and can find ways to show up and speak up. My talents are words, both spoken and written. Our intuition guides us -- if we will allow the words to come forth. Hopefully, you have learned how I showed up and spoke out and it will guide you to do the same and change your life.

It's about showing up

Aggie Kobrin

There are three occasions that stand out in my mind when showing up really mattered.

The first was when I had just started my own business venture and was very busy just keeping my head above water. A friend had to push me to meet her at a Saturday event. It meant that I had to miss my daughter's soccer game, which I didn't want to do. I had already taken time from my family. I really wanted to be there that day. But she was so determined that I did end up going, though very reluctantly. I was very glad I did. I met someone who helped me take my company in a direction I would never have imagined had I not 'shown up' that afternoon.

That was the day I got involved in a little film, "The Secret" which became a huge success. I met some of the leading voices in the motivational and spiritual space. I had the opportunity to work with some of the best and sadly, some not so good people. These were very exciting times for me and my business.

Another time, a friend said, "Come meet me in San Diego for an important meeting." I told her that it was late, and since it was Valentine's Day, I should be home with my family. "You can do both," she said, "come for an hour or two." I went, and this too was a life changing meeting, although I didn't know it at the time.

I met a group of people from the National Space Society, and since that day, they became one of my most important clients. I am totally embroiled in the space world, meeting some of the most incredible people, including astronauts, shuttle pilots, politicians, and the richest man in the world, whose direct line is in my phonebook.

Since that meeting in a hotel in La Jolla, more than seven years ago, I've been involved with a group of movers and shakers. I have helped organize dozens of events for thousands of people and they have entrusted me with the publication of one of the most critical space magazines. I have attended major world events and have earned respect in a male-oriented scientific arena as I watch, close up, the future of space travel.

My life changed because someone knew where I needed to be and made sure that I got there...whatever it took.

Recently I got a phone call from an acquaintance I had known only by phone, from a project we worked on for a very short time. It was another one of those slightly crazy media projects that I sometimes had the displeasure to get into. But this one was different. He described to me something that took advantage of some new and exciting technology. It sounded viable and very appealing. He reached out to me because the project needed my many well-honed skills. Within a few months, we raised seed money and created a media platform. We've amassed thousands of hours of content and an audience of hundreds of thousands who tune in every month. This is another space that's available for people to distribute content that informs and educates. The world is in an upheaval and new voices need to be heard. This new company can provide that platform at affordable pricing. I'm very excited about this because it not only offers a valuable service, but it also makes it possible for me to continue to help people make their voices heard.

I wanted to share my stories because our dear friend, Robbie Motter, has shown us that when we show up, things change.

Sometimes we're too busy or too tired to get out and meet someone, attend a meeting or just hang out with a friend. Home or the office is not where things happen. People make things happen. Most of us can recall when we showed up and the trajectory of our life changed. I'm not saying anything you don't already know... I'm just reminding you.

Show up with us if you're interested. It might just change your life.

Finding Opportunity in Chaos

Wendy LaDuke and Pamela Moffat

*"A pessimist sees the difficulty in every opportunity,
an optimist sees the opportunity in every difficulty."*

Winston Churchill

Wendy and I met by pure serendipity. We hit it off immediately and discovered we were both at a crossroad in our careers. After earning big incomes in the corporate world, we had both been working our tails off for start-ups with the promise of something bigger. Ah, the lure of a brighter future. Funding dried up for both start-ups and so did our incomes. *Now what?* There was no one to fall back on and no cushion. We either had to figure it out or…we weren't sure but thoughts of living in a cardboard box kept creeping in.

Returning to the corporate world was not a possibility. We were just too old. And we didn't want that life anyway.

At first, we had no idea what we wanted to do. What we did know was we wanted to make a difference. We wanted to give back. Then we started thinking about everyone we knew and their struggles. And we had an idea.

Everyone we knew was overloaded. Overloaded with responsibility, stress and anxiety. No one we knew was getting a decent night's sleep anymore. And with Covid-19, things just got a lot worse. And a lot more stressful.

We saw the potential in CBD and knew it could help a lot of women feel better. The more we learned, the more we were convinced that the right kind of CBD had an amazing potential to heal—to rebalance our bodies, realign our minds, replenish our spirits.

We didn't worry about the "how." We knew nothing about the business, had no contacts, didn't really know where to start. It was at times overwhelming. We didn't have a clue how to make this happen, but we just kept showing up until one opportunity after another showed up for us.

People magically started to appear to assist on our journey. It was mostly amazing women and some incredible men—many of whom had dealt with their share of challenges—who were so generous with their knowledge, insights and time. And through it all, our friendship kept us going. Despite late nights, lots of meetings, panicking while putting together spreadsheets we sucked at, and our continual search for the best CBD, we always found a reason to laugh and enjoy the journey.

We just kept showing up and good things kept happening.

We started Verdania Fields, a subscription box company committed to providing the purest, most effective CBD to help women find a better alternative for their health and wellness.

We found a seed investor—again by complete serendipity—and we launched our first box with three products: Anxiety Relief, Deep Sleep and Immunity Boost. We were lucky—again—to find a medical expert to develop these amazing formulas! We had tried more products than we care to remember before we found the winning formulas.

It made no logical sense to start a business during the pandemic and the economic collapse it created. But we kept going because we knew we could help people get through this crisis a little easier.

Now that the stakes were higher, we all yearned for the basics: A good night's sleep. A little less stress. A feeling of well-being.

And that's what we've committed to deliver. Every day.

JUST ASK!

Gillian Larson

"Just ask!" These two words may be hard for you to act upon, but you have nothing to lose and much to gain, and in my experience both people gain from the interaction.

"Asking" is the key to opening the door to many possibilities and opportunities. It can be a one-time ask or the start of a relationship that lasts for years. Don't be concerned if you get turned down. It really doesn't matter. The power is in the actual act of asking, and this rests in both the timing and the situation.

For me, an excellent example is my relationship with Robbie Motter. Our 30-year friendship and collaborations started with an "ask". I was planning a "High School Grad Night Over Night Lock-in Party" for my daughter's senior class and I needed help. I "asked" my daughter to "ask" her best friend to "ask" her mother Robbie if she would help me. She graciously agreed and the Grad Night party was a huge success, as is our relationship to this day.

It's important that you show up even when you're not convinced that you should do something or be somewhere. Just do it. You just might meet someone who can help you or bring someone into your life who can. I've found that many 'asks' lead to mutually beneficial collaborations and when they don't, it was simply the wrong time or the wrong person. So what?

You've lost nothing. When you meet new people, ask who they are and what they need, then ask if there's anything you can do for them. Offer it. So, show up, speak up, stand out, show that you care, and be remembered.

I've spent my life giving and asking but I want to tell a story about what happened when I didn't know *why* I was asking. At the time I didn't understand how many doors would open for me, and how much I would be able to benefit hundreds, perhaps thousands, of people… just because I 'asked'. This was an ask that took 8 years, and my showing up 20 times. It took that long for my 'ask' to become the right "fit". Timing is everything!

In 2000 I learned about a new Reality TV show, "Survivor," and an inner voice told me that I needed to get on that show. I honestly didn't know why, and when I learned more about the show, I didn't find the concept especially exciting. But I do love a good challenge and I liked the challenges it presented to contestants. What I didn't know was the tremendous challenge of getting selected.

As soon as I decided to do this, the next day I started my 'ask'. I asked how to get selected; I asked about what they expected; I asked how to create a strong application video; I asked friends to critique my applications; I kept asking questions of others and I kept asking myself what I needed to prepare. I kept showing up everywhere and I spoke to everyone whom I believed would help me get on Survivor.

I had a family to care for and I was working more than a 50-hour week as a registered nurse, but I gave this mission all the hours I could find. I prepared and sent 19 applications asking to be considered for a spot on the upcoming season of Survivor. I was rejected 18 times, but it didn't discourage me in the least. I was determined, and recognized that if I didn't keep asking, I would definitely not succeed; that every 'no' got me closer to a 'yes'. I also knew that the time I spent on the preparation was not wasted. It taught me persistence and I learned to deal with rejection without becoming disheartened. But most importantly all the preparation helped me become more fit and consequently improved my health. I was getting older and I wanted to be able to keep up with young people.

My unique quest was taking a lot of time but not money. I kept showing up and standing out to help build up my story for Survivor. I asked people to take my picture, and if they knew an agent or anyone who knew someone associated with the show, connect me with them. I put my photos and story on YouTube and called it "Gillian's Journey to Survivor".

More than 60,000 people apply every season and knowing that I still continued to show up and ask. In 2008, after 8 years of persisting, and after submitting 19 applications, at the age of 61 I arrived at an open casting call and all the asking culminated in being chosen for the show. The timing was right. They were looking for an adventurous granny for Season 17 in Gabon in Africa and they saw me as that adventurous granny. Luck is the intersection point between preparedness, opportunity and timing.

I can't explain what drove me on this mission, but it turned out to be the best path for me and I'm glad I took it. It didn't go as well as I had envisioned since I was on for only 6 days and eliminated by the second round, but I did lose 12 pounds and enjoyed a 5-week sequestered vacation. Most importantly, I've been able to use this incredible opportunity to open many more doors. It was all worth it.

When I heard those difficult words, "The Tribe has Spoken," meaning that I was eliminated from the game, the first question I asked the Survivor handlers was what opportunities exist for those who have done their time on Survivor? I learned that some of the contestants get together for fun and to raise money for good causes.

My flame in Survivor was extinguished, but the flame of what became the "Reality Rally, Fun for Funds" fundraising event was lit, and this flame continues to be mine and cannot be put out.

After spending 5 weeks walking 5 hours a day in the jungle training for a 60-mile walk on my return home I found an unexpected gift. While on these walks I started to ask myself, "I've just been given a great opportunity, what can I do with it?" I wanted to make a real difference and I recognized that I've been given the opportunity to do just that. The gift of Survivor.

The answer was that for me, the afterlife to Survivor was going to be better than being on the show. I was now an alumnus of the Reality TV world and a fan of this amazing new and popular genre. And I knew there were lots of fans out there. Just look at the tens of thousands of people who apply to get on these shows every week. I was fortunate to meet many of these people and knew I could do something with that. I came up with the idea of giving the stars of Survivor and the many other Reality TV shows, the opportunity to do something worthwhile with their "celebrity" status to raise money for good causes. I selected Michelle's Place Cancer Resource Center in my hometown Temecula which provides support for cancer patients. It was named for Michelle, a 19-year-old who found a lump in her breast and was told that it was just a cyst and that she didn't have to be concerned about it. A year later she was told the same thing. At 23 she was about to join the Peace Corps and during her physical they discovered that her "cyst" was stage 4 cancer. She fought the disease for 3 years but, sadly, lost the fight. While she had the love and support of her family and friends there was no one else she could turn to during her fight, and she felt alone. Her dying wish to her family was that they create a center to help others going through the fight of their lives. They kept their promise and established a marvelous center that for over 18 years provided cancer patients and their families with free services. They have served the Temecula area community and beyond and have provided support services, hope and love to more than 160,000 people. If you or someone you know can benefit from this wonderful organization, please go to www.michellesplace.org and just ask.

Reality Rally was born in 2011 with the help of hundreds of dedicated volunteers, including Robbie and many members of N.A.F.E. For 9 years, thousands of people have enjoyed 3 days of fun and raised thousands of dollars for this wonderful and generous organization. I owe its success to me having the courage to continue my quest to be part of the Survivor family… And what a family it has been.

For more information, please check us out at www.realityrally.com

And that's not all that came out of meeting challenges head-on. I learned some basic life principles and have had hundreds of opportunities to share these with audiences everywhere. "Dream it, Believe it, Prepare for it, and DO IT!" is a message I've delivered at more than 450 speaking events. It's a Survivor message that can be applied by anyone at any age. Many doors have opened to me since my Survivor experience, and I continue to organize and host many events as well as collaborate with The Gary Sinese Foundation with a Color Run, and the military. Now, at 73, my life is so much more than I could ever have imagined, and I owe it to 'asking' and showing up.

To quote the wisdom of Dr. Seuss, "Oh, the places you will go." He should have added, "**If you just ask.**"

SHOW UP, UP, AND AWAY

Florence LaRue

It was a beautiful California summer afternoon, and I was having a relaxed visit in my backyard with a girlfriend. As we enjoyed our iced tea party, we were sharing our dreams, and fantasizing about how we would make them materialize. She dreamed of marrying someone rich, tall, dark and handsome, and living happily ever after in a big beautiful home with their two children. My dream was even bigger. I dreamed of becoming a rich and famous movie star. The problem was, we were young and naive and neither of us knew what the first step was toward making our dreams come true. But we enjoyed fantasizing. After a fun afternoon of daydreaming, we decided on a plan of action: She would dress in her finest and lunch at exclusive restaurants where she would meet her prince charming, and I would enter beauty contests where movie producers would surely be in attendance looking for talent for the big screen!

Fast forward a few years. Mary became engaged to a wonderful retired government worker. (By the way, they are still happily married with two lovely children and live in a beautiful (medium sized) home!) I was blessed to win several titles, including "Miss Coppertone," and "Miss Val Verde." However, I had not yet been "discovered" to be on the big screen. I spent most of my time in college working toward getting my Bachelor's Degree in Education while also working as an electronic assembler at Hughes Aircraft forty hours a week. I soon grew weary of the beauty contest circuit and decided to first focus on my studies and after I earned my degree, peruse a career as an actress. Besides, it was the 60's and I ran into much prejudice which is why the contests I entered were always for Black females. As a matter of fact, I was not allowed to compete in one beauty contest because I was Black. Also, I had never seen any Black movie stars on the big screen. But my mother encouraged me by assuring me that if I worked hard and had faith in God, I could do anything I wanted. Although she supported my dream of becoming a movie star, she encouraged me to get my degree first.

Later, I was to have an experience I will never forget. My mother and I attended a performance of Lena Horne in New York City. Afterwards, Miss Horne very graciously met with us after the show. My first encounter with a Black star!! Among the things I treasure most are the photos of the three of us.

From that day on, my dream of becoming a star seemed more possible, but I put it on the backburner. I didn't pay much attention until one day Mary told me there were auditions for contestants in the Miss Bronze California Beauty Pageant. I wasn't really interested. I had a full schedule of college and work, but she kept persisting, wore me down, and I put in my application. I SHOWED UP and was accepted as a contestant.

It was mandatory that each contestant demonstrate her particular talent. I didn't know what to do, because there was no talent competition of any of the beauty contests, I had previously been in. Although I played the violin in my school orchestra, reached toe in my ballet lessons, and often recited poems in church, I didn't feel confident enough to perform any of these in the competition. I was also quite shy, so I decided that singing would be the easiest thing to do. I had enjoyed singing in my church and school choirs, and I felt I could "hide behind the song!" As fate would have it, I was introduced to an older jazz musician who heard me sing and offered to coach me (similar to what the coaches do for the contestants of The Voice television show). He became my mentor and did he push me!! ~~~Often to tears. Now that I reflect on the sessions, he was actually verbally abusive! But he was a very knowledgeable and experienced teacher. Among other things, he taught me vocal technique and how to use a microphone correctly. He also taught me how not to "hide behind the song," but to interact with the audience and the judges, while telling the story. It was a very exhausting undertaking, because I studied with him while still attending college and working full time.

The pageant was an amazing two days. It was the largest I had ever been a part of. I was shocked when the last night of the pageant I was announced as the Grand Talent winner. There were girls whose voices were much better than mine, and I'm sure that to this day they, like I, are wondering how I won!! It wasn't until much later that I realized the value of my vocal coach and all that he had taught me and without charging a penny! Not just about singing, but the whole package. As my mother would say about preparing a good meal, the presentation is as important as the ingredients!

As I left the stage clutching my trophy in disbelief, a young photographer at the contest approached me and told me that he was a member of a vocal group. Since not much was happening for the group, they needed to replace one of the female singers who left to accept a well-paying "real" job. I thanked him and explained that I was not interested. Also, I was not a singer and I only sang because it was required that I display some type of talent in the pageant. Besides, I was in my last year of college and working full time and did not have time to attend rehearsals. He wouldn't take no for an answer. He nagged me until I accepted and began rehearsing with the group! I did earn my Bachelor's Degree in Education and quit my nine to five job! At that time, the group he sang with, called themselves "The Versatiles." Shortly after I joined, the name was changed to "The 5th Dimension!" The rest, as they say, is history.

I had been singing with The 5th Dimension for a few years, when after a show as we were signing autographs, a gentleman approached me. He said, "I know you don't remember me, but I was one of the judges in the Miss Bronze California Beauty Pageant when you won the talent. When you walked on stage wearing that white suit and big white hat, carrying that hat box and sang "April in Paris" in French, Eartha Kitt, who was also one

of the judges, turned to the rest of us and said, 'Now, there's your winner!'"
I always had my own fashion style and never followed the crowd. When all
the rest of the ladies performed their talent wearing their gowns, I changed
into a beautiful white suit a large white hat and carried an old-fashioned
hat box. Who knew my unique personal style would have such an impact?
It goes to show, you should always be yourself.

Because I SHOWED UP for the audition, the rest of my life has been and
continues to be "Up, Up and Away!" The original 5th Dimension members
were only together for ten years and I am the only member who has
remained with the group for over fifty years. As I reflect on those years,
I am reminded of many wonderful memories: Performing at the White
House three times~~~ appearing on major television shows (including five
performances on the Ed Sullivan show)~~~Winning six Grammy Awards
~~~Starring in the touring presentation of the musical , "Ain't Misbehavin"
But the biggest professional pleasure for me comes each time we shared
our music with an audience, no matter where it is. I am still very proud to
be a member of a group that performs music that brings such pleasure to
our audiences. It touches my heart when someone comes up to me after a
show and thanks me for bringing back memories of good times in his or
her life ~~their wedding~~graduation, or some other memorable event.

One event that resonates with me the most is the memory of The 5th
Dimension representing the United Stated on a state department sponsored trip to Eastern Europe which, at that time, was Communist. There
were armed guards with dogs backstage to make sure there would be no
rioting. At the end of the show, we were shocked as the audience rushed
the stage. They just wanted to touch us, their connection to a free world.
The guards ended up shaking hands and asking for autographs. This was
just one example of the importance of music and how it can soothe and
bring people together.

What happened to my dream of being in the movies, you ask? Well, I did
have minor roles in two television shows. I enjoyed the working in front of
the camera, but I learned from those experiences that I prefer performing

live. I wouldn't turn down the opportunity to act in a motion picture, but I really prefer communicating with a live audience.

In 1995, I did take a brief time off from the group twice to star in musicals in Canada. Now THAT'S what I enjoy the most. It affords me the opportunity to both sing and act.

I don't want to infer that my fifty years in show business has been a piece of cake. Like any other career there have been ups and downs. The most difficult thing for me was having to be away from my family so much, especially my son. I was blessed to be able to take him on the road with me until he started school. He had his first passport when he was three months old, and I nursed him on planes, trains and buses for six months. I took a nanny with me when we traveled in the United States and hired a nanny in each country in which we performed outside of the States. Because he was a gifted child, I often took him out of school to be with me. Now a grown man, he tells me he really enjoyed his childhood and would like to do the same for his children!

AN AFTERTHOUGHT

I am so very grateful to have had the opportunities I have had and the life I was afforded ~~~That I SHOWED UP, listened to the advice of a wise coach and continue to study my craft. (Yes, I still take vocal and speech classes!)

We all have a talent that is unique to each of us and we all have dreams ~~ Fear is the thief of dreams. Be willing to take a chance ~~SHOW UP! I learned that we cannot accomplish all God has for us if we don't SHOW UP.

As a younger woman, my goal for getting into show business was strictly for fame and fortune. But as I matured, my desire has become to share my experiences to educate others ~~~ To inspire them to dream bigger dreams and encourage them to keep those dreams alive, not bury them, but to fearlessly use their God given talents to reach their destiny. While I do speak to young people, I am especially interested in encouraging our seniors to keep living~~~Don't stop dreaming and don't just exist! We may have to adjust our dreams as we age, but that's fine. Use your wisdom to help someone else. SHOW UP ~~Even if it's on the computer or telephone!!

It's All about Showing Up

Dr. Cherilyn Lee shares how showing up and asking molded the journey of her life!

Dr. Cherilyn Lee

I t's been more than fifteen years since I was invited to a meeting of the National Association of Female Executives (NAFE). I showed up and my life changed. There are not enough words to express my heartfelt gratitude for the transformation that occurred when I showed up and met the incomparable Robbie Motter and discovered this incredible organization NAFE and then in 2017 her nonprofit GSFE (Global Society for Female Entrepreneurs), and the trajectory of my life was transformed.

My Comprehensive Alternative Family Practice was already bustling. I was confident as a Board-Certified Natural Healthcare practitioner, but I didn't have the self-esteem I needed for a career in public life. So many tumultuous circumstances stirred my passion to combine my knowledge of Western and Eastern medicine and integrate mind, body and spirit. I was healing my patients one at a time, but my dream was to expand my reach to as many people as possible. What stopped me was my shyness and a painful self-consciousness that was the result of the experiences and painful conditions that I've endured throughout my childhood. But I also recognized that it was that pain that gave me a unique perspective that motivated my search for ways to help and always do more. Robbie gave me the support to step outside my comfort zone and share my astonishing story; my illnesses, having flatlined twice, and survived two incidents of comas. For my audio autobiography, "Written Before I Was Born," I received the 2019 HerStory

Award from the Women's Federation for World Peace USA, where I also serve as an Ambassador.

It was always so easy for me to advocate for, and speak up on behalf of my patients, but I could never ask for what I truly needed...love and acceptance. My parents were divorced when I was two months old, and two years later, my mother remarried. I don't recall my stepfather showing me any love, and my biological father was absent from my life. I recall my mother telling me that her mother-in-law didn't want her son to marry a woman with a child. I felt even more unwanted because she didn't just have a child, but a sickly one. Our relationship was cold and distant, as I watched how much better he treated my younger half-sister.

I especially remember one incident when, while in elementary school, I asked my stepfather for 10 cents, so I can buy myself something at the neighborhood store. My stepfather looked down at me and said, "I don't have any money for you." The way he said it, I understood that he didn't have any money. He didn't sound harsh and I didn't really feel bad as I walked away, but before I left the room, my sister walked in and also asked him for 10 cents. He reached into his pocket and gave it to her. That was a huge shock and it affected me right to the core. Why would he give money to her and not to me? This created in me deep-seated feelings that I'm not as good as others, and, from that moment on, I could not speak up or ask for what I wanted. My spirit was crushed. I was determined never to ask anyone for anything.

I started working and earned my own money at a very young age, and never again asked anyone for anything. That was who I was. The hurt, loneliness, rejection and the many disappointments I felt from both my biological father and stepfather plagued me for decades and became integral parts of the fabric of my life.

The pain of being disappointed by a parent can set off trust issues; however, when children are given a voice, are empowered and free, revolutionary change can occur. Showing up to NAFE and GSFE over the years and receiving the unconditional support from dynamic and sincere women, gradually helped my inner child reclaim her voice. As a young girl, I always felt I was being punished for being ill. I had several food allergies that often made me sick and prevented me from eating the same food as my family and school mates. I watched everyone eat delicious meals and that persuaded me to learn everything I could about nutrition. I had to change my diet because of eczema, a skin condition linked to allergies and emotions. Like so many chronic health conditions, my eczema had its roots in emotional pain.

Lack of attention and affection, and constant bullying undoubtedly played a role. Children are not born malicious. They aren't born to hate, but unfortunately, they learn both and take pleasure in tormenting children who are different. Kids would throw dirt on me, push me, tease me, torture me and call me names like "raccoon" or 'lizard girl" because the skin around my eyes and mouth was dark, scaly and peeling. The treatment I endured daily was damaging and harsh because I had no way to defend myself and no friends to defend me. Emotional healing, releasing resentment and forgiving injustices liberates the pain we internalize, weighs us down and destroys our lives. External injuries fade away, but internal scars remain beneath the surface. Understanding this encouraged me to record my meditation "Detox the Mind and the Body will Heal." I released my audio meditation to heal my mind, body, soul and spirit.

My peers saw me as successful because I had a thriving practice, the NuWellNess Clinic. However, my emotional scars were still healing. The internal residue leftover from years of abuse fueled my determination to spare others the pain and provide the education they needed to counter all the misinformation they were subjected to. I prayed to receive the knowledge that could shed light on debilitating diseases that plagued me and others. Unbeknownst to me, I was going to be catapulted into the media spotlight. Little did I know that in 2009, I would be sharing my gifts with the King of Pop and in turn be helped by him to deal with the media. He showed me how he blocked out the public scrutiny that he experienced since his days as a child star. It would eventually give meaning to my actions and my choice to fly with the eagles because my destiny was written before I was born.

The world knows Michael Jackson as a brilliant icon, but I knew him as the man who flew with eagles. XXX One night, I thought he would be a nervous wreck and saddened because the news was reporting his cherished possessions were being auctioned off. When I arrived, he was a delightful father, as usual, interacting with his children, as if nothing were happening. He taught me to remain in high spirits any time there was gossip, jealousy or resentment. He looked at all the negativity as baby chicks chirping. He chose to fly with the eagles, above all the chatter. If you're flying with eagles, you don't have time to tweet and lower your vibration to those who do not appreciate you. He was a musically talented human being. His attitude to fly with the eagles and raise his frequency enabled him to share his beautiful music with the world.

Although I was blessed to know the real man in the mirror, when the world lost a mega superstar, the media ignited its fury at me. As Michael's practitioner, I became a witness and lost my anonymity and my privacy. When Michael died, it became difficult for me to leave the house and I found myself pulled in many directions. I was about to be interviewed by Nancy Grace on CNN, and Robbie reached out to her and shared with her my personal story. She described to her that I was a solid member of NAFE and GSFE; a woman of impeccable character, compassionate and dedicated to healing others.

While growing up my mother was constantly in and out of hospitals with me or I was at home confined to my room with either eczema or asthma. The drugs didn't work well in those days and had adverse side effects. I couldn't understand why I was having so many health problems, including wheezing with every breath. Asthma was like an off-tune musical instrument in my head all the time. My parent's second-hand cigarette smoke contributed to my asthma. Eventually, my mother quit smoking, but my stepfather didn't. Even if he smoked outside, it still affected me when he came back inside the house. Asthma landed me in the emergency room, unable to breathe many times, and as a result, I created a wellness designer mask, "Just Breathe EZ". This is not your typical surgical mask. It's a 4-layer activated carbon filtered mask with a proprietary silver complex to effectively filter out indoor and outdoor environmental particles such as dust, grass, mold, pollen and pet dander.

This is an ultra-lightweight mask, ideal when cleaning, petting animals, handling paper or fabric, gardening, painting, exercising, sleeping or walking in the open air. It's designed to correct face seal leakage. Pure bioactive silver is infused into each mask, which helps control antibiotic-resistant superbugs as well as 500 different disease-causing pathogens. I wanted to serve and educate people on the importance of health and well-being, which inspired me to write a book under the same title and motto, "Just Breathe EZ."

Throughout the last decade, I showed up to N.A.F.E events, and since 2017 to G.S.F.E events. I gathered the golden nuggets that spurred my growth, pushed me beyond what I thought was possible and enabled me to lead by example. I continue to be on the cutting edge of new alternative modalities. My nonprofit, the NuWellness Developmental Foundation, offers the only cost-free Thermography, a Painless & Radiation Free Breast Cancer Screening to men, women and teenagers using the CRT diagnostic machine.

Robbie's enthusiasm and encouragement prompted me to expand my center with advanced technologies and perform Free Beauty Shop Stroke Screening. I also offer a quick three minute Cardiovascular and Autonomic Nervous System Screening, using the FDA approved medical device, Max Pulse. My healing-oriented treatments incorporate conventional medicine with accredited, scientifically proven holistic methods, and yield exceptional results.

I am a highly sought-after Integrative Practitioner and global media personality. I host and produce a weekly TV/Radio Show, "NuWellness TV with Dr. Lee," heard live on iHeartRadio, iTunes/Apple, Spotify, Google Play,

Castbox, Deezer and Stitcher. My podcast is seen live on my YouTube channel "NuWellness" TV/Radio with Dr. Cherilyn Lee every Wednesday at 11-12 am PT. The acclaimed series explores advancements in natural health, physical fitness, nutrition, integrative medicine, human rights, well-being and self-discovery with leading experts, many who are referred by Robbie. Robbie honors me by sharing my NuWellnes program with her vast networks.

I have been honored by several U.S. Presidents with Lifetime Achievement Awards for my volunteer work. I have received numerous awards and recognition from government branches at every level, including the City Council to the State Department for the humanitarian work at my NuWellness Developmental Foundation, Inc., a 501(c)(3) nonprofit. I couldn't have done any of this if I hadn't found my voice, believed in myself, and learned to ask for help. I became resilient and resolute to show up and received "the treasures" and embraced the mutual support of the members of NAFE and GSFE, who continue to share my journey.

It's All about Showing Up

HOPE ATTAINED BY SHOWING UP

Jeannette LeHoullier

April 26, 2018 was a momentous event, a remarkable day that changed the trajectory of my life forever. It brought a positive change and occurred exactly when I needed it. What happened was I met Robbie Motter, the marketing and collaborator extraordinaire.

I decided to attend my first NAFE (National Association of Female Entrepreneurs) meeting in Murrieta, CA at a great local Italian restaurant. The lunch meeting had already started when I made my late appearance, signed the meeting roster, paid the meeting fee, and found myself a seat near two interesting business ladies. One was the "Tea Diva" who had bright red hair and an intriguing personality to match and an author. The other woman was a NAFE newbie with years of corporate experience and a passion to help other businesswomen. I swallowed my shyness and embarrassment down as quickly as I could manage, and then tried to blend in with these dynamic and driven women. The meeting format allowed each of the 20 or so ladies to give a brief introduction of themselves and a summary of their businesses. We got through the round table introductions at the beginning of the meeting, before our guest speaker, Claudia Cooley, made her presentation.

As Robbie Motter reminds all NAFE women "Show Up" – you never know who you will meet and what opportunities will occur. My "Show Up" opportunity was given to me very quickly as I introduced myself (next to the last person). The attempted one minute "elevator pitch" introduction included my reason for coming to the meeting (I have wanted to join NAFE for 20+ years). Just being in the presence of remarkable Robbie was an incentive and an instant motivator, however, it became even more exciting after I finished my intro. My presentation skills were a bit rusty since I hadn't spoken at public meetings for over 8 years. I was giving myself pep talks inside my head, just praying that I did not embarrass myself too much with my meager abilities and aspirations. My standing up and introducing myself that day garnered many smiles and eye contact from some that seemed to say "hey, been there, done that, just keep going with your story and you'll be okay".

So, the synopsis of myself went something to the effect: "Hello, my name is Jeannette LeHoullier." (imagine it with a French accent). I am so happy to be in this meeting, as I have considered joining NAFE for over 20 years. Currently, I am a volunteer at the Kay Ceniceros Senior Center in Menifee, offering "Tech Time" services to seniors wanting assistance with their cell phones, smartphones, tablets, and laptops. I have been volunteering there for about a year and I really enjoy what I do. I am a former CEO of The HealthCare Foundation for Orange County, and have experience in websites, computers, and administrative support. After volunteering, it became evident that Seniors need someone in the community to offer private tech sessions, as the ½ hour free appointment at the Center is often too little to accomplish what the seniors need. My business is DJ's Virtual Management, a Senior Tutoring and Administrative Support services business. I have done a lot of volunteering and now it is time for me to make some money. Oh, and I am also a former Board member of a Women's Shelter in Orange County." I was tired, frustrated, a little nervous, and unclear how to promote my business. Oh my, I was thinking, what have I done now?!

Well, I love to tell the story and try to mimic the serious voice and persistence of Ms. Robbie that day, because her amazingness challenged and motivated me like no one had done before. Robbie had folded a newspaper in half, stood up across from my table (4 feet) and said "Before you sit down, I need you to send me a bio and a photograph, and I need it today. I have a deadline for tomorrow." Okay, I thought, I have not updated my bio in 10 years since I was a CEO in Orange County, CA, but hey, I can do this. Not to worry that you will not be home to begin writing until about 8:00 pm. I thought, I'll meet the deadline and I'll have an article written about me in the local newspaper by Robbie ... and ... the article will help promote the new business startup "DJ's Virtual Management/Senior Tutoring" as well as give me a huge boost of confidence because someone sees value in me as a person and in my new business services.

So, I sat back down, the last lady finished introducing herself, and then the guest speaker was introduced by Robbie. Claudia Cooley was a bubbly, dynamic powerhouse with a fun and interesting way of presenting her topic and motivating her audience. What I remember was being relieved to hear Claudia share a little of her life and thinking that she was probably a woman of faith, which resonated with my worldview. After just a few minutes, I heard Claudia mention me, and say, "Who wouldn't want to help a woman like this?" She even bounces when she talks, which shows her passion and excitement for everything she does. Wow, I thought, she just met me. I felt so blessed to be recognized by Robbie for a feature article in the Menifee Buzz newspaper and to be mentioned several times by Claudia in her presentation.

What these ladies had no knowledge of at that time, was that I desperately needed to plan for my financial future, and to earn enough money to live on within 1 ½ years, as my monthly spousal support would cease. Without a steady revenue stream to replace the monthly income, I could potentially be homeless in a year or so. Living on limited Social Security income would put me deeper into poverty.

So, my future was looking bleak, thus prompting me to get going on a business venture. I also had some personal family issues at the time that I knew would alter my life and lifestyle instantly. My 89-year-old Aunt would soon relocate from Central California to live with me in Southern California. She had dementia, was not being cared for properly by her drug addicted grandson, and unfortunately was also being financially abused by him. I felt compelled to bring her home with me, as her own children did not care enough to help her.

Now, back on track regarding that impetus April day at my first NAFE meeting, with Robbie Motter and guest speaker Claudia Cooley.

"Hope deferred makes the heart sick: but when the desire is fulfilled, it is a tree of life." (Proverbs 13:12) This verse represented a part of what I was feeling in 2018 when I first "showed up". Yet, my hope lifeline was strengthening.

I left the meeting feeling very excited that two people believed in me, valued me, and had interest as well as respect for me after just a couple of hours. Still recovering from a devastating divorce, loss of my dream house and a thwarted future during my retirement years, I was struggling. However, I had a spark of confidence generously given to me that day and it was helping to bring back some of my lost JOY. No, I was not walking on cloud nine, but I sure felt lighter and hope was renewed.

So, I pulled off the deadline, submitted the biography and photo via email to Robbie at 11:58 pm that same night with 2 minutes to spare! My bio included my business and personal background, and I was excited and apprehensive to share my personal story with the public. I was full of anticipation, not knowing what was to become of my new business venture.

Robbie could not have been easier to work with. She assured me the newspaper would print and distribute around the first of May. I eagerly awaited being "discovered", my business getting a strong boost, and help with an early launch.

When the article was published, Robbie hand-delivered copies of the paper to me and gave me specific instructions to get out of the house and "be seen", as this would also help promote my business. Her guidance was and still is very valuable and gratefully received by me. Although I had been suffering from migraines, I did my best to "show up" that evening, enjoying a Frank Sinatra sounding performer at a local restaurant. Robbie's infectious "go get em" attitude was sparking joy and motivation in me.

Robbie had written some lovely things about me in her article, as well as encouraged me to write future articles for the Menifee Buzz. This was a bit of shock to me because I had never been invited to write professionally. I was thrilled and honored to be considered, as I have had a desire to write for a long time. This too became a wonderful outlet to share information with our senior community and their families. Since then, I have written articles such as "Senior Social Media - Nothing to Fear, But Fear Itself", "Flipping Out Over Flip Phones", and "Family Caregivers Using Technology".

Curiously, I am known for my unique laugh that seems to make people smile and laugh along with me. However, many people did not decipher the sadness deep within – the feelings of despair, unworthiness, and low self-esteem. Aha, yes, it is true! Although I created the name JOYFUL DIVA for GSFE Diva Membership, that Joy came and went far too often than I wished it to.

Do you know how it feels to be buried under anxiety, depression, self-focus, and discouragement? Of course, many of you do. This describes some of the ways I felt in April 2018, although I covered it up well with a smile and intentional half upbeat enthusiasm. I walked into my first NAFE/GSFE meeting and met beautiful, heart filled women who offered business support and encouragement. They just did not know how badly I needed it!

I was still recovering from a devastating divorce, trying to rebuild my life from brokenness to one of survival, success, and happiness. The business process trajectory had begun 1½ years ago by volunteering as a technical tutor to seniors. Easing back into the business working world was the focus of volunteering. It brought not only happiness in refocusing my saddened life by helping others, it also brought an avenue for me to redirect my life as a senior citizen who had to establish a new career for financial stability. The idea to alter my business concept to one that includes specialized tutoring for seniors spurred me into reaching out to more than the seniors at the center.

What does the focus on HOPE have to do with Robbie's theme of "SHOWING UP" – and how that may have changed our lives? Well, let me share with you.

"If you treat an individual … as if he were what he ought to be and could be, he will become what he ought to be and could be." Goethe

This rings true to the human capacity of compassion and acceptance. When Robbie showed that she believed in me at our first introduction, she propelled me forward in a way I was not familiar – non bias acceptance. I did not have to prove myself; I was just accepted for who I was and who I was becoming.

From that very first meeting, I decided to join the GSFE Divas, and attend the fun launch party within the week. I also chose to attend Claudia Cooley's Women Leaders in the Sisterhood day retreat also within the week. Within the month, I attended two additional NAFE meetings (Murrieta & Menifee) and was on my way to gaining focus and building networking skills.

I eventually met another NAFE member, Mercy Noland, founder of VERIDIVA, a female women business network. Each of these 3 women (Robbie, Claudia, and Mercy) have helped mold my life into a more beautiful one. Their business expertise, knowledge, support, and encouragement have given me a strong base as I continue to rebuild my life and build my business.

When you get someone's voice in your thoughts and mind, it is often difficult to get them out. Fortunately for me, Robbie, Claudia, and Mercy's wisdom tidbits resonate and renew me often.

Surprisingly to me, I have met many women within the communities I engage in who have written books. These are dynamite women: Robbie

Motter, Kelly Bennett, Esq., Jami McNees, Barbara Berg, Dr. Barbara Young, Shelly Rufin, Claudia Cooley, Jennifer Crosswhite, and others. This alone has encouraged me to continue with my own writing goals, never giving up my desire and passion.

Getting to know people has been exciting and rewarding. As I mentioned in a Menifee NAFE meeting, being involved with NAFE helped me to "come alive" again. I have become more confident, happy, and experienced good will shared by the businesswomen I meet. Leaders and members bring their skillsets to meetings all the while encouraging and motivating us to be successful.

Each new woman I have met during the past 2 years, shows such strength, wisdom, and aptness in their fields. It is remarkable how each of us are unique and special in ways we do not always recognize within ourselves. What is great about showing up and engaging with fantastic women is sharing – ourselves – our talents – our stories. The unique business groups I have shared in have not been limited to only women and have also included the Temecula, Murrieta and Menifee Chambers and other meetings that have garnered many opportunities.

Sitting at home does not provide enrichment and happiness. Showing Up, as Robbie Motter encourages hundreds of women, is such an awesome concept. It is simple yet takes effort when you are not feeling it. I am so pleased and grateful that I met Robbie, and happy to continually take a leap of faith and push myself to show up. Believe me, it is worth every ounce of effort – the possibilities are unlimited.

Showcase Your Enthusiastic Power

Diana Londyn

S ince the dawn of time, it seems opportunity fell upon my lap. It was
though an array of offers, were presented to me on a prism platter.
Several I accepted and many I turned down. Who knows, maybe I regret
several I let slip through my fingers.

This formerly shy to a fault Pennsylvanian gal missed out on many chances
to grow, therefore many avenues of advancement. I couldn't keep up with
the gifts of challenge. Nowadays, I welcome all opportunities that knock
on my door and for those that I seek.

Pickle Ohio

One day on location, our boss asked us if we would like to jog three miles at
a popular trail in the forest in Pickle, Ohio. I thought, even though I was in
great physical shape, was I really up for it? I wasn't a jogger. Could I pull off
the required endurance with no previous training? I decided to decline.

The next day, he asked us again to join him and if we did, a bonus would
be waiting at the finish line. That incentive motivated me to accept the
challenge. A few of us chose to go. We all jogged light on our feet at a
steady pace, yet not too fast. We completed the task and polished off the
three miles. There was such beautiful scenery surrounding us. What a way
to start the morning.

We each burned 350 calories, which was equivalent to a piece of chocolate cake. I thought, Wow! That's a good bit of exercise in exchange for a dessert. Is the dessert worth the work behind burning the calories? We all received a bonus of five hundred dollars. The achievement, the goal, and our incentive mystery bonus made our day. I learned to never underestimate the power within oneself. Most of all, stepping up and out was a new beginning of confidence and it sparked a fire underneath my core. What possibilities could happen if I spoke up for what I need? Hmmm…. They say, "the squeakiest wheel gets the grease."

I set forth approaching management at a marketing firm. Inflation set in, and I much needed to raise my income. I had my statistics prepared just in case I would need to access them. I asked and not only got what I asked for, but an advancement as well. I was amazed how quick my request was granted. I say, "Just go ask for what you want or need."

ORIGINAL ENTERTAINMENT

I was looking at starting my own business. A couple I knew owned an entertainment booking agency. They planned on moving to Oregon, after years of being in this industry in California. They decided to sell their business. Kevin and Meg approached me since they knew I was a performer, perhaps I would be interested. It wasn't my first choice, however I checked out the variables and analyzed this may be a great livelihood. After all, they were the first in Orange County California when they started. Original singing telegrams were billed as #1 in O.C. and had preferable placement in the yellow pages.

The purchase price included my training, rights to all of their personalized songs, costumes and equipment. I found the thought of booking shows intriguing. Now it's time to get a business loan. I had a small savings however, not enough. I could have gone to a bank or family, but someone stood out in my mind. A restaurant owner who openly discussed investing in several companies during our patronage. He may like the idea of entertainment in the restaurant as they have featured bands, strolling magicians and look-a-likes.

One day, I mustered up the nerve to ask the owner if he would consider the investment and he did. I am so glad I asked. Original entertainment was my choice to call my new pride and joy. This brought so much laughter with such a sense of independence. I met more magicians, singers, comedians, dancers, Broadway icons, famous look-a-likes, children's favorite characters and vaudeville artists. It was one of the best decades of my life.

Family History

Family is a big part of my life. We have such a big family with a massive number of cousins to keep me busy through eternity. Even so, my curiosity took it one step further. To dig deeper into our roots. I had documents and heirlooms from Grandparents and predecessors. How many more pieces to the puzzle shall I find? Since we spent more time with nearby family on my Father's side, it was time to meet more folks on my Mother's side.

This exciting voyage started with me, literally calling relatives out of the phone book that I never met before, yet recognized names spoken. My first call was to Beryl who was happy to meet with his wife at a local restaurant. They surprised me bringing another cousin, Rebecca. They were all my Parents age. We all had our information packets that we brought to the table. I was elated and we had a delightful time. Rebecca worked extensively with our family heritage since the 1970's prior to Ancestry.com was even thought of. Her collection dated back to the 18th century. Her stash included courthouse records, newspaper articles, photos and recordings of songs. Many loved to play piano and sing. She invited me to stay with her. The home office looked like a library. I had access to shelves of historical books of the counties and all her work to date. It was the first time in years, both hands were rotating the wheels of an old-fashioned microfiche reader using microfilm. We took turns searching names in decades of archived census records. We made a great team. This was genealogy heaven at its best. Both of us set sail to discover more family mysteries like a treasure hunt. We found relatives at the American Legion Hall, Churches, picnics, political events, an Alpaca sanctuary and an Indian pow wow. We toured and listened to stories in graveyards.

My great grandparents' old farmhouse, acres of land and barn was my next quest to seek. The drive along the countryside was so picturesque. I knocked on the door to introduce myself to the current owners. They gave me a tour and encouraged me to take pictures inside and outside. We have kept in touch and visited occasionally with other family members to go horseback riding. We also enjoyed bonfires and cook outs. This farm and barn are one of the 3 preserved and registered in the National Historical Society in Pennsylvania.

The last and most significant hunt led me to a 10-year-old cousin, Daniel. At 15, he came to California and stayed for a decade. He called me Angel Mom. This all transpired with my willingness to ask and get out of my comfort zone.

PUT YOUR PRIDE ASIDE

Once pride is in your genes, it's hard to kick it. I found the thought of asking someone for anything to be very difficult, unless for directions. I have spent more time stressing over asking than simply asking. The phone can become very heavy. It's time to take a deep breath and exhale all the apprehension built up and let it right out. It's silly in a way, so just go for it and ask. One way is to ask for a favor for another's benefit like an organization. That is an icebreaker. I was involved with a scavenger hunt for a children's center. The mission motivated me. One of the items on the list was a receipt from a specific destination. I had one, however not in the correct time frame. Our team needed this to complete the task to win. I put my thinking cap on and phoned three ladies in the area. Perhaps one of them could fill the quest. Two of the ladies didn't have what we needed yet, offered to share with others. I was appreciative for the help. Folks feel good to help out when they can. This lessens the hype knowing the sense of making others feel good about being of assistance. The third striking lady, I met at a Chamber of Commerce event. Believe me it took a lot of nerve to ask, yet I did. She looked into her records and low and behold she located the treasure the same day. Third time's a charm. I was excited to meet her. I treated her to coffee and took her a gift for her trouble. We spent 3 hours talking and sharing ideas for a book and marketing concepts. She inspired me to write an article for her online magazine. I gave her insight on what to do with her tourist biz possibilities and who to talk to. I later sent her leads in her vicinity to get sponsors for the magazine. She was just as grateful as I and told me, "Boy am I glad you contacted me. "

Mention your Invention

It 'twas a drizzling misty early morning at 5:45 am standing in line at Universal Studios for a few hours. Why would anyone do that? My friend and I went to the "Apprentice" show auditions. Charlotte wanted to be on the show and as for me, I had a different goal entirely. Mr. Trump approached our table of 8. When he got to me, I told him I am not here to audition, rather to share my invention idea and handed it to him in a priority envelope. He said, "Thank you and now I have it. "Mr. Trump's attorney, George Ross, senior counsel of the Trump organization, explained to me that they are backed up on projects for 2 years. Time was of the essence and they needed to strike while the "Apprentice "show was hot. In a few years it may not have the same appeal. I had a trademark attorney to seal the deal. I made sure to cover the non-compete clause and agreement.

The creation is of the Twin Towers as an alarm clock. When the alarm goes off, it plays," Money Money Money "song by the O'jays represented by Red Entertainment. It goes off twice. If one hits the snooze button one more time, Trump says, "You're Fired! "This is ingenious for stockbrokers waking up so early in the morning. It is great for New Yorkers or anyone who fancies a unique clock. I planned to give a percentage of the sales back to the Twin Towers. This was to help rebuild New York as well. Red Entertainment, the O'jays and the Twin Towers gave me the stamp of approval. I shared with the Trump organization how national and international sales and marketing were key with a few other trade secrets. Time ticked away and this deal was placed on the back burner. I may still be on their radar for future endeavors.

The perseverance taught me a lot about following through. By the way, while standing in line that early morning during the rain, I made new connections. I was on the prowl for new candidates for my recruiting biz. It's exciting leading to endless possibilities. Never give up!

Enhance Your Magical Moments

Magic Castle is a historical and private club for magicians, enthusiasts, and guests. It is located in Hollywood, California. The ambience is incredible, the dining is exquisite, not to mention the sleight of hand and shows. I frequented as a member received numerous invitations by magicians that I booked for events through my entertainment company. I was invited one evening and nearly declined as I was spent. I pulled it together and chose to show up. The evening was enchanting. I met an eccentric costume designer by the name of Silvia Bouke. She was visiting from Germany and hoping to get contacts in the industry. I helped her with several possibilities. A well-known magician invited Silvia and I to an academy award gala the following week. We accepted his offer to attend. I picked her up from the Magic Castle Hotel and chauffeured her to Otto Rothschilds restaurant. We went for an early dinner downstairs from the Dorothy Chandler Pavilion where the awards were taking place. During our dining, a kind gentleman introduced himself as Gerry Conlon. Now, Gerry Conlon was one of the Guildford Pub four that were wrongly convicted to 15 years in prison for being a Provisional IRA Bomber. He wrote a book, "Proved Innocent "in 1990. In 1993, he was the lead character in the movie, "In the Name of the Father "portrayed by Daniel Day Lewis. I was a true fan of Mr. Day Lewis's acting, as he took on a colorful array of roles. Mr. Colon invited us to the "In the name of the Father "party held at Jimmy's Irish restaurant in Beverly

Hills. The movie was up for several awards. Did destiny play a part in this or was it pure magic? I had a dream a week prior to the Magic Castle where I attended a St. Patrick's Day party and Daniel Day Lewis was there. We attended our first gala & then off to Jimmy's we went. I had a chance to tell Daniel Day-Lewis, we were rooting for him since he was truly the "Last of the Mohicans "in the "Age of Innocence" and I swear to it, "In the Name of the Father on my Left Foot ". He had a big smile and laughed.

So many opportunities came about from the magic of showing up.

The Story of Sue Lopez

Sue Lopez

I was living in North Torrance, CA in a small 3 bd, 1 bath home, built in 1954. My children were grown, and the Watts Riots had just passed. Things were starting to settle down, however my children were still worried for my safety. Then the local jewelry store, about a mile away, was robbed and the owner was shot. That's when I started to think that I should sell my home and move closer to one of my children. My oldest daughter lives in Temecula, my son lives in Santa Ana and my youngest daughter lives in Canyon Country. I also have a brother in Temecula, a sister and a brother in Hemet. So, I decide to move near my oldest daughter, not because I love her any more than my other two children, but because I have more family in the Inland Empire, and homes were more affordable than in the other two places and Sun City. Menifee was one of the fastest growing cities in the US and I knew that I could get more value for my money.

It was 2006 and the housing market was at top dollar, so I sold my home in Torrance at a great price. I found a newer and more beautiful home in a gated senior community in Menifee. In 2006 this area was called Sun City. About 4 years after I moved there, Sun City became part of the New City of Menifee. Since then things have taken off. It is now one of the fastest growing Cities in the U.S., and the 7th fastest in California.

Before that happened, homes had lost a lot of value. At one time, my new home was worth about half of the price I paid. I didn't panic because I knew prices would go up and I wasn't going anywhere. Today my home is worth much more. Menifee has its own Mayor and City Hall along with 4 Council persons. Menifee now has its own Police Chief and they are building a Police Department. We are getting our own Movie Theater and Bowling Alley. New homes are going up on practically every vacant lot. Hooray!! This made me think about property values and job opportunities.

Over the years, I learned that networking is how you meet people and survive financially. So, the first thing I did was to get involved in the community. I joined the Chamber of Commerce, attended networking groups and met many people. I served on the Board of Directors for the Chamber of Commerce, joined BNI, National Association of Female Entrepreneurs (NAFE) now known as (GFSE), the Murrieta Breakfast Club Lion's, The Menifee Women's Club and was part of the Core Group to develop the Menifee Valley Lion's Club, where I'm still the treasurer. I learned how to use my "Sphere of Influence" to meet and work with people.

I met a wonderful friend, Robbie Motter, by showing up one night to an event that neither she nor I wanted to go to. A mutual friend invited both of us separately, to an event in North Hollywood. It was a weeknight and we both had work the next morning. It was an event about "The Secret". Which, I have adapted in my life as it has changed my way of thinking. People call me the luckiest person. I always win because I believe.

Through Robbie, I met many people who have become good friends. Robbie has so many connections and is a connector. Because of her I was able to go to Dr Phil, the Emmy's and the Academy awards. What a blast! If you need a connection for something you have always wanted, just ask Robbie. One of my secret ambitions was to sing. Not necessarily professional, I know I'm not that good, but I did want to perform. So now I sing Karaoke whenever I can. Robbie has had me sing in a couple of her Extravaganzas. I felt very privileged. Robbie is now one of my best friends. Like she says, "It's all about showing up".

One of my first jobs in Menifee was selling marketing materials. It helped me get by for a while, but I always wanted to get my Real Estate License. So, when I saw the real estate potential in Menifee, I knew that it was time to fulfill a long-term goal. I continued to work and took the home study class and three months later took the real estate test and passed. I continued to focus on networking, which, as I said is the best way to meet people and grow your "Sphere of Influence".

Through networking I became friends with the Stamper's, owners of Rancho Plaza Realty. Their office that specializes in Property Management. I met the Stamper's at a Chamber mixer and for several months we would sit together. They would introduce me to people in the industry and helped me grow. They called me one day and asked if I knew anyone who might be interested in a receptionist position at their Real Estate office. They knew I was studying to get my real estate license, but they were reaching out to their network to find the right person for their office. I realized that being in their office would get me closer to my goal. So, I suggested to them that I take the job until I got my license and I could make a living as a licensed agent. They gave me the job and I worked as a receptionist for several months and continued to study. Hooray! Not much later, an opportunity came up for a Property Manager with the company and they offered me the job. It wasn't a sales position, but it was a start, and I did very well and was making good money. After nearly 6 years as Property Management I realized this wasn't for me and I needed to move on and do sales. There's lots of stress in Property Management dealing with irate tenants, some of which kept me awake at nights. I had to show the homes to prospective tenants, do credit and background checks, type up and get the leases signed and keep track of renewal dates.

I also had to work with the homeowners, taking in homes for rentals and then managing them. This required me to prepare the management agreement, get it signed, take pictures of the home, and put it in the MLS. I also had to manage the move in and move out inspections. If a tenant had to be evicted, I had to call the attorney, and go to court for financial disputes. After 6 years of this and all the work on my plate the next day...call a plumber for this one, the AC guy for that one, pest control, it started to take a toll on me. When I fell and broke my foot while showing a property, I was off for three months and during that time, I started to feel less stress and decided it was time for a change. Selling homes was my original goal and now it was time to get to work on it.

I cashed in some of my investments, paid off all my bills, and called a broker whom I had met through networking and told her about my situation. Barbara Caley of LCL Realty and Property Management welcomed me into their family. The first sale I made was with one of the property owners whom I had worked with on his rental. He wanted to sell his home and his tenant was interested in buying it. It was an easy sell, but it helped me get acquainted with the process from the selling disclosures all the way through escrow. I was on my way... That first year I sold 7 homes. If you sell 6 homes in a year, LCL pays your MLS fees, which is a nice saving. So, bingo, they paid my fees the 1st year and every year since I'm there. In two years, I was their #1 Salesperson.

When attending a networking event, you're asked about your goal. I always said that I wanted to get a Million Dollar transaction. I've worked hard, with lots of marketing and it has all paid off. I didn't just achieve my Million Dollar Listing...I got a listing for over Two Million Dollars.

So, happily I'm still at LCL Realty and have a passion for helping people get into a new home of their dream, and helping sellers get a good price for their home and move on. I'm still working with owners to rent their homes, but I'm glad that after I find them a good tenant, I can hand them over to the Property Management department at LCL.

I have made lots of friends at LCL and feel like I'm part of a family. We'll go for lunch and enjoy time together away from the office. I've even become close friends with a couple I just happened to meet at an Open House, and they decided to buy the house I was showing that very day, Kathy and Dave Leidike. Another couple of special friends are, Mary and Neil Snooks, I've known Mary since the Second Grade and were inseparable in our youth. They wanted to move to Menifee a few years ago and I found a lovely home for them with RV parking and everything they wanted in a home. John Neihouse, whom I worked with for years at a T-shirt Silk Screening Company, has now moved to Menifee. We get together often and have a great time and have gone on vacation. I'm so blessed to have made so many good friends in Menifee. I wish I could tell you about each one.

I have 3 Children, Kimberly who is married to Beto, Tom is married to Gavi, and my youngest Theresa is married to Cheo. I am very proud of them. They have all been married for almost 30 years. I love their spouses like my own children. We get along well… At least I think so! LOL….

I have 10 wonderful grandchildren: Alex, Billy, Dominick, Charles, Victor, Amber, Crystal, Cheo III, Emily and Steven.

My 11 great-grandchildren are: Derek, Shane, Savannah, Danny, Isaac, Able, Stevie, Matthew, Ava, Lexi and Cheo IV. I feel like I am the luckiest person in the world. It does get expensive for Christmas and birthdays, but I love the giving. It's great to see the joy on their faces.

I love spending time with my Children, Grandchildren and Great-Grandchildren. Family and friends are very important to me. What more do I need? I just ask the Lord to give me many more years to do just that.

The Story of Two Loves

Debbie Love

N ever in my wildest dreams could I have ever imagined my life going down the path where I find myself today. I did not set out to be a martial artist, a self-defense instructor or an advocate for women's safety. It is what I was compelled to do after the life of a family member was tragically and brutally taken. It had a profound effect on me and would eventually change the course of my life.

Julie Love was only 27, and well on her way to making her dreams come true. A few days earlier, her boyfriend proposed, and she had enthusiastically said YES! The children's aerobics program that she created for the Atlanta schools, was becoming a success. Julie was cute, petite and at under 5 feet tall, barely stood taller than her young students who loved "Miss Julie."

Julie was last seen on Monday, July 11, 1988 at 9 pm when she got into her beloved red Mustang convertible after attending a Career Chat networking meeting. And no one saw her since. Her Mustang was found abandoned in Buckhead, an exclusive suburb of Atlanta, where the streets are lined with old southern mansions and the lawns are perfectly manicured. The car was found just two miles from Julie's condo. To walk or jog two miles would have been easy for Julie. She was in excellent shape. So, where was she? And so, it began …

"Have You Seen Julie Love?" became the rallying cry for the entire city of Atlanta. Posters and flyers were showing up everywhere, on streets and store windows. They were on billboards and on the sides of trucks. A rally was held at Piedmont Park, which was the first of its kind. The entire city seemed to be looking for her and Buckhead residents were frightened; vicious crime such as this had never happened in their neighborhood. Julie's disappearance was the top news story every day for weeks, and then for months. The story caught the attention of national news outlets as well as the Democratic National Convention which brought thousands of delegates and journalists to Atlanta all of them wondering, who is Julie Love and what's all the commotion about? The pressure on law enforcement was enormous. The GBI and FBI were brought in to help solve the case. The daily reminder of her disappearance forced people to confront their own mortality. Julie's case remained the top news story for more than a year. About a year after Julie's disappearance, there was finally a break in the case when a very frightened and badly beaten woman, Janice Weldon, came forward saying she had information about Julie Love. She told police she was in the car the night her boyfriend Emmanuel ("Demon") Hammond, along with his cousin Maurice Porter, grabbed Julie as she walked home, hit her with a sawed-off shotgun and threw her into the car. Ms. Weldon agreed to work with law enforcement and was fitted with a recording device for when she met with Porter that night. He gave it all up. He told her what happened after they dropped her off at home. She had asked to be taken home and didn't want to be part of Julie's ordeal.

Both Hammond and Porter were arrested and taken into custody and both men were charged with kidnapping, robbery, rape and murder. Porter confessed to the crimes and led law enforcement to Julie's remains. In March 1990, after an eleven-day trial, Emmanuel Hammond, the trigger man, received the death penalty and was put to death by lethal injection by the State of Georgia on January 25, 2011, twenty-three (23) years after Julie's murder. Maurice Porter avoided the death penalty by pleading guilty. He was sentenced to two consecutive life sentences and will spend the rest of his life in prison where he is today. Janice Weldon was given complete immunity and was not prosecuted in the case.

Debbie's Story

Julie and I were cousins, born and raised in Birmingham, Alabama. I was about 6 years older. We were both the youngest of our respective families; she had two older brothers; I had two brothers and a sister. We were both under 5 feet, but while Julie was 100 lbs. of bubbly cuteness, back then I was a tomboy, chunky and a solid mass of muscle. We were both athletic, but it was Julie who was the natural athlete. Back in high school, I was good at two things: physical education and typing. When considering colleges, My parents said "NO", to physical education, which left typing. I enrolled at the Atlanta College of Business and set my sights on becoming the next Della Street. Julie graduated from the University of Texas with a degree in physical education a few years later. It was on the late local news when I first heard about Julie's disappearance. In utter disbelief, I called the news station thinking it had to be a mistake. No, it was not a mistake, Julie was officially a missing person. That news broadcast was one of those events that sticks in your mind. You remember where you were and what you were doing. Every detail is stored like data on a hard drive. The next morning, I met up with the family at the home of Julie's fiancé, whose home had been turned into a makeshift operations center. Nothing seemed real. Uncle Jerry (Julie's dad) and his wife Loretta were exhausted. They hadn't slept at all. I stayed with them for most of the day. Uncle Jerry's world was falling apart. There were several police officers as people moved in and out of the house. I didn't know then but I know now it's common for the perpetrator of a crime to show up at the funeral of a victim, or even to volunteer to help in the case of a crime he committed to keep an eye on the investigation. There were dozens of volunteers there to help. The place where Julie's car was found was less than a mile from my office, so I would slip away whenever I could to cruise the areas around where the car was found. Always starting at the spot where the car was found and going in different directions each time. On the weekends, I would set out alone to search further away from the city.Eventually, the searching took a terrible toll on me. For months, I travelled throughout Atlanta armed with hundreds of posters and a staple gun. I would go to community parks and ballfields to search the outer edges. I found a broomstick to use to poke around creeks and ditches and added it to my arsenal. I would search under bridges and overpasses along the highways. For the first few months I was treating this like a second job, which helped to keep it compartmentalized in my mind. But it got to the point that I couldn't do it anymore. When I learned that I was pregnant for the third time – after two miscarriages -- I couldn't take any chances. Because of the pregnancy I was becoming more freaked out and downright scared whenever I left the house or office. Julie was always on my mind. I kept thinking, 'if it happened to Julie, it could happen to me.' Finally, a year after Julie disappeared, there was news that someone had come forward with information about the case; this person claimed to have witnessed Julie being taken near where her Mustang was found. The next day two men were arrested, and Julie's remains were found and identified. Finally, Uncle Jerry could bury his little girl. The funeral was in Birmingham and Julie would be laid to rest next to her mom. Everybody was there. I was eight months pregnant, and as I stood at Julie's graveside, I made a promise to my unborn son that I would always keep him safe. If I was going to keep my little boy safe, it was time to learn self-defense. So, I signed up for a class. I gave it my all, but the techniques were complicated and didn't seem to work for me. Then, I saw an ad for a self-defense class just for women and signed up. Surprisingly, they were teaching practically the same moves to a group of women as the previous class where the group was mixed. No matter how many classes I took, (and I took a bunch), I didn't know much more about defending myself. The common factor in every class was that the instructors were male who probably never considered that women might need a different approach to self-defense.

In 1998, we moved to Cardiff, California. My son Mark was 8 when he started his new school. Mark was not as tall as the other kids and was bullied because of it which was hard on him. To help build his confidence; we tried a karate class and he loved it. I was amazed at how quickly his skills developed. He was getting sharper and quicker and his confidence grew. The sensei (teacher) suggested that I train with him, but karate was Mark's thing and he was good at it. I wasn't going to interfere. At 15, Mark earned his youth Black Belt. That same day a high-ranking Sensei from Colorado asked why I would just sit and watch. Before I could answer, the Grandmaster, who was visiting from Okinawa and rarely spoke, pointed at me and said just two words in his broken English, "You train." That night I asked Mark if he would mind if I started training. His response, "Mom, I've been waiting for you to ask." The next day I bought a gi and joined him on the floor. That was 20 years ago. It wasn't quite as easy as it looked from the sidelines. I felt uncoordinated and lacked some of the balance I may have had when I was younger. Mark became my 'at home sensei' and, even though I drove him a little crazy, he was patient and always made time for me. Keep in mind, he outranked me, which made for a completely different dynamic between us. But he was always humble and kind as he would guide me through the moves, I was trying to learn. I slowly improved and moved up from white to yellow, then green, brown and finally I was testing for my Black Belt. The Grandmaster and the Colorado sensei were there for my test and presented me with the Black Belt. It was common knowledge that my goal in karate was to learn self-defense, and everyone went out of their way to work with me. Some techniques just didn't work because of my small size, while others just needed to be tweaked a bit. When I received my 4th Degree Black Belt, I made plans to open my own studio. I wanted a place just for women to learn skills not found in any gym. In my studio, there would be no sparring, no competition, no intimidation and absolutely no men. A place where women can have the opportunity to learn self-defense or karate, and gain strength, balance and coordination in the company of other women. Heads Up Self-Defense for Women will be a place where confidence soars. It was just three years ago that I left a 40-year career as a paralegal to open Heads Up. Today, I devote my time to educating women about their safety and the safety of their children through speaking engagements, self-defense classes and workshops. At Heads Up, women learn self-defense that makes sense, comes naturally, is simple and easily remembered.

In the 20 years of training, I was the only woman in a room full of men. Of course, there were times I wanted to quit. It could be intimidating standing toe to toe with a man more than twice my size and being covered in bruises, but nothing would keep me from the next class. I just kept showing up. Now, the men I train with are my closest friends and my biggest supporters. It is because of the tragic murder of my cousin that set me on this journey 32 years ago. Julie made a simple mistake that night when she didn't stop for gas and it was a fatal mistake. We've all made mistakes that could have ended badly. Today, a simple mistake might be leaving home without your cell phone and without the ability to call for help if needed. Another lesson learned from Julie is that exclusive neighborhoods do not translate into safe neighborhoods. Julie was in the wrong place at the wrong time. If she had filled up earlier in the day, she would be alive today. I want to remind you to be mindful. Get gas when you need it and keep your cell phone with you all the time. And it never hurts to be prepared. Show up and learn self-defense.

HAVE YOU SEEN JULIE LOVE?

Last seen wearing peach colored shorts & shirt, white socks & white high top tennis shoes.

Her 1983 red Mustang, with white convertible top, was found in West Wesley-Howell Mill Road area.

- 27 years old
- 5 ft. tall
- 100 lbs., petite
- black curly hair
- brown eyes
- Friendly…"Wouldn't hurt a fly."

Her family, friends and pre-school students miss her so badly. If you have any information, please call:

658-6841 (Missing Persons Squad)
or
355-2772

$10,000 REWARD
FUND HAS BEEN ESTABLISHED TO PAY FOR INFORMATION LEADING TO THE RETURN OF JULIE LOVE.

SHOWING UP AND ASKING
QUESTIONS IN NEGOTIATIONS

Marlena Martin

Throughout my career, I have enjoyed asking questions and sticking around to hear the answers. Here are a few of the best questions I've asked:

1. **I wonder if it would be possible to up-level my signature event to a famous and bigger destination hotel and spa?** The Queen Mary, to me, was the big time. The destination weddings on board, the Lady Diana Exhibit, the Tea Room, the Churchill exhibits, the five-star Winston's and the best brunch in town complete with ice sculptures, string quartets, champagne and enough of a food display to rival anything in Las Vegas. Famous for Art Deco weekends, the Scottish Festival, Barbeque Festivals, private events surrounding the Long Beach Grand Prix, and a myriad of other themed events, surely the Queen Mary would be way out of our budget--or would it?

As the prices at the Hilton and the Embassy Suites climbed higher and higher, I thought, "just for fun, I wonder what it would take to hold my event on the Queen Mary?" I called and asked to be patched into the catering department. When I spoke to Michelle,

one of the catering managers, I explained my program of working with women and honoring them through Woman of Achievement. She then asked me the magic question: "What are you paying NOW at your current venue?" I told her the figure and she said, "We will beat that by $100 and throw in some of your dressing rooms for free." Not only did I get an amazing venue upgrade, I was saving money and the ballrooms were huge! I was now able to host more women and raise the entire look and overall vibe of my event. Why? Because I asked "in spite of" my reservations--never in a million years believing they would bid lower than what I was already paying!

I have now moved two other annual events to this venue because I asked another great question: "How can I increase the bottom line?" I was paying top dollar on other locations and I figured if the new venue was willing to work with me on this one event, why not move all my events to this locale? Although the original person who did my contract is gone, I'm so glad that back in 2014 I was not afraid to ask the question: "How can I up-level this to a better venue?" and I didn't let the dreaded "But how could I afford it?" question stop me from at least asking.

Over the years of negotiating contracts, I started to ask another question:

2. **What can I bring with me to this negotiation to give me an edge?** Much of life is negotiation and the more powerful you can appear before opening your mouth, the better. This goes in relationships, salary negotiations, just about everything. Non-verbal edges can be in the credible and advanced elegant communication leading up to a meeting. Edge can be seen in a brisk assured walk when advancing forward and stretching your hand out for a handshake. Edge is mirroring. Mirroring is matching your handshake firmness to theirs, sitting the way your counterpart is sitting, and even in the speed of the communication itself. If your counterpart talks fast, do not talk slow. The more you are like them in subtle ways, the more comfortable they will feel with you during negotiation. Edge is in your walk, your posture, and even in what you choose to wear when attending a meeting. Wearing white around the face with a black, navy blue or darker suit jacket for men

and women, will always highlight the face and make you stand out and command attention. Darker shirts next to the face will make you less noticeable. There are entire books and courses in nonverbal perception that can be translated through the clothes you choose to wear for any given event. The bottom line? Never ever be dressed in less formal attire than those you will be negotiating with! This will at least level the field by saying non-verbally: "we are both professionals here".

Before moving all our programs over to the Queen Mary, I still hosted a Teen Event at a local Disney boutique hotel. We had been holding our event there for two years when the sales staff called again to book us back in for the third year in a row. My rep, Kelly, left me a message on my cell phone stating the price of the ballroom and it was the same price we had always paid in prior years. I accepted, glad to be back, especially when I heard that the pricing for the ballrooms would not be going up!

We agreed on the date and I sent out the invites to my team and mailing list. Weeks later, when the hotel emailed the actual contract, the pricing was *several hundred dollars from what my sales representative had stated on the phone.* When I called the Catering Manager (Kelly's boss) about this, she would not budge. It was the new pricing or else. At this point, I had already advertised my event, made flyers, and many people had already booked their flights into California. I had to sign the contract. My host hotel had me over the proverbial "barrel". I could not cancel but the situation did not sit well with me.

It appeared to be game over. I asked myself another great question: "How can I possibly turn this around?" After mulling that question in my mind, I came up with an answer.

My plan had four steps:

1) Request a meeting with both the Sales Associate and the Manager to chat about the overall event, but not solely about the pricing.

2) Wear my power suit to the meeting.

3) Bring a male Board member to come to the meeting to sit beside me; and

4) Find that voice message and play the recording in person when I get there, (but only after we break the ice), tell them how much we loved the venue, and discuss other items FIRST. That way, I could "sandwich" the problem in with everything else.

It was worth a try.

During this negotiation, I learned some things that have proved true when dealing with most catered or hotel events.

1) When there is an issue and you have to meet at the property or even off-site, hotels almost always bring a 2nd person with them so you will be out-numbered and out-gunned if you meet them alone. (Lesson: bring another person with you. It is better optics and you have a witness if any facts are later called into question).

2) As a woman, I have found that bringing a man (preferably a Board Member, husband or other interested party) who merely sits by my side during the negotiation is a powerful nonverbal deterrent to both male and female Catering Managers fast-talking me into decisions I didn't initially agree to. Perceived power is the real power. Even in the middle of live events when the Catering Manager comes down to re-negotiate something, I simply call my Board Member who is suited up to just stand next to me while I talk. It does not matter how much power you think you have; it is only the PERCEIVED power that counts!

Back to our story. When I played the recorded message on speaker phone for everyone at the meeting, the Sales Manager had to reluctantly agree to honor the verbal price even though the written contract had already been signed! She warned me though that "next year, things might be different." Of course, there would not be a next year. The next year all my events had been moved to our new venue. In a situation that looked impossible to win, with a signed contract already on file, I still won. I won by asking three questions: **"How can I possibly win? Who and what can I bring to this negotiation to state my case?"** and **"What powerful non-verbals can I take into this meeting?"**

Now that I have shared a few ways I have improved my events by showing up and asking, I wanted to share a funny story relating to "perceived power" and how we are viewed when interacting with others:

3. Would she really say that to me if I was a man?

Almost every other day, I go to a local donut shop in my little town. It is run by a family who emigrated here -- the cash register run by the normally very courteous wife of the owner. I do not go to eat the donuts, but they DO have fabulous coffee and because of that, I am a regular customer. Many families go into this coffee shop. Retired men sit in the shop and discuss their grandchildren and family travels while looking out the windows. Parents bring their kids on the way to school. Truckers pop in off the freeway to grab a quick bite. People come in and out, but there are always the regular locals inside. My coffee is about $1.75, and the shop only takes cash. One day, I came in and could not find any dollar bills in my wallet. I was ready to turn around and go home to get the bills when I glanced into my coin purse and realized that I had enough change to cover my coffee. As I counted the quarters as quickly as I could, the wife at the register said to me in a very loud voice: "Next time, have exact change!"

I thought about that for a minute. The more I thought about it the more ridiculous it seemed. I turned around to those who stood behind me at the register and said, **"If I were a man ordering coffee, do you think she would say this to me?"** The answer of course is no because she wouldn't DARE talk to a male customer that way. Gender disparity and how women are often treated by other women is a fascinating discussion for another time, but again, this goes back to non-verbals and perceived power within social constructs.

In closing, I do believe that "the quality of your life Is always related to the questions you are willing to ask". Solutions are like facets of a diamond…we must listen to all opinions to come up with the most colorful, synergistic solutions. This is how we arrive at the best answers. **Keep ASKING!** The ANSWERS are there if you ask the right questions and are willing to listen to all possible solutions, even the uncomfortable ones. **THE QUALITY OF YOUR LIFE IS IN THE QUESTIONS YOU ASK AND THE ANSWERS YOU ALLOW YOURSELF TO HEAR.**

Here is a final question for you: "Is anything TOO GOOD for me?" Hopefully, we all know the answer to that one.

It's All about Showing Up

Sugar Daddy

LuAn Mitchell

Throughout my life, I always showed up and no matter what happened or who was in the saddle, I asked for what I wanted and deserved.

Who am I? My life is in transition. I am undergoing a physical and spiritual transformation.

I changed my hair color several times. Blonde to black... then to something in between. These changes represent a return to who I really am... my authentic and true self.

I dedicate this sharing with love to every woman who has ever felt powerless, used up, or has ever felt that she has nowhere and no one to turn to. We are taking down walls and joining forces in the greatest numbers. We are ONE and I love and celebrate you.

Just exactly how 'blonde' are you?

How has your body changed over the years and how were those changes a reflection of you? Are you blonde, dark, too fat, too skinny, or with just a few extra pounds? Healthy, unhealthy, sad, happy, confident, scared, contented, the roller coaster continues every day. Yes, these fluctuations are what make up the days of our lives.

Whether single or in a committed relationship, what are we really looking for? Do we really believe that our Prince Charming will come along and make everything right? We need to learn to be authentic and true to ourselves. We need to eliminate unrealistic expectations and see our lives for the gifts that were given to us.

Lori Gottlieb's book, *Marry Him: The Case for Settling for Mr. Good Enough;* "Gottlieb, a 42-year-old single mother, caused quite a stir when she wrote a piece for The Atlantic in 2008 telling women to settle for men with shortcomings like bad breath—and not hold out for a big, heart-clenching love. If they did not, she argued, they would find themselves alone and without someone to help with the hard slog of bringing up kids. Marriage, she wrote, was not a "passion-fest," but a "boring, nonprofit business."

I had to find a way to assimilate my internal life with my external look. Inside I felt a lack of identity. I was beating myself up over a failed marriage, even though I knew that I should never have entered into it in the first place. I wanted closure so that I could move on. It felt like I was living in the Wild West. It was time for me to celebrate the "dark side" of all my successes. I didn't know where all this confusion and darkness was coming from. I have accomplished so much and really felt great about my life. I needed to look at myself as I got older and some of the beauty of youth began to fade. I needed to look back with pride and honesty at who I really am and all the good that I still want to do. I wanted to send the message to myself and to my audience that we are all God's children, his greatest accomplishments and in His eyes, we were all beautiful, whatever color our hair happened to be. I felt liberated. The change was extreme, and it felt great. I wanted to explore that feeling more. I wanted to know who I was inside my body. I wanted to know why what I looked like on the outside often mattered more than who I was on the inside. Who am I really? Who is my true self? When did I become the person I am?

My friends and I tossed around many ideas until we found what I was looking for -- faith and emotion. There was emotion! The movies and the headlines led audiences to believe and to engage. That was me at every step in my life journey. I had faith that I will get through this one, and "dodge" the next, and the next. I was always fully engaged in my life. I was always the star of my movie. In everything I did – in my thoughts, feelings, actions and words. If we are "just actors on the stage of life", as Shakespeare once wrote, then I want to be the best actor that I can be. I want to be true to myself. I would tell my lady friends that this is just a passing phase, like puberty, it will serve to prepare me. I will get through this. I am being trained. I am Billy the Kid, or Clint Eastwood. Each moment prepared me for the next big event in my life. With my thumbs squarely in my front pockets, and my palms out, I would walk bow legged and ask my girl friends to: "Go ahead and make my day." This is not my "forever after," not a Cinderella-like silly story line, but a rough and tumble "tom boy" kind of take on life. Without losing my feminine self, I could tap into my masculine side too.

They would giggle and I would wobble in my stilettos, (I love my heels) and happily (or sadly) I knew this (situation) is not the end, but a new beginning! I would tell them that my life is not some "freakin" fairytale! If there is a prince charming out there, he better damn know I want to be celebrated for who I am, all of me, the good the bad, and well... OK... we could work on that "other part" together. LOL

No, not a "bitch session" or a "woulda, coulda, shoulda" moan and complaint department – that wasn't it. We decided that this life is a solid training ground; together we can keep guard to our hearts and minds. Sure, I can do prayer work, or I can meditate; or I can choose to commiserate, whatever, but the truth is there is a bigger picture, and sometimes I may just wanna "pack a pistol," and shoot it in the air just for effect. Of course, I'm a peaceful person. This is just a game...a cleansing. I become peaceful when I remember that this life is just an illusion. It's our personal movie. Sometimes it's a comedy, sometimes a wild western and unfortunately, at times it can be a horror movie. But it's only a movie. Perhaps we're being tested. The "truth serum" technique works for me and I can go to that place inside me, at times and take control of my movie projector in my mind and create my story. We're all the main actors in our lives, so we need to be alert to our personal stories and create the lives we desire.

I realized that I don't have to give away my power because I'm a woman. I don't need to look for some sort of "prince charming!" I know that I'm already protected. I'm already loved by a magical being -- a powerful spirit, and that it all starts with me!

I write the script of my life. I write the "classified ads," for the people and circumstances I attract. Girls, I learned to be bulletproof and you can be too. We need to move forward as ONE body. We are ONE, and there is power in numbers, and we are ready to know the truth.

This is where I was when my husband died, and our struggling business fell into my lap. Until now I had believed that I'd end up working for Revlon or Louis Vuitton or some company in the beauty industry. So I looked up with my hands folded over my chest and said, to the heavens "OK, if this is what you want me to take on as my next challenge to prepare me for whatever you have in store, who am I to argue?" From that moment on, no one was going to stop me from going into the place and kicking some ass so I could take it from the brink of bankruptcy to a $450 million plus company.

What did I learn when I went from one level to a higher level? It can be very difficult to be publicly criticized or to read things about yourself or those you care about, that aren't true. Sometimes, a "headline" can be simply something that was said to me and it stood out as if it were that day's front-page proclamation. I can still pull some of those up in my mind's journal.

After that gabfest with my girlfriends, I spent a lot of time thinking about those things that are not obvious but are strange and inexplicable and why they got my juices flowing and my heart pumping. I came to realize that the villains, the outlaws so to speak, were just paper tigers. They were someone else's script that I was running on the projector in my mind... at least that was all they were to these universal sugar daddy hero dudes – that could slay them all and save my day.

The chatter about paper images all blended together in my memories and in my experiences and in my mind and heart. At times memories would be flimsy, lacking substance; and at times they could be used to hurt someone with harsh words, like 'you weirdo', or the incessant falsehoods; or even registered letters over the years bringing me problems like "the bank called your mortgage." Some of these papers might be laminated or impenetrable. And some might be nothing more than fancy wrapping. Yes, the pretty little "paper thin" bathing beauty pageant girl wins! Many times, I had felt as vulnerable, and as tough as paper, strange but true. So, it really is up to me to tell the truth and to face that truth.

It was clear to me that "love conquers all" and if only I could get that on paper, signed and notarized. Take a closer look and you will see that this theory has two sides. I set my course and I set my intention, no longer just a "well it's not my turn," kind of girl, I set my course by proclaiming my God given right to do so. I called out, "Give me whatever you've got Universe and I will learn from it and I will take it to the world to HELP OTHERS and with gratitude for it all! Yes, I will have a fresh perspective and be grateful for all of IT!"

At the same time, having trust and confidence in the process, I knew that my life would become more unique, wondrous and creative. It could convey a real hope for a peaceful global future. It could bring a heartfelt message and lift up spirits with musical notes; become a delicate cushion for some. I guess in many ways this vibe was also recognized by my girlfriends, there was a bigger picture like a universal sugar daddy watching out for us. This special light was within each and every one of us! I am known as the "Paper Doll," and yes, I have a book and a Podcast series by the name as well so let me explain. Special times with my women friends included some playful paper fights that were fun and entertaining. Whether paper was used for books, origami, puzzles, paper hats, butterflies, a piñata, as legal tender in a transaction, (in God we trust) for mutual benefit (an exchange of love, empowerment and energy, or money) it could bring a new loving image to life. It could make people smile, like when a proud child delivers his or her report card that would illuminate the face of a loving parent whose goal was to prepare that child for a future filled with joy and amazing new possibilities. Or it could advance the cause of peace. We can be cynical but remember that when we all hold hands no one is "cut out" or left out! A paper airplane can take flight. Why not? If properly constructed in our hearts and souls, it can take flight. No matter where we begin as individuals, we can be one global family. Oh, the power of ONE!

We can all take a fresh perspective and look at ourselves and envision the world differently. We can take charge and write our own personal fairytale, our own classified ads and even our movie script. We can demonstrate that every life has meaning.

But buyers beware! It's your movie, your classified ad, your life. It's what you're buying into. Don't let someone else label you or lock you in a tight little box. Let that wild and wonderful person hiding inside of you come out to play and devise your own brand of universal sugar daddy. You can be all that you envision. Set your sail and set yourself free. We're all one and we shall join hearts and spirits. You are not alone. Don't drift away in a prevailing wind; don't be torn by every criticism. Be your very own hero. Learn to dodge the creeps and their bullets. Learn to LOVE and be grateful for it all. When you do, you will soon see that GREATER times and GREATER things are on their way! You just have to 'vibe high' and keep the faith!

What kind of 'catch' will you be? And will you be used as a planter of seeds for good? Or will you be a spectator? Are you plugged in or are you destined to just be a "bullet ridden" victim? Will you realize that you are a hero and defender of the good?

Having achieved your goal, will you close ranks to protect your hard-won gains or will you share your achievements with others? Will you build a fort around your newly found treasures? Will you proudly declare what you learn and plant a seed for good to help others grow... never knowing if what you give will be returned to you? If you are always true to yourself even when you're at your lowest — like a protected seed with your sprout waiting to break out, to break free, to come to life – you are like the spirit of the pioneer that will be there no matter what is happening to you. As a teenager, I couldn't see the bright side of what had happened to me, and it was many years later that I recognized that there was good in suffering a tragic loss. It was then I realized that I was being prepared by something much greater than anything that I could fully understand. Now, many years later I understand that through it all; the hurt, the pain, the happy, and the sad times I was always loved and had value. There was always that bigger picture. I had a universal sugar daddy watching over me, walking with me, showing me, and loving me. I learned that a "pity party" mood was not my best option. Heroes surround us in other women and the men that support our cause. This realization is a cause to celebrate and this is my seed for good, I am the love gardener of that seed to help others; and lo and behold, I have become my own sugar daddy.

much
Success
Robbie
Nolte

Showing Up is Like a Treasure Map; You'll Never Know What Treasure You'll Find or Who You'll Meet!

Robbie Motter

Showing Up and Asking has been and is, the mantra of my life. I can say truthfully, that when I show up and ask, good things happen.

Because I spent many years of my life in foster homes, I learned very early that I would never have anything if I didn't ask for it. It was a good lesson; one that I carried with me throughout. I left the last foster home when I was 14 and took a Greyhound bus to San Francisco for a job with Levi Strauss. Thankfully I looked older than my age and dressed professionally and they offered me a trainee position.

Someone was kind enough to tell me about a boarding house in which I could stay, so I looked up the address and went to see it immediately. I liked the place but didn't have any money. Since I was good at asking for what I needed, I explained to the landlady that I didn't have any money, but that I had a job and would pay her as soon as I got paid. She was kind and must have taken pity on me, because she agreed.

I had a good career at Levi Strauss and several other companies, and I credit my climb up the corporate ladder to always showing up and never being afraid to ask. I asked for more responsibilities, more promotions, and for more money.

Of course, I also faced many disappointments throughout my career, and I saw, first-hand, that women weren't showing up much and weren't supporting each other. Few ever asked for what they deserved or needed, and certainly not for what they wanted. In 1976 I decided how I would live my life, and now, about 45 years later, I'm committed to sharing my insights, and making a point of encouraging women to 'show up and ask'.

Twenty-nine years ago, I started and ran business networks, and although women would stand up with ease at our meetings and describe with confidence what they did, they would assume that everyone there knew exactly what they wanted. I suggested that they add another 30 seconds to their elevator speech about how they could help the group and what they needed from it. What happened next was magical, and they were very excited about the results.

There are several incidents I want to share with you that demonstrates this. One of our members and her husband were big fans of a certain Canadian celebrity who was coming to Los Angeles. To get tickets for this event they needed an American Express credit card. She had the cash but not the card. She stood up at one of our meetings and said, "Robbie tells us to ASK for what we need, so here's what I need today." She described that she needed to buy tickets with an American Express card, and immediately four women raised their hands and told her she could use any of their cards. The member was surprised and from that day forward she believed in the power of asking. She went ahead and bought the tickets and gave the cardholder the cash and at our next meeting she decided to ask again. Her celebrity friend was staying at a hotel in L.A. that was sold out, and she and her husband really wanted to stay there for the night. She asked if anyone knew someone in the industry who might be able to help. The next day three of our members contacted her and she got a room in that same hotel but had to stay for two nights when she needed a room for only one. I suggested she check in and let the hotel know that they had had an emergency and would have to check out early. When she did, the hotel clerk was delighted, explaining that the hotel needed their room and that she was upgrading them to a suite for the same price. The suite was bigger than their friend's room, and after the show they hosted their friend and his entire band; they had a memorable evening…all because she asked for what she needed. Today, she's a true believer in the power of asking, and the resolve to show up.

At another meeting I personally made an ask that I wanted a spaded white female Maltese dog. The next day I got a call from a member who told me, "I have the dog you want. I'm going through divorce and I need to give her up. Her name is Majesty and I'd like to give her to you." The dog was part of the divorce fight for a while, but eventually I got that beautiful dog and couldn't be happier.

These are some of the stories that inspired me to create a book that clearly illustrates what happens when you show up and ask. I wanted to show, through personal and heartfelt stories, how it changes lives and helps people succeed in their careers well beyond their expectations.

We build our careers by showing up wherever it leads us. I was prepared to move wherever and whenever I was given an opportunity. In the late 70's I got an opportunity to work in Hawaii. I showed up at the Hawaiian Village Hotel for a job in Payroll and within the year I was Director of Personnel. Several years later I accepted a transfer to another of their hotels in Washington DC, as head of the Payroll and Personnel division. Next, I moved to Bellevue, Nebraska for a job with Gate City Steel, where I learned about computers, and this enabled me to join a major consulting company in Virginia where I continued to take advantage of every opportunity to learn. I just kept asking for more and showing up! My next move was to an Insurance Company in Houston Texas after which I got a call from D.C. offering me a position with more opportunities and a staff of 800. You see the trend? I saw an opportunity and I showed up.

In 1985 I moved to California and became an entrepreneur, spending the next ten years helping small business owners apply for government contracts. I helped them ASK and was delighted when they got what they wanted and needed. I then got involved in NAFE and took control of it, constantly showing up and asking for what we all needed. I travelled all over the country and watched our members excel in whatever they were doing. As I got older, I wanted to stay put, so I stopped travelling but continued to stay involved. I just kept showing up. I never looked for work. People came and offered jobs to me.

After 30 years running the NAFE networks in a volunteer capacity, I started a 501(c)(3) nonprofit, *Global Society for Female Entrepreneurs*. Like most of my successful enterprises, I didn't do it on my own. I ASKED one of my members, Cecilia Burch, whom I knew was an expert on nonprofits, to help me set it up. Then I ASKED some amazing people to serve on our volunteer board. They came on board and we started doing all our events under the GSFE nonprofit umbrella, and I continued to run the California networks under NAFE.

In April 2020, during the COVID-19 epidemic, I decided to fold the Southern CA networks into the GSFE nonprofit and in so doing, stepped out of the role as NAFE's global coordinator. I treasured my years with NAFE; I was there through many transitions, including buyouts and different presidents, and had met many extraordinary people along the way. But now it's time for me to carry my legacy of being a lifelong champion for women to its ultimate conclusion. I continue to be their cheerleader and mentor, and keep the flame going by SHOWING UP and ASKING for what they want. These are the critical tools for building personal and professional success. At 84 I still have much to do, and I'll continue to SHOW UP and ASK as long as I am able.

It's so important for each of us to step out of our respective comfort zones. I've stepped out many times, but the one that was most critical for me occurred in 2019. Michele Bergquist is the founder of Connected Women of Influence and delivers SUETalks, the highly successful female version of TEDTalks, on YouTube. She's also a friend and member. Since the early days of SUETalks, Michele has been inviting me to become a speaker, but I had declined her invitations. Every year she organizes several events in San Diego, Orange County, Los Angeles, and now the Inland Empire. At each of these events several women and one man share their stories. Now I've been speaking to audiences, sometimes as big as 10,000, off-the-cuff. I use some notes but never memorize my talk. When speaking at SUETalks, one cannot use props or notes. Your 12-minute talk must be fully memorized. I finally agreed to present at a SUETalks and was about to tell my story; a story I have told many times about who I am and what I know. Days before the event I could think only about how I could get out of going. I wanted to quit. But I have always told my members that quitting is not an option, so I had to take my own advice. On the night of the event, as I looked out at the audience during the sound check I couldn't even recall the title of my talk; I was so nervous. The room filled, the lights went on... and everything came back to me. I delivered my talk to a standing ovation. This was an experience I will always remember, and I thank Michelle for her tenacity to get me to do it. And once again, the importance of SHOWING UP was reaffirmed.

Always showing up can benefit you when you least expect it. Attend a small group meeting and speak to the group whenever you can. Speaking to small groups eventually opens doors to bigger venues. As an example, I got a call to speak at a technical school in San Bernardino, CA a few years ago. I SHOWED UP and spoke to a small group of students and staff but a few months later I was invited back as the keynote speaker at their graduation of more than 10,000 at the LA Convention Center. That was an awesome experience that happened because I SHOWED UP for the small group.

There are so many coincidences in life, and I've experienced more than my share. A member will call me asking about someone I might know that they would like to meet, and the next day the other person also calls, and I'm able to introduce the two effortlessly. One such incident occurred just the other day. I received an email from a former DC member who had developed a curriculum and was looking for someone who might be able to help her get CEU's (Continuing Education Units) for it. That same day I received an email from a guest who was scheduled to be on my *Diva Strategies for Success* radio show and while going through her bio I learned that handling CEUs was her expertise. So, I sent her my member's request and asked if she could help her. Or occasionally someone would say, I'm looking for a job and I'd get a call asking me if I know anyone with the exact skills needed. Or they're looking for a speaker on a particular subject and I go through my members list and find exactly what they need. Once you make SHOWING UP and ASKING a priority, magic happens. The stories in this book have validated my beliefs time and time again.

As a businesswoman (or man) make a commitment to include SHOWING UP in your strategic and marketing plans, or better still, create a "SHOWUP and ASK" PLAN and list and track ways to employ this strategy. You never know where your ideal customers will also show up.

Begin by ASKING yourself questions about what you want and let that list become your roadmap to the treasure chest of success.

I always SHOW UP but the power is in the ASKING. I've learned to ASK for everything and when some say no, I ask "WHY NOT?" My events are always successful because I invite successful speakers and entertainers. I ask for sponsorship, I ask for donations for our opportunity baskets, and I learned that people like being ASKED. So, my challenge for you is to SHOW UP and ASK, and I'm here to help you discover your SHOW UP Plan. Connect with me rmotter@aol.com for a free half-hour consultation to get you started on the path to greater personal and business success.

Robbie Motter, CEO/Founder GSFE (Global Society For Female Entrepreneurs), Distributor Bemer Group USA ID Number US 70131, Premier member Connected Women of Influence, Los Angeles Chapter, Director of Long Beach, Menifee, and Temecula GSFE networks, Co – Director, Riverside and San Fernando GSFE Marketing/PR Consultant Certified National Speaker, Author & Event Planner, Radio & TV Show Host, writer for Menifee/Murrieta Buzz and E, The magazine for Executive Magazine and Western Region GSFE magazine

It's All about Showing Up

My Love Affair with Paris

(Excerpted from the "Diamonds of Wisdom" Book by Mercy Noland)

Mercedita (Mercy) Noland

My love affair with Paris began long before I went there to visit. I have read much about the City of Lights and the City of Romance. Reading many books rhapsodizing about its allure made me dream intensely of the day when I can visit it. From these books, I remember two quotes about Paris most vividly, words that have made such an impression on me that I memorized them. I share them here because I feel that they are relevant, inspirational, and set the tone for this narrative. The first quote is by Gertrude Stein, American novelist and playwright who said, "America is my country, but Paris is my hometown." The second quote is by George Sand, French novelist and memoirist who wrote, "I know of no other city in the world where it is more agreeable to walk along in reverie than Paris." Both women, although born nearly 70 years apart were known for their fierce independent spirits. So fierce and fearless that with the sheer power of their words and the way they lived their lives, paved the way for many women to be elevated. They challenged the old and obsolete adages that women were weak, and therefore inferior to men. Then and now, I wholly and unequivocally support their philosophy – That women, although created differently, are equal to men.

In my lifetime, I have traveled to many countries and to many cities. I have been enthralled and wowed by many of them. Being a perpetual optimist and an inveterate romantic at heart, I always look for the beauty and charm of the place I am visiting and take pleasure from each place's individual charms and enjoyed them to the hilt. No other city, however, has captured my imagination, nor can compare to the nearly indescribable bliss I experience whenever I am In the "City of Lights". Paris appeals to and resonates with me on so many levels. This resonance is at once sensual and intellectual, buoyant and melancholic, flamboyant and cerebral, and always, always provocative and profound!

Fall 1989, was my first visit. When I first "showed up" in Paris. I was invited as part of an incentive trip for travel coordinators (one of my main responsibilities working for a multi-national company) to see and to experience the city. The trip was sponsored by Air France and its related hotel properties. The invitation was for a 6-day all expenses paid trip, that included business-class and first-class round-trip air fare. Luxury hotel accommodations at Le Meridien Montparnasse and Le Meridien Étoile, tours and meals! The invitation came at a time when I was completely broke and emotionally broken. Having been recently divorced, uprooted from my beautiful home, and forced to move to a different city, with my three-year-old son, I was a woman in deep survival mode. Despite my "default" attitude to look brave and bright, I was crying inside. This was one of the reasons, I demurred from accepting the first time I was invited. I had no spare funds for a trip anywhere, least of all for a trip to Paris! In the end, gracious pressure was exerted for me to decide because timely arrangements had to be made with both Air France and Le Meridien hotels. After much painful deliberation, and successfully arranging for my son to be watched by my Great Aunt Flor (who encouraged me to go), I finally said Yes!

That year, the Eiffel Tower was celebrating its centennial year. She was 100 years old. Every night that I was there, it was lit up in all its glory, so beautiful and so scintillating. In the quiet hours of the night, when my life's challenges fully hit me, the Eiffel Tower became for me a beacon of hope – quite literally and metaphorically. She has endured, and so shall I. During the "free days" when we were not required to travel as a group, I walked all over the city, traversed the streets of the Left Bank or "La Rive Gauche" and the Right Bank or "La Rive Droite" of the Seine – the river that divides Paris. During these walks and, as George Sand had written I was utterly lost in reverie! I went both in the daytime and nighttime. Sometimes alone, and sometimes with 2 of the guys who were in my tour group – John and Paolo. At one of our solo jaunts, John and Paolo "confessed" to me that they were gay. When I simply raised an eyebrow and unshockingly and unperturbedly asked them, "And your point is?" They immediately granted me their friendship and loyalty and adopted me as a surrogate sister of sorts.

We walked and found adventure everywhere! The Right Bank or "La Rive Droite" is also known as "posh Paris" – fashionable, attractive and with the famous Avenue des Champs Elysees, Avenue Montaigne and the Place Vendome, represented all the "joie de vive" that France is known for. This is where all the haute couture and globally iconic design houses such as Chanel, Dior, Louis Vuitton, and Hermes – brands that are synonymous to French elegance - are located. Many of the ladies in the group shopped at these designer boutiques, where I would not even dare go inside because I knew I would not be able to afford anything! I distinctly remember our beautiful host, Isabel, purchased a gorgeous crystal vase from the House of Baccarat. She hand-carried this treasure on the plane with her all the way home. It was a singularly stunning work of art that represented to me something to aspire to. I promised myself that the next time I visit Paris, I will be able to afford and purchase a piece of Baccarat crystal.

Here at Rive Droite also are the Louvre Museum where 3 days is not enough to soak up the entirety of the story of the world's civilization, the Pantheon – the penultimate monument to the French nation's democracy that loudly proclaims "Liberty, Equality and Brotherhood" on its front facade, and of course the Palais Garnier and the Bastille Opera – the 2 most prestigious theaters in the world.

The Left Bank is what I call the "Artsy, Intellectual Paris". Historically known for nurturing the creative (and often tortured) souls of literary legends such as Ernest Hemmingway, Henry Miller, Anais Nin, and Gertrude Stein, to name a few. It is where for decades, street artists performed on the streets for tokens practically every day of the week. The Right Bank and the Left Bank are the geographical representations of the cultural paradox that is Paris! Along its boulevards and cafes are an untold number of soul-stirring stories – lived and created by its inhabitants and the expatriates who are drawn there like bees to honey.

As earlier mentioned, at that time of my first Paris trip, I was a newly divorced, broke, emotionally unravelling and a struggling single mother of a three-year-old son. I accepted a position with a fairly-sized company as an administrative assistant and one of my main tasks was as a travel coordinator – a position far below my skills set and educational level – where one of my daily responsibilities was to arrange and coordinate all the travel requirements for the company's top and mid-level executives. I was in deep survival mode reeling from a violent breakup of a marriage that I thought would last forever and struggling emotionally and financially. My job provided me with enough money to pay for my cost of living while raising a child, but by no means had any extra for any kind of luxury. When the Paris trip offer was made, I eventually accepted realizing that it was an opportunity I may never have again. It was one of the best decisions of my life because I finally met a city that embraced me in all my brokenness, all my yet unfulfilled dreams and all my promise!

Fast Forward to Spring 2009. Exactly 20 years later, and a million other stories of struggles and triumphs in between, I have attained a moderate amount of success as a financial advisor. I got engaged to Rod - a lovely man who has been my best friend for 7 years before we became romantically involved. After living together for 5 years, he presented me with a beautiful diamond ring, and he and I agreed to exchange vows in Paris! We booked our plane, paid for our hotel in advance, and through a dear friend of mine, Sister Nenita Patena – arranged for a wonderful Catholic Priest, Father Marcelo Manimtim - to bless our vows! After all these arrangements, we belatedly found out that couples are required to live in France for at least 60 days to be granted a marriage license! My fiancé and I looked at each other, said "bleep" the license, we are going ahead with our plans without an official marriage license! We exchanged vows on a beautiful spring day at the Luxembourg Gardens, surrounded by centuries-old sculptures and monuments to saints, and the countless botanical marvels the gardens were known for. Our intimate ceremony was witnessed by our two gay friends – Roger and Edwin - my very own "Gays of Honor". Afterwards, we went for a delicious lunch and champagne, and in the evening celebrated at the George V, Four Seasons Paris.

We spent 10 glorious days in Paris, mostly reprising the things I did when I visited in 1989, as well as visiting the places I did not get to see. We made special memories just for our post-vows-exchange! We walked around the Trocadero, visited the Eiffel Tower, spent an afternoon there where we met a nice old lady named Jeannette at a café kiosk at the park. I gave Jeannette a bar of Nestle chocolate crunch which she opened slowly and with such elan, savored with such gusto with her cup of coffee. She told us she is a grandmother of 4 and lives not a mile from the park. Every morning, my Sweetheart would get up and go to the nearby café, pick up café au lait and croissants and bring them back to our room. After about a week of that, he made friends with the café owner – Pierre, who would tell him where the best local places were to eat. We followed each of his recommendations and it was well worth the adventure.

We attended on Sunday, a solemn high mass at the Notre Dame Cathedral, a service conducted in 3 languages – French, English and Latin! Afterwards, we had lunch at Ile Saint Louis followed by standing in a long line to Bartholomew's for a taste of the world's most famous ice cream.

We bought a day-pass to the Louvre, where I met an 8-year-old boy who was on a field trip with his class. We were both checking out the "fountain of Medusa" an enormous red granite fountain dating over 500 years with a fearsome bronze sculpture of Medusa at the center. In my rudimentary French, I explained to him that Medusa was a mythical figure whose eyes turned you into stone. The little wretch looked at me with all the arrogance of a prince and told me in perfect English, "I know Madame – I am

French." I was so flabbergasted by the response – I think I was simultaneously impressed as well as shocked by his attitude, so I simply raised my right eyebrow and dryly said, "Good for you." Afterwards, I recounted this to anyone who would listen, and had a great laugh! Father Marcelo said that the "French do take great pride in their children's education." So, really Kudos to them!

Rod and I went on our own for a day trip to Versailles (his first and my second visit). This time, I served as Rod's tour guide, and explained things to him while we walked through Palace of Versailles' Senate Room, the Queen's chamber, and the Hall of Mirrors which provided a remarkable view of the gardens outside. We walked in great wonder and admiration around this beautiful garden with its parterres, trees, orangery, groves, and priceless sculptures. I, of course took lots and lots of photographs for posterity. The spectacular garden whose design and renovation were entrusted by Louis XIV to the famous architect, Andre Le Notre is a living legacy of France's glorious (and violent) history.

We walked, and ate, and of course, shopped. We shopped everywhere – at the "festival des arts creatifs" where many artists and artisans proudly sell their wares and attended by many American store buyers who were on the hunt for fresh designs and fresh talents. This is where I met a lovely, artist named Chloe who designed gorgeous hats and fascinators. I did not want a hat, but I fell in love with a large hand-made silk flower in fuchsia! I asked her if I could just purchase the flower because I needed to wear one for my hair. She agreed, she took it out of the hat, and created a beautiful hair piece right before my eyes. In her own words, "It has to be perfect"! I still have that silk flower and have worn it on my hair and as a brooch on many special occasions! It still looks as fresh and beautiful as the day I purchased it!

It is important to note that by this time, I can afford pretty much anything, and so at one of our shopping expeditions, we went to the Baccarat boutique at Les Printemps where I purchased a Baccarat crystal wine carafe – a promise I kept to myself in 1989. I also indulged in Mariage Freres teas, purchased a dozen glossy tins to give to tea-loving friends in the States, as well as bags and bags of luxurious and heavenly smelling "Orchidee de Minuit" (Midnight Orchid) bath salts wrapped in elegant silver grey bags with silver ribbons and silver Eiffel Towers to special girlfriends. These bath salts were made from pure essence of midnight orchid that the luggage I brought them in smelt of it for months!

Since that time, I have been to Paris 2 more times – in 2015 with my friend Annabelle to celebrate our milestone birthdays (with a 5-day London trip prior to), and in 2016, for a combined vacation and wedding celebration of my one and only son, David to my precious daughter-in-law, Lana!

The year 2015 represented to me the year of becoming! Having achieved success in my profession as a financial advisor and having successfully raised a wholesome, healthy, and wonderful son, this year marked for me the beginning of the next chapter of my life. When I was no longer responsible (at least financially) for my child as he has completed his college education and professionally situated, I decided that now, I will focus on every dream, every goal I have long ago set for myself and put aside during my years of living in "survival mode". I am now in "success mode".

During this trip, we stayed at one of the most iconic 5-star hotels in Paris - Le Royal Monceau Paris. We were accommodated in a special suite with a "salle de bain avec miroirs sans ombres" or a suite with a "bathroom with mirrors that has no shadows". Designed by French architect Philippe Starck – who is famous for his elegant and utopian ideal of creating and designing interiors and various useful everyday items not just for the upper-crust, but for everyone. This suite, in of itself, was an architectural and technological wonder. Somehow, the room temperature and the lighting were always perfect, regardless of the weather outside, or the time of day. Our suite overlooked a compact but elegant patio adjacent to the Michelin starred restaurant, Il Carpaccio where we had our dinner the first night we arrived. It was framed by boxes of colorful flowers. The suite was a perfect marriage of utility and comfort, and the perfect place to inhabit after full days of shopping, dining, and sightseeing. We made friends with the Lady

Concierge, Margaux, who was literally our personal go-to lady during our stay there. Margaux was the quintessential French woman – she was slim, elegant, and very gracious to us. I fulfilled another promise to myself – I purchased expensive luxuries as such as- my first Chanel necklace and first Fendi purse at the boutiques in Avenue Montaigne, and a one of a kind Italian silk scarf with 3 kinds of furs on the collar from Leclaireur.

As of this writing, I celebrated yet another milestone birthday, but no matter where I am in life, Paris will always represent the fulfillment of promises I made to myself – the most important promises to keep.

About the Author: Mercedita Noland – Mercy to her friends - is Founder and C.E.O. of VeriDiva Women's Business Networking Group, an elite women's business networking group. She is a registered financial professional. As of this writing, she is affiliated with one of the most prestigious Broker-Dealers in the United States. Also, as of this publication, she has written and published non-fiction narratives and finishing her first solo book

It's All about Showing Up

Show Up in a Different Direction

Katherine Orho

I n 2007, while I was in California State University Fullerton studying Asian American Studies, I had a class project where I had to do a presentation about family values. I had my team of classmates to work with. I came up with an excellent idea to include the interview of people in performing arts. We did an interview of the band, Far East Movement. But I thought we could add more to it. I found out that there was an Asian American Film Festival in Riverside county. I begged each of my teammates to go with me to the film festival to see if we could interview one of the film makers. I guess it seemed like too much effort for little to no chance of getting the interview. Each one of my teammates refused to go with me. At the last minute, I decided to go alone.

Upon arrival, I spoke with the manager of the theater to ask his permission to interview some of the performers. He was surprisingly kind and cordial about it. He gave me his blessings and even seemed to be excited about the project. That night the movie I decided to see was Ping Pong Player, starring Jimmy Tsai and Jessica Yu. It was fabulous! After the movie, I asked the manager if he would talk to Jimmy Tsai to see if he would do an interview with me. I couldn't believe it when the manager came back to introduce me to Jimmy. He showed us to a relatively quiet area where we could film our conversation. I did the whole interview with Jimmy, who was not only the star of the film, but one of the writers and directors of the film. It was an amazing experience. The interview went smoothly; I spliced it into the rest of our video project. The whole project got an "A", too.

In 2013, after leaving my job, I was left with free time on my hands. I always say that "If what you are doing does not work for you, go in a different direction." So, I decided it was time to see how I fit into the tech field. I started out small, by joining The Riverside Robotics Society robot club in Riverside county. I found the group on Meetup.com. During my first Meetup with the group, I inadvertently suggested to the founder about something that I can no longer remember. Thomas Messerschmidt turned to me, and what I later came to know was true Thomas fashion, said, "That's a great idea. Why don't you take charge of that?" I was blind sided and could not get my mind to function. This was my first time meeting the man. It was my first day in the group. I didn't want to look like I was incapable of taking on a challenge. So, I stuttered out a weak "Okay".

About three months later, I was elected as Secretary of the club. I held that position for one year. To this day I still hold an honorable post on the Leadership Team. I left Riverside Robotics the following year because my body was not doing so well with the weekly meetings, and long drives. Also, I was presented with the opportunity to go from Secretary of The Riverside Robotics Society to being one of the Founders of another robotics club. That's right; I jumped from that position to being one of the Founders of The Techroom Robotics Club. I actually came up with the name for the club, too. We located the club in San Bernardino, California. I still hold that position to this day. I am listed as Human Resource Manager of the group, because I realized that I am most comfortable in an administrative capacity.

In 2014, I was diagnosed with stage 3 breast cancer. I won that fight in 2016. About two years after my last radiation treatment (2018), I picked up the phone and called Jill Eaton, the director of Susan G. Komen Inland Empire. Their grand opening of the Riverside office was the next morning. I left her a message asking her if I could volunteer to help them out 'tomorrow'. I emailed her a resume and quick cover letter. Who does that? I was sure she would say no and think I was a crazy person. She returned my call that night and told me that she would love to have me come and help out. She was genuinely welcoming. That floored me. Again, I showed up and have not left. I have volunteered for each Murrieta Race for the Cure (now the More Than Pink Walk). Eventually, I started coming in to volunteer in the office every Wednesday. Right up until the Covid pandemic, working in that office once a week was a complete joy.

At the beginning of 2019, I also joined the Inland Empire Software Developers Meetup group. I convinced the founder of the group that they needed a Board of Directors. I immediately applied for a position on the Board of Directors. I nailed it, since mine was the ONLY application.

Showing up also means putting yourself out there in new opportunities. My whole life is about showing up. Showing up in new fields, new positions, and new relationships. I really stand by my saying that "If it's not working, go in a different direction." That means that in the face of failure or loss, I can pick myself up and dust myself off and move on.

By 2019, prior to the Covid 19 pandemic of 2020, I was sick all the time and majorly depressed. I had survived stage three breast cancer, but my body was not recovering a smoothly as I wanted it to. There were family issues that I could not ignore. I felt like the walls were closing in on me every day, then the pandemic hit. I was devastated – at first.

I eventually decided to take my own advice. This will be the most crucial test of my saying: If it is not working, go in a different direction. In order to do that I had to figure out what wasn't working and what did work for me. I came to the realization that I am not very good at studying technologies, programming languages and I no longer felt good about the prospects of robotics. It has some very helpful applications, but I do not feel comfortable with some of the directions predicted about robotics and the future of employment for the average American. It truly bothers me that to think that after this pandemic, businesses might seize the opportunity to displace many workers who desperately will need their jobs by replacing them with robots that will work more efficiently and for less cost to a company annually.

I have not been sleeping at night. So, what direction can I go in? Simple! I started studying in my bed throughout the night and into the morning hours. What did I get out of that? I improved my Spanish by leaps and bounds. I started studying Chinese again, too. But the most significant new direction is that I started taking courses on Executive Assistant and Administrative Assistant with Alison.com, LinkedIn Learning and the American Society of Administrative Professionals. I have acquired certificates from Alison.com for Executive Assistant and Administrative Assistant this week alone.

Already, I've been contacted by another student of the Chinese course I am taking on Edx.org on LinkedIn.com. Surprisingly, he is a software developer. I thought that was ironic. He will be my Chinese language pen pal.

In a text to my son I spelled out the importance of showing up by doing:

> *"Look, you and I both are good people, but we lack self-confidence. This is a whole new world we are walking into, post covid. It is a major game changer. Things were getting desperate BEFORE this pandemic. But it has really forced everyone's hand. Survival is the mode that we are in now, not success. It is now "___ OR GET OFF THE POT" time, as my mother used to say. The two of us have to be adults, realistic grownups.*
>
> *Step up your game, Babe. Your smart, your capable and you've got this. Carry full loads from here on out. Otherwise, you are selling yourself short.*
>
> *Kisses."*

It is the truth. When the economy opens up it is going to be a whole new world of competition and struggle for many people. We will have to shed whatever was holding us back and go in new and strange directions. It doesn't happen if we do not show up.

Do not think that I am saying that I don't have a long way to go. I know that I have barely started to redefine myself. But I challenge you to show up. So, what changes do you need to make? Show up and go in a different direction.

There are ways to network with like minded people without even leaving your home now. Since 2002, Meetup.com has been in the business of connecting people to people for hobbies, work, opportunities and so on. It is a great place to start to look for clubs, organizations or events. For technology alone, Meetup has over 7,000 groups worldwide. And if you do not find what you need, you are welcome to create a Meetup group for whatever you want to network in. Designing a Meetup group is a great way to utilize leadership skills, management skills and even project management skills.

Did you know that LinkedIn has a section called groups, where you can get involved with clubs or organizations/associations that share a similar or new interest as you? LinkedIn has been in business also since 2002. Many people utilize it for professional networking and job search as well.

Then there are nonprofit organizations like Susan G. Komen, which is a national breast cancer foundation. Fifty-six percent of donations that are allocated for research goes into finding more effective treatments. Komen has a walk or race every year. It is one of their largest fundraisers. And it is so much fun. If you are a survivor, you really get the feeling of being in good company when you are in that walk and look around to see all of the smiling faces that are walking with you. There are more men who take part in Komen festivities than you would suspect. The truth is that men can get breast cancer and they need support just like everyone else.

Susan G. Komen welcomes volunteers. Volunteering with them is a practice in leadership, event planning, and administrative tasks. Not just Komen, though. There are more than thirty cancer related nonprofits, just in California alone. They really need help and welcome volunteers.

There are many more non cancer related nonprofits that you can get involved with. Whether in your state, nationwide or globally you can find a nonprofit who wants you to volunteer with them. Check out VolunteerMatch.org. This platform links people to volunteer positions all over the world. Volunteer Match has been in business since 2008. I love how their site says, "Our aim is to build services that overcome the barriers that keep volunteers and nonprofits from finding each other, working together, and developing strong relationships." What a beautiful goal!

Improving on a skill is a good way to demonstrate that you are capable of showing up. It shows that you care about your skills enough to expand on the ones you have, review or learn new skills all together. Alison.com offers free courses with an option to purchase a certificate or diploma upon completion. Alison started doing business online in 2007. It is an Ireland based company. LinkedIn Learning also offers a certificate, but you pay a monthly fee to gain access to the courses that you want to take. LinkedIn recently acquired its competitor, Lynda.com, giving LinkedIn Learning more courses to offer the public. EdX was founded in May 2012 by scientists from MIT and Harvard. Its founders included Gerry Sussman, Anant Agarwal, Chris Terman, and Piotr Mitros who taught the first EdX course on circuits and electronics from MIT. Today, Edx provides more than 3,000 courses to offer from universities all over the world. More than 2,000 of those courses are self-paced.

All of these organizations and platforms mentioned provide ways to change the direction you are going in. So, again I say, I challenge you to show up. Figure out what changes you need to make. Then get out there to show the world your skills in leadership, event planning, teaching, public relations, performing arts or arts and crafts. Show up and go in a different direction.

It's All about Showing Up

Been Showing Up Since 16
(Knowingly AND Unknowingly)

Kisa Puckett

The moral of the story that I am about to share with you is to Show Up. My name is Kisa Puckett. It's spelled K. I. S. A. but pronounced with an "h", so it's Keesha. I am an eclectic, creative entrepreneur at heart and have been since the age of 16 years old. I've had my share of small triumphs, huge successes, and plummeting failures. But, even within the failures, there's always a lesson so it's never really a fail. Instead, it's an opportunity to get better, pivot, or build on the foundation of new knowledge. I started off very young tagging along with my dad to network marketing conventions and meetings. I can say at first, I wasn't too pleased when being the fill-in partner. I was too young to really take advantage of anything I was hearing, but what it did for me at that time was to instill the burning desire that I have now for entrepreneurship. It gave me a sense of what freedom was like, how dreams come true when starting from a place of passion and tenacity, and how I could achieve whatever it is that I wanted to achieve in life with creativity and the ability to allow myself to actually dream and live out every zone of my genius. So in essence being exposed to this at a very young age although it had to grow on me, which it eventually did, was the most pivotal part of my life that paved the way for where I am today. Years later I would experience working in the legal system as a Deputy Court clerk. I would also experience owning my own restaurant and entering into my first licensing deal with a large chain restaurant at the age of 23. I would then go on to experience my first stab at creating a fully mobile business in the spa and beauty space and launching my own beauty product line. Having the privilege to consult businesses and entrepreneurs in over 50 industries in the areas of marketing and branding over the years, has been nothing short of amazing.

That is when I truly discovered the power of showing up. Fast-forwarding into recent years I began to really understand the importance of being present and showing up in everything that I do. One of the most pivotal moments in my life that demonstrated the power of showing up was in the year 2019. This was also the first year I heard Robbie Motter and her message of showing up and asking for what you want. This made the biggest difference in my outlook for the year and the direction of my business.

2019 was the most exciting year, I have had in a very long time. It was full of surprises. After working for local government for over 10 years, I had finally decided to step out into my business again full time. This came with a flood of emotions from excitement to fear of the unknown to pure empowerment. I have had several businesses prior to this, but this was very different. It was at a time where I had been within a system that was very restrictive and didn't really encourage out of the box thinking. Thankfully, I always had a side business or entrepreneurship venture that kept my attention and fulfilled my burning desire to create and share my genius with the world. Although I was there in this system for over 10 years, I never allowed it to extinguish my creativity, joy, or the excitement that came with bringing new ideas to the table and expanding old ones. However once the end of 2018 came, I knew that I needed to do something different, more fulfilling, and to really serve within the space that God ordained for my life. It just wasn't enough anymore to continue to work outside of my purpose in a system that was designed to be something very different then I needed in life. That was my moment where I decided to first show up for ME. I ask myself the questions: What is it that I want to do? How do I want to impact the world that I live in? How can I serve others to help them be better and grow into all they were meant to be? I was forced to be honest with who I was, what I brought to the table, and what I needed to do next. Showing up for me was imperative and for me to see what I was truly made of. It was also the opportunity I needed to continue a legacy that would bring my life full circle and allow me the chance to live out every dream that I had ever dreamt. I had always been a believer in chasing after your dreams, doing it scared, and giving yourself the space to be creative, innovative, and free to make choices in life that would allow you to truly experience life to the fullest. For me crossing over from 2018 to 2019 was once again me giving myself permission to show up and step into the greatest version of myself. Once I was able to make this transition, the ride of excitement and Discovery began. 2019 was full of uncertainty, excitement, and some of my most creative innovations and experiences to date. I continued to show up all of 2019. I continued on the theme of creating experiences around my zone of genius, shaking hands with new people, hugging on those I already knew, and stepping into different situations and experiences that I had never experienced before. I created and launched over 20 events by the summer of 2019. I showed up for each and every one of them. I met and mingled with so many incredible people. It was like a year-long networking and engagement intensive. However, I always networked with intention and leveraged the connections to the highest degree of engagement. I never took any relationship for granted and I was present in these moments to truly capture the true essence of the beauty and value that it would bring to my life and my new fledgling business. Out of these many events and engagements, I was able to build a business around trust, relationships, and community. Just as importantly, I SERVED. It was not just about me and what I was going to get out of these new relationships, opportunities, and ventures that I encountered. My most important asset in all of what I did in 2019, was service. It's what God used to bless me from all of the showing up. The fact that I didn't come into a place or space with my hand out on every occasion but was willing and ready to serve, offer value, and be present in the moment was one of the greatest gifts that I was able to give in all of my showing up. Although there were obviously times that asking was also important, my showing up never was without service. With this, true and authentic connections happened. These connections led to an incredible amount of business, amazing opportunities, and very lucrative ventures. Showing up and being prepared to meet new people, experience new things, and allowing myself to operate authentically in my zone of genius is what created the space for me to thrive. It's what allowed me to create business when little opportunity was available. It allowed me to turn ventures that were dry into running wells of water. It's allowed me to meet people that would add additional value to my life spiritually, mentally, and emotionally. It's created new friendships, deeper relationships with those that I admire, and an opportunity to turn ugly circumstances into beautiful experiences and valuable learning lessons. Showing up for my business and people is what changed my life from uncertainty and fear to excitement, hope, and joyful anticipation. The showing up that I was committed to in 2019 is what brought me abundance with all of the things I touched in 2020. With this abundance, it has meant more lucrative opportunities, expansion of my territory, and a new level of myself within my space in this world. Everything that was built in 2019, all of the challenges that I experienced ending out the year in 2018, and my decision to show up for myself, my family, and the people I serve was what sustained me, and allowed me to continue to grow into who I was meant to be. In the course of all of this showing up, I came into agreement with God that if He would show me the way, connect me to the right people, and provide the opportunities, then I would show up and see them through. It wasn't always easy and was most times quite challenging, but it was always worth it. Today, what I have learned more than anything is that trusting God and having him lead me in that, showing up has been one of the biggest blessings I could have ever experienced. You never think that showing up and being in agreement with yourself could create such an amazing success. It has been proven in my life that trusting God and showing up has been the connecting points for my success today. During a time where people are losing their jobs, business is slow, and an economic downturn like no other has been experienced.(due to COVID-19), my showing up all of 2019, has provided me the blessings that I have today with a thriving business during the pandemic and a continuously impactful set of ideas that continue to carve out room for me and my future successes. When you're showing up, it not only blesses you but blesses those around you, your community, your family, the people that you serve, and the places that you go. It is the most fulfilling life story that could ever be told. My showing up has done exactly this. I started with a traditional marketing agency model and event producing business. In this space, I have helped many become highly visible in their zone of genius and create the success that they desire. I have grown my business from a traditional marketing agency to a full-blown creative and digital ad agency that encompasses a house of brands. This house of brands now includes a global barter exchange designed for professionals, business owners and entrepreneurs, a digital ad agency, event production and media distribution company, and a signature educational program for entrepreneurs and business owners. From my showing up I have been able to take uncertainty, a huge transition in my career, and the fear of the unknown and turn that into a marketing and media empire that I will continue to build for years to come. I have gone from being in business for only a little over a year as a solopreneur to hiring an entire team to support our ever-growing company and forever clients. We now have adopted the model and built a culture and methodology around attracting your forever clients. It was in all of that showing up and building those relationships that meant the most for my personal life and business. It has allowed me to see that attracting your forever clients through showing up and taking action are the secret sauce behind launching, growing, and scaling your business astronomically. Scaling for me has meant launching my own TV Network and media distribution across Roku, Amazon Fire, Apple TV, and Android TV. This is now allowing me to carry on my legacy of supporting people with positioning them to receive high visibility and next level profitability. It is allowing me to create not only the space but the stage for messages and movements to be shared globally. I'm able to do what it is that I love which is passionately serving people and supporting them to birth their greatest dreams. It has meant me serving my clients and giving them access to ways to truly accelerate their business and activate their dreams and goals. It has allowed me to equip the people that I serve with the knowledge, skills, and preparation to fulfill their God-given purpose. Showing up has meant a difference in my relationships, my income, and my life experiences that I will be able to now pass down to my children. What I have learned in all of this is that you cannot create magic, receive tangible gifts, or be blessed with the invaluable treasure of connection if you never show up.

So again, moral of the story? Show up. And after you've done all that showing up, ASK for what you want.

It's All about Showing Up

Showing Up Will Change Your Life

Lori Raupe

I t was 2014, some high school friends and I got together in Old Town Temecula (Southern California) for lunch. It turned out to be a very long and enjoyable lunch. We shared the highlights, and some lowlights of our lives since we left school 42 years before. Dawn Elders (Strickland), described for us a life of a nurse who travelled the world on medical missions. She had joined the US Navy after high school, being elevated to Major before returning to the private sector.

Her adventures were many and the people she met were extraordinary and for me very inspiring. I regretted not having traveled much. In fact, I had only been on a vacation to Hawaii back in the 1980's. Dawn's life had been full of adventures. Dawn told us that she was preparing to go to Africa to provide medical care at Helping Hands Orphanage in Malawi. She was so passionate, and her passion was palpably contagious. She's been at the orphanage at least 15 times and she and her husband had adopted a young boy, Hastings, and helped him get a college education. I was hooked by her stories of compassion and generosity of spirit. When she spoke about Malawi, I could feel it calling me. The timing of her next trip was not convenient for me, but I committed to going sometime soon. Another classmate, Leonard, did join Dawn on her next trip, and I loved seeing the Facebook posts from their trip. His smile in the pictures spoke volumes and I regretted not going with them. That day, that lunch was a turning point for me. I was determined to do more traveling and broaden my experiences.

I never seemed to have time to travel. Working and raising my family was the fulfillment I focused on for most of my life. We did take a lot of "power" weekends for boating and off-roading. I especially enjoyed trips to Victoria, Canada, but I felt that these trips were just vacations. I've always given generously of my time, especially for church activities.

Don't get me wrong, I wasn't judging myself. I had a full life, that included my personal tragedies, but no matter what happened to me I was always there for others…be it my family, friends or anyone in need. I helped out in the community as much as my time and energy allowed. But that day I realized that I wanted to do more, and Dawn had opened the door for me to contribute to my community. The time was right. I was about to retire, and my daughter had a family and was building a wonderful life for herself.

There was a time in my life when I had been so consumed by grief that I could barely make it through the day. My younger daughter, Jennifer, or Jenna as we called her was killed in a car accident. She was only 16. In those days, when I lived in pain and despair, I turned to God. He in His wisdom showed me hope and a future so I can bring hope to others.

I still don't know how I managed to put one foot in front of the other, but I managed to walk though that pain and committed to helping other parents whose lives were also shattered by the loss of a child. I met many on an online platform, webhealing.com. I attended Compassionate Friends and met many people who needed healing and connected with many more on the online platform, webhealing.com. And, over time, I began to heal. It took a long time for my broken heart to begin to recover. But the seed that was planted showed me that I can heal by helping others and this became my soul's journey and passion.

Then came the California Cedar Creek fire in 2003, when our home burned to the ground. I stood there looking at the ashes of what we had worked a lifetime to accumulate. It was a humbling experience as I picked out a few trinkets, but they were also charred and almost unrecognizable. I grieved again for my losses, not for the things, but for the memories. Grief can be all consuming, causing some to stay stuck in it. Others come to a place of healing, where the pain never goes away but they're able to find some happiness and joy again. When a love one dies, grief hits you in such a devastating way that your heart seems to stop at times and it's almost as if your life has ended. Then something happens, and you realize that you can get through this. The pain I've experienced was more than I believed I could live with, but then I discovered just how resilient we human beings are, and the importance of taking our grief to help others survive the way we did.

We lost nearly everything in the California Cedar Fire, but I was grateful to be alive. We had a few belongings, our cars, and Dee-O-Gee, our Springer Spaniel. The fact that we got out was a miracle. As the fire raged all around us, I filled the cars with everything I could collect quickly and prepared to evacuate. I never imagined that we would come back with nothing left of our home. The mind cannot comprehend such devastation. Of all that we lost, the most important were the precious tangible reminders of Jenna. It was like losing her all over again.

The loss was immense. How were we going to start over? Where will we live? There was no time to grieve, we needed to recover fast and rebuild our life. It was so devastating. It wasn't just our home, everywhere you looked was like a war zone. The look on our neighbor's faces were of despair. I wanted to hide under the sheets and never come out, but I didn't.

I was determined to help others with information and encouragement. To show them that they weren't alone. I had experienced this need for myself and people were there for me when I needed the support. They were there for me when Jenna had gone to be with the Lord. The grief group was there for me. I reached out to my neighbors and worked with them so that we could recover together and lessen the load for each of us.

In 2016, it seemed like a good time for me to retire from a very demanding job in Corrections and begin the next chapter of my life. It was now two years after our golden girls' luncheon, and I had thought about Malawi often. I had joined the John Maxwell Team and had learned a great deal about leadership and other business theories from John Maxwell. I had embraced one of John's quotes as my own. "I want to make a difference, with people who want to make a difference, doing something that makes a difference, at a time that makes a difference." I knew that I wanted to join him as a speaker and coach.

So, the time was right for me to join The John Maxwell Team and teach his incredible truths that once applied, can transform your life. Learning and working with such an inspiring man, gave me a new purpose and now I was in business for myself, but no longer alone. There are more than 30,000 members on this amazing team. The team culture was labeled JMTDNA, which are the initials of attributes assigned to team members worldwide. It's a model of life lived intentionally and with valuing others. We share our knowledge and our experience freely with each other and the world.

After seeing Dawn on that wonderful spring day and hearing her inspiring story, I had the pleasure of getting to know Hastings Kajomba Bwanali on Facebook, and FaceTime. Hastings is one of the Directors of Helping Hands Orphanage. He was the young man Dawn and her husband have helped to become the man he is today. He has a wonderful wife and two beautiful daughters, Hope and Grace. They live in Blantyre, Malawi. There are four sites where they provide food for 500 children, most of whom are orphans, as well about 300 elderly people who are alone. When the children are older, they are partnered with an elderly person to help and care for. Their greatest gift is spending time with them and listening to their life stories. The young people benefit greatly from the wisdom they share.

Timing is everything and is part of God's design for our lives. So, when the time is right you must act. I started to pray for the HHO and made a sign that I always carried with me to speaking engagements. The sign read, "I work for food." I would hold it up and smile, then explain that I wasn't asking for food for myself but for children at the Malawi orphanage.

In 2017, I had the opportunity to join the John Maxwell Team on a trip to Asuncion, Paraguay. John's teachings were both inspiring and transformational and the opportunity to teach these transformational principles around the world was my honor and blessing.

The trip to Paraguay was amazing, to say the least. I met a lot of beautiful people and had the opportunity to facilitate the teachings all over the country, including the Department of Commerce and Trade. John's teachings are helping to transform countries. One of the highlights of the trip was meeting the Landfill Harmonic kids. These are kids who live in the landfill just outside the city of Asuncion. A very talented and gracious man has made instruments for the children out of materials they found in the trash. Their music is like nothing I've ever heard. Their smiles are beautiful, and they enchant their street audience with their songs. They live in poverty that is unimaginable to the children in our wonderful country, but you can see that they're happy. We brought with us gifts and the look on their faces when we gave them new backpacks would melt any heart…it certainly did ours. They were so grateful and couldn't stop hugging us. We handed out some juice boxes and I took some pictures of them as they drank, with the mounds of smoldering trash behind them. It rained that day, so they told us that the trash didn't smell too bad. We looked sadly at them because the smell was terrible. I'll never forget those kids, their music and their smiles. I have a picture from that day displayed in my living room to remind me of that day and the people I met. We went to change lives and in the process our lives were changed.

In 2018, I went on another transformational trip to Costa Rica, with The John Maxwell Team. After several days of teaching and speaking, we visited a center where the kids had been rescued from the streets. They had been exposed to sex trafficking, drugs, prostitution…unthinkable things. They were finally getting the help they deserved. The volunteers we met were compassionate and the look on everyone's faces was love and hope. After those two trips I was determined that this was what I wanted to do with my life.

I woke up in the middle of the night with a dream and a vision to create a learning center in Malawi as a legacy of my daughter, Jenna. I saw a place where kids can be safe from the harsh weather and to recover from the traumas of their lives. They would be free of disease, drugs, sex trafficking and wars. They would be taken care of and loved. They would no longer be victims of the evil that surrounds them.

I envisioned building a Jenna House at Helping Hands Orphanage. I asked God for His help and miraculously the house was built, but I didn't see it for a while. Money was in short supply so I could spend it on a trip, or I could send it to feed the children. I chose the latter.

Dawn gathered another group of friends for lunch at the end of 2019. She told us that she was going on another medical mission to Africa and to visit the Helping Hands orphanage in Malawi in the Spring of 2020. On my drive home, I knew that I needed to be on that trip. I wanted to see the Jenna House, meet Hastings, his family and the kids in person. On many nights, I dreamt that I was already there and during the day I wished I was.

I organized a birthday fundraiser in January and raised all the money I needed for the trip. I was ready to go. I bought my ticket, reserved accommodations and started collecting all the things I wanted to take with me. I met with Dawn to get more information about the trip. I asked John Maxwell to autograph a copy of the John Maxwell Leadership Bible for Hastings. I was excited and apprehensive. They say everything you want is on the other side of your comfort zone, this certainly was for me.

Then sadly, the trip was canceled. Like I said, timing is everything. The world pandemic hit, and flights were cancelled. I was terribly disappointed. I have my transformational work, a country I have fallen in love with, and along with its people. Now may not be the time, but it will be soon.

I'm used to disappointments and whenever I'm down I reach out to help others. The program I was taking to Malawi was the John Maxwell iChoose program. It's a wonderful introduction to the far-reaching and to John's transformational work. I've been able to introduce this program at several locations in my community, including my local high school near my home.

Whenever something troubles me or there's an important decision I need to make, I'll wake up in the middle of the night with a clear and open mind and the solution appears. Recently, I must have been thinking about what more I could do to help the kids at the orphanage. It wasn't long before the idea of pen pals came to me. I had a pen pal through Girl Scouts while in elementary school and I smiled as I recalled how much I enjoyed it and what a wonder experience it had been for me. I knew, at that moment, that I should start a Pen Pal Project for the kids who were now at home because of the pandemic. It would also help parents who were looking for a meaningful experience for their children while at home. I didn't doubt that it would also be a tremendous experience for the children at the Helping Hands orphanage.

It occurred to me that I might be able to get more funding too for the orphanage. I was so excited I could hardly wait until the morning light, but I did manage to go back to sleep with joy in my heart. I reached out to Hastings immediately and he was also excited by the idea. I started The Pen Pal Project Facebook group and asked friends to ask their kids to participate. The rest is history. A few weeks later we had 60 matches, 120 children are writing to each other. I can only imagine the sharing and the friendships that will come from this.

We all experience disappointments and sometimes, tragedies, but with God's help we find a way out of it. I'm certain that, when the time is right, I will be going to Malawi soon and the trip will be everything I imagine it and more.

When I look back and think, I almost missed that lunch in 2014. My dad had recently passed away and I wasn't ready for small talk. I was thinking of cancelling, but I'm so glad I showed up and it changed my life. I want to continue to help those who cannot help themselves.

My life is so much better today…filled with meaning and is significant. As my mentor, John Maxwell, says, "Once you taste significance, mere success will never be the same." After all my tragedies and those that I have learned about from the children and people I've been fortunate to meet, the beauty of their smiles and the hope in their eyes gives meaning to my life. I am forever grateful.

Let me know if you know a child who would enjoy writing to a child in Malawi.

It's All about Showing Up

Showing Up

Reanna Ritter

In August of 2018, I decided I could not take anymore. I hated my job and quit, with a fair amount of debt and no savings, I was just hoping I would make enough money to avoid foreclosure or collections. This was not exactly a lofty goal, but the stress was affecting my health. For more than two years, I had been thinking about starting my own consulting business and had started working on building up my administration infrastructure, but had trouble launching into sales. I have to be honest, that part of the business was intimidating. I had no idea how to connect with clients. My father-in-law had introduced me to some successful accountants who had started out the same way I was planning to. They talked to me about their networking strategies before the concept was known to me and I must admit, it sounded awful. I'm an accountant. Networking is not in my skillset, I thought. I knew marketing was necessary, but an effective marketing strategy was elusive to me. I also recognized that my community did not stretch any further than my neighbors. I needed to figure it out, fast. Without networking and marketing, my business would be a failure before it even started.

What I learned, and value now about networking, is the knowledge I gain from the people I meet and the wonderful friendships that I now enjoy. I expected every networking interaction to lead directly to business and therefore believed it was worth my time to show up to them. But I was wrong, not all do. Often, it takes months or years to attract a client, and sometimes, it doesn't happen at all. Of course, this is very discouraging, and a lot of entrepreneurs avoid showing up and networking, not realizing how much they miss. How many times did I think that showing up to a networking event was a total waste of time and my self-talk was, that I won't get any business or maybe I'll attract the wrong kind.

Every relationship is an opportunity to learn valuable lessons that will lead to new growth, and more success. It's up to us to make showing up work. I found that most relationships did eventually lead to at least one referral. Showing up and asking has been difficult for me. I prefer interacting with people one on one or in small groups in order to build more meaningful connections. I am used to doing things for myself. I don't ask for help. Well, at least that's how I felt a year ago, but I don't anymore. Now, I know for certain that showing up and asking is the only way a business can succeed. It took me over a year to learn this truth. It's not about asking people to buy your service, but to get to know and trust you and if they, or someone they know can benefit from what you have to offer, to keep you in mind. I learned that it is easier to tell your story and make a personal connection than to sell.

I started to search for community groups that would be good places for me to meet potential clients. From what I learned, I decided to join the Murrieta/Wildomar Chamber of Commerce. My first networking meeting was a casual lunch the Chamber hosts every Wednesday. I walked into a room full of strangers who were small business owners. Most were in business by themselves. I was hoping to find large companies with big outdated information systems. I was looking for companies that had a healthy budget and wanted to go paperless. The small business owners I would meet here were the DIY (do it yourself) types when it came to accounting, and mostly involved tax preparation. I doubted their IT know-how. But I was there, and I was going to make the most of it. Perhaps some may need bookkeeping help. I smile when I look back on my mindset because I know now that my attitude wasn't helping me.

We went around the room and each person stood up and introduced themselves. I was shaking when my turn came. I stood up, tried to appear confident and project so the room could hear me. I could feel my voice shaking. I spoke too fast, repeated myself a couple of times and sat down quickly. I didn't do well. My audience smiled graciously, and I was determined to be better prepared next time.

After that day, I started going to every networking event I could find time for. I still had my full-time C-Suite job, a husband and two kids to look after. Over time, I got better at speaking, smiling, and meeting people. As people became familiar, I got more comfortable. So many times, I found myself to be the youngest person in the room. At first, I found this intimidating, thinking that everyone there had so much more business experience and were surely smarter than me. After showing up at a variety of networking meetings for about two months, I had some luck. At a breakfast meeting, after we made our introductions, a man about my age came over to me and asked me to help him with his project. I was so excited, and we talked about his project for a while. He said he was happy to give a startup a chance. We agreed on the approach and price and I got started. This was now my second client and the project turned into a monthly retainer and a long-term client.

At a different event, I met Bryan Caron a graphic designer at Phoenix Moirai, who invited me to his networking group, Business Network International. I was surprised to learn that this was the largest networking organization in the world. It was an early morning meeting (my life was very busy in the morning), but I was excited about the group and agreed to show up. I immediately liked the group. It was smaller, around 20 people, and they met weekly. So, I could get to know the members better and could build stronger relationships.

I joined the group and the referrals started to come in from both within and outside the group. Later, a friend I had made through the Chamber, Virginia Earl, invited me to a networking group called NAFE. This was an only women's group and I found this group friendly and very accommodating to new people. The stories the women shared were both inspiring and encouraging. I met Robbie Motter, founder of the Global Society for Female Entrepreneurs. What tenacity she has. Robbie is a giving person who offers the women in her network opportunities to show up, get out of our comfort zones and help each other succeed.

It was at my second NAFE meeting that I met my first business coach, Candace Gruber. The speaker at the meeting told a heart wrenching story, and I confided in Candace about my worries that a similar tragedy could happen to me. As she wiped away the tears caused by the speaker, she told me that I could not go through life thinking that way. We had several helpful conversations over the next couple of months, she invited me to join her in a collaborative marketing presentation. She was an excellent speaker and got her message out effectively, so that people could appreciate the value of her services. I cringed at the idea but decided that it was something I had to do eventually, so why not now? We worked on a presentation and invited a few people, and some showed up. She was great but I lacked the confidence to follow up. I needed some coaching to move to that level and she, being a great coach, worked with me.

I was feeling that my business had plateaued, and I had to find out why and create a plan for moving forward. We talked about what I was struggling with and it became apparent that there were some emotional obstacles that I needed to address in order to move to the next stage of growth. I had to work on my low self-esteem and recognize the value I bring to my clients. I must convey that value, when I speak and get comfortable asking for compensation based on my real value. I did believe in myself and my skills and now I had to find out what belief system was getting in my way.

I wanted a lifestyle that would allow me to spend more time with my family, travel, and especially be happy to get up each day and work. I was getting caught up just working and networking and had little time for my family. We were barely getting by. I was prepared to change what I had to change because I didn't want to live this way. I stopped showing up, and my business stopped growing. I still had work, but my referrals dropped off dramatically. I took time to take care of my needs, exercise, and find space just for myself. One evening, my friend, Virginia Earl came over. We explored my fear of changing what I felt I was worth. In her pleasant way, she reminded me that I was starting to sound like a broken record. I knew she was a medium and she told me that I should schedule a session with her. That was silly. I didn't really believe in that stuff. But I went and it was not silly at all. She helped me identify the sources of my negativity, see them for what they were, and begin to put them in their place.

I was relieved that I was starting to get some answers and was ready to dig deeper. I read some amazing books that reinforced for me that my past created patterns of negative thinking that were engrained in my subconscious and have been there for most of my life. The books that had the most impact on me were; "Girl Wash Your Face," by Rachel Hollis', "The Year of No Nonsense" by Meredith Atwood, and "You Are a Badass" by Jen Sincero. Candace, Virginia and these books taught me the practice of positive thinking. I learned to meditate and started to appreciate its enormous power. I learned that my thoughts control my circumstances and not the other way around. I learned that I had taken some childhood experiences and in my child's mind, magnified them, and made them my core beliefs about my self-worth. Now that I knew, they seemed trivial and I knew that I could create new and more accurate core beliefs.

A few months later I showed up to a QuickBooks conference and ran into Loren Fogelman. I had seen her at a NAFE meeting I had attended and heard her introduction. I had wanted to meet her then but instead I had to rush out of the meeting because I had filled my schedule with some low value tasks that I should have delegated, she pointed out to me later. Or perhaps I was afraid of the change, meeting her would bring. I learned that so many of us fear success, and don't even know it. I recognized Loren and approached her. She is a profit and pricing coach. That's exactly what I needed at the time. Once I became aware of the harm that my past had done, I was ready to move forward and knew that creating my future was up to me. Positive thinking takes practice and I had to be prepared to focus on it. When Loren and I talked, I explained that I believed that to attract business, I had to give away my services for free or at a steep discount during the first year in order to build trust and credibility. She said, "No, you don't." Her response made me angry...at myself. I've wasted so much time and wasn't getting anywhere. Loren gave me her card and we went our separate way.

A few weeks later I received an email from Robbie Motter that Loren was offering our network a bootcamp session on pricing. I was really worried about cash flow, but I remembered that the universe is abundant and it's our fear that holds us back from getting some of it. I signed up for Loren's course and learned so much that my financial situation improved immediately by changing my pricing and collecting structure. I also invested in her coaching for the year. I've learned so much from Loren about pricing and contracts. I am confident that I will never have to work for anyone else again.

My business is thriving because I asked all the people who came into my life for help and acted on their advice. I learned that it was the lack of alignment between who I was and my goal that defined my future. I no longer fear failure or my ability to provide for my family. I had stepped out of my comfort zone and with the help of my network, I can now control my thoughts and choose actions that help and not hurt me.

If I had not shown up at conferences, I wouldn't have met all the awesome accountants who are still in my life, and I would have missed out on friendships that have brought so much into my life. My courageous and giving friends have shared insights, frustrations, compassion and have encouraged me when I needed it. They are valuable allies and assets. If I had not shown up at that first Chamber of Commerce lunch meeting, I would not have learned how kind and supportive the small business community is and I would have remained afraid to ask. I would not have many of the friends and clients I have. If I had not shown up to BNI, I would not have many of the friends and clients I have today. I would still not understand networking. If I had not shown up to NAFE, I would not have met Candace Gruber, my first coach, and I would still be controlled by my negative thoughts. I would still feel unfulfilled and overworked. If I had not shown up at my first Thursday Mixer with the Murrieta/Wildomar Chamber of Commerce, I would not have met Virginia Earl. I would not know what past experiences and current attitudes had been holding me back. I would not be moving forward. If I had not shown up to NAFE, I would not have met Loren Fogelman and I would still undervalue myself, my knowledge, and my skills. I would allow perfectionism and procrastination to immobilize me and get in the way of my success. I would still be chasing money. If I had not shown up to NAFE and the Global Society of Female Entrepreneurs where I met Robbie Motter, I would have missed out on events that lifted my spirits when I was discouraged. I would not have become aware of the need to make time for myself to fill my cup so that it runs over and benefits others.

My story would not be in this book.

In my first year in business I made more than I made in my corporate job. While not having a steady paycheck that takes some getting used to, the fact that my success is entirely up to me is exhilarating and builds confidence. I have met amazing people and learned about many industries. I have employees and have become better at delegating...difficult when it's your own business. I didn't know what resources and help was available to me when I entered the world of entrepreneurship. To succeed in business and in life we just need a burning desire, humility and understanding that the way will open to us. If we do not try, we cannot succeed. If we do not understand what we need to build relationships and learn from others, then we are not really trying.

My skills were a major factor for my success, but without showing up and asking, I would not have achieved the success I enjoy today.

Exciting Things Happen When One SHOWS UP and ASKS!

Dr Iris Rosenfeld

" Showing up is like a Treasure Map; You Never Know What You Will Find." This is a stand that our Regional Director, Robbie Motter, has been sharing with us for years.

As a Doctor of Chiropractic and owner of the Rosenfeld Wellness Center in Laguna Hills, California for over 30 years, the topic of "showing up" has always played a major role in my professional and personal life. For me, it has been about establishing and nurturing long-term quality relationships in social and business situations. In the first years after I opened my practice, I was able to participate in multiple networking opportunities to help me catapult my business forward, and lay seeds for continuous speaking engagements, Health Fairs, and other professional activities.

As the years passed, I continued to meet with colleagues in many related fields in the areas of wellness and medicine. This would give myself a goal of meeting with a minimum of 2 to 3 other specialists per month to exchange relevant information and thereby develop a network of professional support.

At times, showing up became very time-consuming. So consequently, I directed my efforts toward learning exactly where I wanted to invest my time and energy. My goal was always to develop my skills, stay current on the latest trends, meet mentors, prospective partners, and build my business, while still giving back to my community, and continue to support other business owners.

Sometimes, showing up became difficult and draining, even for an extrovert like me. My calendar was overloaded with work obligations and family commitments. However, having built a strong professional network, I had a competitive edge throughout the different stages of my medical career. So, I recognized that it's alright to prioritize my available time without feeling guilty.

"Being rather than knowing requires showing up and letting ourselves be seen. It requires us to dare greatly, to be vulnerable." Brene Brown

I have noticed throughout my profession, inviting my staff to join me at local networking events was always advantageous for my business, for each of them personally, and we benefited exponentially as a team. A new energy was also regularly brought to our Staff Meetings. Much of that brainstorming, has contributed to improved communication and well-defined business opportunities.

Very often when I attend an event, I do not know what to expect, but I go with an open mind and anticipation. I set goals for how many new connections I'll meet and with whom I'll reconnect with from prior meetings. I always follow up through Facebook, LinkedIn, a text, an email, a phone call and sometimes a more personal hand-written note. These follow-up communications are vital to building a strong, long-term support network of professionals. In addition, I search opportunities where I can provide value and assistance to people in my networks, which warms my soul. Even more, I have learned so much about other Industries that have been shared with me through many groups both personally and professionally. This has contributed indirectly to finding ways to expand my business to new levels.

"Instead of showing up to let everyone know how great we are, show up to find out how great everyone else is." Simon Sinek

One example stands out in my mind. A few years ago, I was invited by a fellow business-owner to attend a networking group, where I met this fascinating and captivating woman who is known as the "Networking Queen". We continue to support each other in business and spiritually. Her insights and contacts are unlimited, and she has significantly contributed to my growth as a professional leader in my community. Through the connections I've made by networking and showing up, I've created enormous opportunities to speak at events, meet new and stimulating people, learn about the fascinating world of business, and keep growing and evolving as a health professional while building a flourishing medical practice.

"Showing up" is not only about business success, it is also even more about the friendships and relationships that I have built. I am especially grateful for my friend the "Networking Queen." Even though she recently moved out of state, we are in touch often as we will continue to support one another for many years.

Showing up is like a Treasure map. Why a Treasure map? By definition, a treasure map is a "map that marks the location of buried treasure, a lost mine, a valuable secret or a hidden locale. More common in fiction, than in reality, pirate treasure maps are often depicted in works of fiction as hand drawn and containing arcane clues for the characters to follow."

So, as you show up, think about the people you meet as if they were precious gems and how each person contributes to the instrumental success of the whole group. It is the concentration of each cherished jewel that is valuable in a sea of undiscovered wealth. Being open to showing up and rediscovering something new about someone you have known for years or meeting a new face, can recreate a buried treasure chest of valuable riches that you may not have ever been able to imagine. It is even possible that you may meet your next "treasured" lifelong friend.

In summary, I have always made networking and showing up at events enjoyable. Not even trying may be a mistake and you might just be missing out on fun, learning, advancing your career, and a treasure-chest of opportunities.

It's All about Showing Up

The Importance of "Showing Up" and the "Power in Asking" for what you want.

Shelly Rufin

Forty-Seven years ago, at the age of seven, I was placed in foster care.

Forty-Five years ago, I was searching for stability and acceptance in a new home and school.

Thirty-Six years ago, I moved for the 16th time and to my fifth school district with no future. My story will unfold, of a little Italian girl, searching for acceptance in a world I didn't understand, to find a world of possibilities and opportunities.

Thirty-Five years ago, I was accepted into college, with little social and cultural capital, but with great ambition to succeed. In college I was offered to show up and serve as an Assistant in the Financial Aid Office helping students and parents; I loved it.

Thirty-One years ago, I moved to Hilton Head Island, S.C. for work. I met the man I married and with whom I would share my life, dreams, goals, and raise our three boys, (30, 28, 19). I discovered the meaning of family and a home to call my own. As a military wife for 33 years now, we were consistently on the move. This was something I was really good at, having grown up in foster homes, my sisters and I were bounced from one home to another. Our first home was in Arizona, and then we moved to Okinawa

Japan for four years. In Okinawa, Japan, I was 25 years old raising two little boys, (2 and 4 years old). I accepted the opportunity to serve as an English teacher to local Japanese nationals and served as a Case Manager for the American Red Cross serving soldiers and their families for four years. I learned about being a mom, the military, Japanese culture and customs that was very different from my own.

Nineteen years ago, while working as a Financial Aid Officer at a U.S.-based college, I was always showing up and asking to attend conferences and workshops. I sought out advancement and professional development; my desire to achieve success for myself and being an inspiration to my children; something that I didn't have growing up. I showed up, went the extra mile, attended training seminars, and workshops. I received several certifications from the U.S. Department of Education Federal Student Aid School Relations Division, Title IV Funding Administration, National Association of Financial Aid Administrators and Western Association of Student Financial Aid Administration: Student Loan Administration.

I was promoted to a Director of Financial Aid and Scholarships. I was accepted into Bellevue University while working full-time and raising three boys. My thirst for knowledge was on fire and I wanted more in life. I received a dual Master's Degree in Human Services as well as a Master's Degree in Clinical Counseling and Neuroscience; my personal and professional growth was on steroids.

Twelve years ago, I resigned my position, withdrew my 401K and started my own business. I took a huge risk. It was 2018, and the economy was on the brink of disaster. My husband is a graphic artist and with help and support, I created a dynamic marketing plan with my son as my assistant and a staff that included; an IT Systems administrator, Outreach Coordinator, and external resources. As founder and CEO of EDFIN College Planning Experts, (a College Prep, College/Financial Aid Planning Company), I started out with a handful of students and now, 28 years later, my company is the leading expert in the country. EDFIN helps students navigate the rigorous requirements of applying to Ivy League colleges. Having served as a Director of Financial Aid and Scholarships with U.S. based colleges for fifteen years, I learned so much from the families and students I worked with. I developed a greater understanding of their needs and applied it to my business. This is how EDFIN College Planning Experts was born. As Founder/Owner of EDFIN College Planning Experts, we work with the best and brightest kids and help them achieve their higher education and career goals. To help my clients, I wrote '*Nine Key Decisions of Better College Planning, Better Life: Making College DREAMS a Reality*',

This book is a straightforward approach with proven strategies that educate families from around the globe.

Developing my unique niche' as an Independent Educational Consultant, I've seen the words Independent Educational Consultant defined numerous ways over the years. Is it their education and experience? What makes an Independent Educational Consultant? Passion? Is it all about the situation? Is it meant only for the chosen few who rise to the top? Or, is there a different story?

It's showing up, the power in the asking, perseverance, determination, and never giving up on your dream. This same year in 2018, I was accepted into the Ph.D. Psychology Industrial Organization program at Capella University. I spent summers expanding EDFIN's College Prep programs, by helping students through a rigorous college-prep summer program.

Ten years ago, I learned networking with community leaders and astute business moguls. I showed up at high school events, college fairs, and asked how to serve in my community. It became my new way of doing business and I continue to make a difference in the community. This led to being recognized for volunteering service at local high schools and serving as an advocate for the advancement and acceleration of women in business. I received the President's Award from Women of Connected Influence, State of California Senate Community Service Award by Senator Mike Morrell, Community Service Award by State Senator John Moorlach, 37th State District, Congressional Community Service Award by Congress Karen

Bass, and Senate Award for the 67th District Melissa Melendez. I have been recognized for educating students 8th through 12th grade and parents on the importance of early college planning.

In 2017, after the success of EDFIN College Planning, my next venture was to make a difference in my community by starting up my own EDFIN, TV show. With almost three decades of being an Independent Educational Consultant, I have helped with college planning, speaking, and most importantly, real-life in-the trenches college experience and knowledge. I share with listeners, educating the public as an Independent Educational Consultant. Helping families and their kids pursue their dreams of higher education is a passion of mine; may it be vocational, certificate, community college or attending an Ivy League university. College Planning is for everyone. It's one of the most important decisions you will make in your life. Here I interviewed Mayors, Community Leaders, small business owners, parents as well as students who shared their inspirational stories. During one of the shows, I had the opportunity to interview Robbie Motter, former Global Leader for National Association Female Executives (N.A.F.E), and now CEO/Founder of Global Society for Female Entrepreneurs (G.S.F.E). Little did I know, my future was about to change for the better again when I joined (N.A.F.E). Serving as the Co-Director of the Temecula group would lead me to many more opportunities to show up. This Temecula group as of May 1, 2020 now operates under the name Global Society for Female Entrepreneurs (G.S.F.E) a 501 (c)(3) nonprofit. Their mission is to empower, inspire, educate and connect women so they can become successful entrepreneurs and enjoy fulfilling, productive and abundant lives.

Three years ago, I accepted the N.A.F.E - ACE Award by the National Association of Female Executives (N.A.F.E) for EDFIN College Planning, for the advancement and acceleration of women in business. By accepting this opportunity and by showing up, I unexpectedly was able to meet with and sit on the panel of 15 Fortune 500 companies: Proctor & Gamble, Johnson & Johnson etc. I ended the year as a published author of '9 *Key Decisions for Better College Planning, Better Life: Making College DREAMS a Reality.*'

Three years ago, by reaching 4,000 hours of volunteerism in the community, (I volunteered my time to help local high school students by guiding students and counselors through the college prep, financial aid planning processes of preparing 8th through 12th-grade kids for college), I was awarded two Life Time Achievement Awards by President Donald Trump and President Barrack Obama.

In 2019, I was accepted to Harvard University Business School. I learned from the best and the brightest CEO's, Department of Justice, students from all walks of life and business owners like myself.

This year, I pioneered the C.I.A.M. and led 20 M.B.A students through three research projects, guiding each student to meet their specified requirements for the projects.

Remember, showing up is the first part of a successful journey. What you do with it is up to you.

Showed Up... For Me

(Chasing Freedom on the Frontlines, Finding Red Letters in The Valley)

Dawn Kelly Schultz

B y the time I was ten years old, I knew that something was wrong in
my life. I was often at a friend's house or attracted to people much
older than me. I also had trouble sitting still in school. Things were going
on in my home, behind closed doors that wasn't spoken of, but the package
looked good from the outside. My mom worked as a waitress and my dad
was a machinist. I remember being hungry for their attention. I remember,
as a four-year-old, putting red lipstick on the cloth face of my Raggedy Ann
doll, and then trying to wake up my mom asleep on the couch to show her
what I did. By the time I was in my teens, I had seen violence in our home.
I loved my mom, but she couldn't love me back the way a young person
needs to be loved. My dad, the person who was supposed to show me how
a man loved and honored a woman, left us when I was 15 and never came
back. He couldn't stop drinking and eventually chose booze over his wife
and three kids. Mom didn't take her wedding ring off for 20 years expecting
him to come back. He never did.

I know now that since I didn't have a healthy and happy childhood, I spent
my life looking for love. Anyone who would give me attention and affection.
That which I missed getting from two teenagers, when they had a little
girl, named Dawn. They were about 17. I was hungry to hear them confirm

that I was a good girl or that I was wanted or appreciated. Instead, I got scolded and punished for things I didn't do or do well enough. Nothing I did was good enough for them. I wanted so much to prove to them that I was worthy. My mother would say that I made her sick and tell me that I'd never amount to anything. She gloated over other children's accomplishments and treated them better than she treated me. I couldn't talk to her at a time when I really needed her. "You ought to be ashamed of yourself" were just some of the terrible words that stayed with me for decades. I carried those words and so many others for so long…they were my reality. I spent years chasing the love and acceptance that I craved and began a life of people pleasing, codependency. I had no one to support me so I became a target for a string of unhealthy and abusive relationships, both friends and romantic partners.

I dreamed for that perfect family but would realize that there was no such thing. Throughout my childhood and young adult years, I learned to compensate for my unmet needs; I learned to put on a smile on the outside while I was broken inside from the pain and trauma. I walked through life feeling I wasn't good enough and I'd never measure up. I learned to say yes when I wanted to say no. I was going at full speed, non-stop, my schedule always full, and underneath it all I carried the guilt and shame that created my belief system. The messages that I wasn't good enough. That I wasn't seen. Or loved. Or accepted. I used to imagine that I died and when I looked down on my parents at my funeral, I would see their tears, and finally know, at last, that they did love me.

One day the weight of it all became too heavy. All my life, I had shown up for everybody and everything, and made sure everybody was happy, fed, clothed, nurtured, protected. I served my community at the church like a good Christian. In the process of living this façade of a good person, I left myself behind. I began bandaging my pain with alcohol and food -- anything that would help stop the pain, the overwhelming feelings of exhaustion, guilt, shame, and fear.

Years later, my life in a downward spiral, it took one more bad relationship, that allowed me to break through. It was an imposter, a narcissistic- socio-path, who claimed to be someone he wasn't. He stole with military valor and false love. He was so good at putting on an act that he cared about me and my children but had ulterior motives. He was someone else.

My disbelief and denial brought me to the lowest point in my life. There were no answers. My life and dreams were shattered. When I could go no further without hitting a wall, the only place left to look for love was up. And I showed up and when I did, God met me there. Sure, I had 'played' going to church for years like so many codependents and others do, but when you're living a facade, most of the time, you don't recognize it. I had gone to church most of my life but didn't even realize how disconnected I was.

It was at that moment, when my hands were empty, and my heart was broken. I had nothing to offer but myself. Jesus showed up in my life and I could feel His presence stronger each day. He was always there, but I had left Him. I wouldn't be alive today if it weren't for Him. He never gave up on me even when I gave up on myself. And I was inflicted with trauma by others, that he wept. How often I survived, when I shouldn't have, as if by miracle, He and His angels were there. He brought me to my feet again and sat me down on a rock. And when I had fully surrendered, He, through people and spiritual forces, taught me what it meant to be a daughter of the King, and taught me to love who I am, I mean REALLY love who I was becoming -- not just saying, but feeling it. And TO SHOW UP FOR ME -- FIRST, because you can't pour from an empty, broken cup.

One of the things I struggled with most was that my whole life was dictated by how YOU felt about me; I was caught up in a battle where my joy was dependent on how others felt about me and about my external circum-stances. Everything I did was mechanical. I just wanted to get through the day. He taught me to understand how deep His love was, and that it didn't matter what others thought about. What mattered was what I thought about myself. He taught me that people struggled to love themselves and often weren't capable of the love that I felt.

I had work to do! It was a long process and I still work each day to be in alignment as so much gets in the way of my joy. He taught me how to expect hope. Expect healing. And to expect miracles on this side of the veil. And today I do. Today I can be an example to my children, family and even to strangers. There are so many people who need love or support, and it costs nothing to give them. Kindness is free. Imperfectly perfect. And forgiveness. Forgiveness doesn't necessarily lead to reconciliation. I have forgiven my parents and those who brought ill- will to my life. God has restored the relationship between my mother and I, with loving boundaries. Today I am the founder of a nonprofit organization called The Dresses and Dreams Project where we help teen girls deal with their hardships and difficult circumstances. I want to be the person for them that I needed growing up.

I dreamt big from a very young age but didn't know how to achieve them. I didn't have the bridge between point A to point B. I know that young people today face similar challenges. We help these young girls go to proms and celebrations by giving them free formal gowns through an annual event, Operation Prom Girl. We've dressed more than 1200 young women.

I work as a freelance makeup artist with 25 years of experience. I provide on-location special event makeup services. Since showing up for my own life, I have dreamt of much more. I've dreamt about going back to school soon to study counselling so that I can help young children who are trauma survivors of human trafficking. I want to help them live productive lives and to know that they are loved, regardless of the wreckage they've experienced and despite their circumstances. I've shown up for my own life and I know that with God all things are possible. I'm alive today because He has a bigger plan for me…. much bigger than I can see today.

"Share your story~ It can make a difference in someone's life and impact the future!"

It's All about Showing Up

The Power of Showing Up

Rhonda L. Sher

Showing up is a concept that can make the difference between meeting someone spectacular or missing out on a life changing opportunity. For me, there have been many times I showed up when I did not want to, and the results are what makes my life so amazing today.

Have you ever been invited to an event and felt like you had to push yourself to attend because it was out of your comfort zone, you were tired, or just did not want to go? Those are the times that SHOWING UP can bring you the most unexpected and miraculous gifts. At least that is what has happened to me on more occasions than I can count.

Even though I am an extrovert, a professional networker, and LinkedIn expert who is known as a connector – there have been many times when I did not want to SHOW UP – and yet when I did – my life changed in such positive ways that I could not have ever imagined.

In my personal life, I got divorced after 28 years of marriage but never stopped loving my husband – in fact, even though I got engaged to someone else after my divorce, I still secretly wished that I could reunite with my ex-husband and remarry him. My ex-husband and I had a friendly divorce and have two amazing daughters together (now 28 and 30). During the time we were divorced, we both did some personal development work. Shortly after I broke up my engagement – my husband (not knowing I was single and me not knowing he was also single) invited me to a Community Sunday which was an event through Landmark Education, a program we both took separately during the time of our divorce. I remember that day clearly since it was Mother's Day 2015 and our daughters were out of town. I was not sure I wanted to attend – there were 200 people there and I was going as a guest of my "ex-husband" or wasband as I called him. I decided to go even though I knew I might feel uncomfortable since we both knew many of the people there and had not attended an event together as a couple in a group of friends since our divorce. I SHOWED UP (even though I was nervous) and when he introduced me to the group of people there, (which was part of the program where you have a chance to introduce your guest and tell them what they mean to you). Bob introduced me by saying I was his ex-wife, but in his mind, I would always be his wife and he still loved me. I told him I loved him and 200 people including us were all crying with joy. Because I SHOWED UP, the opportunity to create a new beginning opened. Fast forward to Feb 13, 2016th. We remarried in Las Vegas with Elvis. I now say, because I SHOWED UP, I have a husband I adore, a wasband - I did not have to change my name and the kids are ours. SHOWING UP that day was one of the best decisions of my life. Our marriage is great – filled with love and laughter and we now say we are married 40 years in October with six years off for good behavior.

In my business as a LinkedIn expert, I remember being invited to a local BNI meeting a couple of years ago. I work from home and get most of my business from LinkedIn, so going out and socializing at a physical networking event was something I had been doing less and less. In fact, the only place I really was SHOWING UP was online, on LinkedIn, which was isolating since Zoom really is not a replacement for meeting in person. I pushed myself to SHOW UP that afternoon and as a result, I met my client and now friend, Misty Cogdill, a Bob Proctor coach and handwriting expert. Because I SHOWED UP that day, I met Misty and became her client, I learned how to change my handwriting so that miracles have occurred in my life. My relationship with my daughters which was fractured during the divorce, got repaired from changing my handwriting. My business increased because I learned how to eliminate blocks and my health has improved as well. I am so grateful for the invitation to that BNI open house and to my friend who "pushed me gently" to SHOW UP and get out of the house and attend that meeting. I now have an amazing new friend – Misty – a new relationship with my daughters and a tool that allows me to get totally different results in my life simply by changing my handwriting in a way that eliminates blocks. Check out Misty here: https://www.facebook.com/groups/AlphabetAlchemy/

Another event where I SHOWED UP happened over 10 years ago. I was gifted a ticket to a James Malinchak Big Money Speaker Event. It was a 3-day event and I really did not want to go. I used to attend this type of training all the time and remember thinking not another pitch fest and *rah-rah* event, but the person who gave me the free ticket encouraged me strongly to attend. I remember thinking I really did not want to go and in fact, I SHOWED UP on day 2, (thinking I was 30 minutes early on Day 1) not knowing it started a day earlier, only to walk into a room of 500 people and being an hour late since the day before, they had decided to start at 8:00 am instead of 9:00 am. They found me a seat in the third row (That was way out of my comfort zone in those days since I liked sitting in the back) and I was seated next to a nice man from Canada who I ended up hanging out with for the next three days of the event. We had much in common and knew many of the same people. John was a top sales professional who was venturing into the world of entrepreneurship and was looking for marketing and speaking mentorship skills. We both ended up joining the $15,000-year long Mastermind with James Malinchak. The best thing that happened from SHOWING UP at that event was my friendship with John Pyke. John became my client for many years, my friend, and is still a colleague. I regularly refer business to him, since he is one of the world's best recruiters. I am so grateful that I SHOWED UP – albeit a day and an hour late – because I would have missed out on one of the best business relationships I have made in my career. John has sent me many clients and I have done the same for him.

The last story I want to share about SHOWING UP is when a client of mine, Cindy, told me about a Bootcamp her mentor was having about Neuro Linguistic Programming (NLP). I have always been fascinated with understanding people and NLP and never gone to any classes about it. Cindy told me to SHOW UP in Fullerton at the Pivot Point Advantage Boot camp and I would love it. I trusted her and I went. That day changed everything. I signed up to do the entire course with Pivot Point Advantage, became certified as a Train the Trainer NLP Coach and met a community of people I NEVER would have met if I had not SHOWN UP at that boot camp. In fact, my income doubled the month after I did the first course called "Prac" and I have an incredible community of friends in the Pivot Point Advantage training. If you are curious about NLP, check out www. PivotPointAdvantage.com and Stacey O'Byrne. It may change your life like it changed mine if you SHOW UP.

I am so grateful to Robbie Motter for teaching me the power of SHOWING UP. It has helped me remarry my husband, grow my business, have a great relationship with my daughters and meet people I would not otherwise have met. Whether you SHOW UP in person or online, remember to always have the mindset of how can you can serve others and ask yourself, – what can I do to help and even if it feels a little uncomfortable, SHOW UP anyway, You never know what miracles might happen.

It's All about Showing Up

The Struggle is Real, So Is the Victory!

Kelly D Smith

I made a career decision in my late thirties that I wanted to become a special education teacher. Little did I know that it would take me over a decade to realize this dream.

While growing up, going off to college and graduating, my parents did not encourage or instill a love of learning in my siblings or me. My parents didn't go to college, although, my mom did attend a local vocational school. My dad struggled in school and graduated at the bottom of his class. I struggled with math and nearly missed graduating from high school. I failed math and had to pass a math proficiency test to complete the final year. I didn't pass the test and had to retake it again, but I finally passed and graduated. Because of my difficulties with math I grew up thinking that I just wasn't smart enough to go to college. I didn't believe in myself or that I could achieve anything.

I got married when I was twenty-two. My mom always worked but my husband's mom stayed home taking care of the children and the household. My husband and I talked about having children and whether or not I would continue to work outside the home. After we had children, my husband didn't want me to work and I didn't want to either. We decided that it was important for me to be home with our children. So, I didn't see any reason to go to college and pursue a career. I was contented and happy being a homemaker. But this decision didn't prepare me for the unforeseen future.

After twelve years of marriage, my husband I separate. I don't have a college education, work experience or job. We then divorce, and I have to find a job. Everything I find is low pay or part-time.

I find work as a special education teacher's aide. It's part-time and the pay is low. Not even enough for me to make it through each month. I end up working three part-time jobs to make ends meet, while raising two young daughters. There are times when I don't have enough money for food. I'm fortunate to be able to pick up food from the food bank at my church and other food pantries. Family and friends bring us food, shampoo, deodorant, and other hygiene and personal items. I'm hopeful that it won't always be like this, and often I reflect on the Bible scripture, where in the book of Jeremiah 29:11 it says, *"For I know the plans I have for you," declares the Lord, "plans to prosper you and not harm you, plans to give you hope and a future."* (NIV).

I'm not able to pay my electric bill and I pray for God to help me. I attend church, sit down and wait for the service to start. An usher walks over to me and hands me an envelope. I open it and see that there's enough money to pay my electric bill and have some left over. There's no name on the envelope, so I don't know whom to thank, and I'm so thankful.

I work as a teacher's aide with special education students, and I love my job and feel fulfilled. I get so much satisfaction when I see a student who has been struggling, finally get it and a smile appears on his or her beautiful face.

I was still working as a teacher's aide when the *No Child Left Behind Act* passed. This Act required teacher's aides to have 48 college units or an Associate of Arts degree or to pass a district-wide test. I was worried about keeping my job. Years later I realized that this was the best thing that could have happened. I was forced to go to college.

Of course, I was nervous and excited at the same time. I was thirty-seven years old when I started college and having struggled with math earlier, I was worried about the college assessment I had to take. I took the test and learned that in order to have sufficient credits transferred to a university, I needed 48 credits, and that included six math classes.

I recall my last college algebra class. The teacher had his back to the class demonstrating an equation. I raise my hand, say out loud, "I don't understand." He turns around and says, "What don't you understand? I just explained it." He turns back to the board and keeps writing. I know that this is going to be difficult for me and I have doubts that I can do this.

I did pass all my math classes, except for this algebra class and I have to take it again, making it a total of seven math classes. It's a long, hard road. I stay up late many nights studying. I go to the math lab after work and study with tutors until the lab closes. I drive to my brother's house on the weekends, and he and my nephew work with me on my math. Many times, I want to quit and complain to my dad, "I'm going to be fifty years old by the time I get my degree." He says, "You're going to be fifty anyway. You can be fifty with a degree or fifty without a degree. You might as well be fifty with a degree." I agree and keep going. And the hard work finally pays off. I pass.

My dad was so proud of me and that made it so special. He didn't go to college, and how proud he was when he announced, "three of my four children will have college degrees." Unfortunately, he didn't live to see me graduate.

When I completed my 48 units, I start to think about the Associate of Arts degree and since it meant only twelve more units, I thought I might as well continue. It takes me six years to complete all my classes because I'm a single, working mom, and I only have time to take one class at a time. I finish and graduate with distinction.

My accomplishments give me confidence and I see that just because I'm not good at one thing, like math, it doesn't mean I'm not going to do well in other academics. I now know that I can do anything I put my mind to. I would get a bachelor's degree, which would qualify me as a teacher, and I do it.

Before I start my bachelor's degree, I meet a wonderful older man, Dan, who is a pastor. I never thought I would get married again, but in my prayers, I would ask God, "Where's my Boaz?" Boaz is a Biblical story in the Book of Ruth. He's an older man who sees Ruth picking wheat that was left in the field after harvesting. He doesn't let anyone touch her. He takes care of her, feeds her and watches over her and marries her. Dan asks me to marry him. One day I have lunch with a senior pastor and his wife from our church and he says to me, "You know who he is? He is your Boaz." I never told anyone about my prayers, so I see this as a confirmation from God. Dan and I get married. Later when Dan asks why I went out with him, seeing that he was older than me, I tell him, "I liked your kindness, and your gentleness won me over."

I continue to study for my bachelor's degree and find that I need another math class. It's easy, just a refresher course of elementary math for teachers, but nonetheless, it's another math class. It doesn't deter me. I complete the course work and get my degree. Another achievement, and I'm not done yet.

Next, I want to get my teacher's credential and decide that I might as well combine it with a master's degree. A part of the credential program includes state tests. There's the California Basic Educational Skills Test (CBEST), which is done in three parts, and can be done together or separately. Of course, there's a math component. I decide to take the math portion separately.

I study and my husband helps me. To my surprise, I pass the first time. The next test is the California Subject Examination for Teachers (CSET). This test has three parts, which can be taken together or separately. Since this test also has a math section, I take them separately. One section of the test is a combination of math and science with multiple choice and two essay

It's All about Showing Up

THE POWER OF ASKING

Maryann Ridini Spencer

C hange and growth are essential to living authentically. How do we align our actions with our true selves? By using the *power of asking*, listening to our gut, and traveling our life's journey with an open mind and a loving heart.

"What should I do?" was the question I "asked" my mother that started me on the path to an exciting and successful life. It was the summer break before my high school sophomore year, and I wasn't yet old enough to join the workforce but found myself bored and out of sorts. My mother was aware of my creativity that showed up in the thrill of dressing up and putting on theatre skits with friends. She recognized my passion for theatre and suggested I join my school's local summer theatre group.

Joining the troupe was the foundation to everything that happened to me in my life journey. I met life-long friends, performed in musicals and dramatic productions. I put all my creative talents to work by also working behind-the-scenes. I learned about set design, props, and costuming. It was an incredibly fulfilling and rewarding experience and I stayed with the ensemble every summer for the duration of my high school years.

Theatre became my passion and I continued to major in it in college. I auditioned for and landed several apprenticeships in Equity and Non-Equity theatres.

However, during my sophomore year I was becoming restless. While I loved the theatre, I didn't enjoy the performer's lifestyle. I loved to "tell" stories, not just deliver lines. After some careful consideration I changed my university, my major, pursued television, film production and communication.

My father was a college professor and guided my applications for scholarships to offset my tuition and boarding costs. I was grateful and fortunate to be one of eight students to receive a full scholarship in the Communications Department at Hofstra University in Hempstead, New York. One of the requirements was to take on teaching assistant roles in the university's state-of-the-art television studio. I became co-program director of the college television station.

Going to Hofstra was a great opportunity. I had access to a massive, state-of-the-art studio and drawing on my theatre experience, I produced taped-as-live dramas. I got to write, produce, direct, run cameras, stage-manage, and every behind-the-scenes job available. I directed productions of "The Miracle Worker," "The Rainmaker," "The Valiant," as well as news broadcasts and so much more. This learning experience was instrumental in landing a series of excellent jobs after graduation.

After graduating, I landed a secretarial position at a top Manhattan ad agency, but before long I was asking myself and others, *"How can I break into my first love, making movies?"* The answer — *Go West!* — had me packing up and moving to Los Angeles. With my meager savings, I found a temporary home in the living room of my sister's friend.

I landed a series of short assignments on the Hollywood studio lot where Norman Lear filmed his iconic comedies. The jobs were temporary and would dry up, so I was always on the lookout for the next opportunity. One day, while in the studio office, I asked for a complimentary ticket to a local concert that was headlined by a performer from my hometown of New York. I got the ticket and was told to enjoy myself. I had a feeling, a strange feeling that this was going to be a special concert for me and a new opportunity. My car was in the shop, so I convinced a friend to drive me.

My intuition proved to be correct. I met a young man, wearing a New York Yankees baseball cap with the CNN cable television crew. I said *"hello,"* to my fellow New Yorker, and we chatted for a few minutes and I said, *"If you hear of any jobs around town, please let me know."* To my surprise, he replied, *"Actually, we're looking for a writer/producer with a television background, why don't you interview."* And he handed me a piece of paper with a phone number. This was my big break! I went for the interview and got the job. I was the only woman on staff. Working as a writer/producer at CNN was a fantastic experience.

During the day we filmed on location at various events, celebrity interviews, and other industry-related news. I met everyone who was anyone in Hollywood. In the afternoon, we'd edit the segments and write the evening's taped-as-live program that was aired from 10:00 to 11:00. I loved to write, so I asked an associate who freelanced for magazines and newspapers, *"How did you start writing for publications?"* This question led to us writing together for a while and started my writing career as a lifestyle journalist, which is still going strong to this day. I write for magazines such as *Palm Springs Life, Desert Magazine, Ventura County Star*, to name just a few.

Another turning point in my career came when I befriended a woman who was an agent and we booked many of her celebrity clients. Our first meeting led to lunch and friendship. She told me there was a publicist position in her company and she recommended me because of my experience as a writer and television producer. After three productive years at CNN with a grueling, 24/7 work schedule, I was ready for a change. Publicity proved to be the answer.

During my time as a publicist, I worked with a lot of celebrity clients, network television shows, feature films, nonprofits, government, environmental, health and wellness, and many more. I became Director of Publicity at Miss Universe, Inc., overseeing titleholder press and coordinating publicity and marketing for the Miss Universe, Miss U.S.A., and Miss Teen U.S.A. Pageants. I also helmed press rooms involving 80+ countries globally. Later, I became Senior Vice President of Stephen J. Cannell Productions and

The Cannell Studios, overseeing publicity for the five TV network series as well as movies that the studio produced in Los Angeles and Vancouver, British Columbia.

I never really aspired to my own business. However, an opportunity arose in 1990. I was approached to take on several lucrative contracts. I jumped at the chance and opened the doors to Ridini Entertainment Corporation. By opening my own shop, I was able to do it all. I would work with P.R., marketing clients and also carry on with my passions to write and produce. I was getting closer to my dream of making movies.

As fate would have it, my first production deal came through one of my PR clients. Impressed with the publicity I was generating for one of his movies, legendary film producer Roger Corman asked me to work for him. On the spot, Roger offered me a first-look production deal if I agreed to also coordinate his studio publicity.

Roger was the best. He knew what he wanted and made quick decisions. My duties in the co-production arrangement required that I acquire appropriately themed projects with partial funding attachments. If Roger liked and approved the projects, he would complete the funding, and we'd go into production. I had the great fortune to work with Roger and produce several movies for his Showtime movie deal.

After several years of working with others on their film projects, I really needed to find my own voice and write the movies I would make. I was looking for an idea for a screenplay but couldn't focus. Then in 2002, a wonderful opportunity presented itself. A friend approached me with a novel she thought I would love, "The Lost Valentine." The author and his manager were looking for a writer to write the screenplay, and she asked if I was interested?

I read the book and loved the story. A deal was struck. I bought books on screenplay writing and began my next fascinating journey in this fairytale industry. The film's message was that of lasting love, a love that transcends time, people helping people, finding themselves, and the importance of family… I was hooked and put pen to paper (or in my case fingers to the keyboard). A year later at a client's public relations anniversary celebration, I happened to overhear two producers looking for quality, family entertainment scripts. I waited patiently until the conversation ended and I approached the producer and asked if I might pitch him my script. He invited me to his office and a deal was struck.

The film that I wrote and co-produced was based on the Pratt novel, "The Lost Valentine." It was sold to Hallmark Hall of Fame in 2006. It went into production in 2010, and the film premiered on CBS-TV in January 2011.

When I learned that *"Betty White will play the lead."* I was ecstatic! I've always admired Betty White, and she was perfect for the part of Caroline, a widow, who, each year for 65 years, returns to Union Station on the anniversary of her husband Neil's departure to fight as a Navy Lt. in World War II. Hearing about Caroline's touching story — honoring her husband declared missing in action by visiting the station every year at Valentine's Day — Susan Allison, a TV journalist played by Jennifer Love Hewitt, begins to investigate what happened to Neil 65 years earlier. During her research, Susan is led to address her relationship demons, and it's through discovering Caroline and Neil's love story that Susan and Caroline's grandson Lucas, are led to find lasting love as well.

The night it premiered, "The Lost Valentine" won CBS-TV the night in ratings with *over 15 million viewers* tuning in. It held the position of the network's highest-rated film for five years. It also became Hallmark Hall of Fame's highest-rated movie in four years. Receiving critical acclaim and was nominated for several awards. In 2012, the film won a "Faith and Freedom" award for inspiring American values and ideals at the nationally televised, star-studded, 20th Annual Movieguide Awards (February 2012). The film has since gone on to become a Hallmark Classic, airing each year on the Hallmark Channel in February, and is now part of Hallmark's Gold Crown DVD Collector's Edition.

Eager to get more scripts to screen, I realized that sometimes it takes a village to mount a production. So, to keep occupied and to continue to tell stories that entertain, inspire, educate, and uplift, I decided to write novels. It was another dream I had for years and talked about a lot. I started to toy with an outline for a book around 2013. A title came to me, "Lady in the Window." *Okay, now what's the story?* I asked. I revised the outline many times before I sat down and wrote a few chapters. It wasn't working out well, so I set the manuscript aside.

On a trip to Kauai in the summer of 2014, I knew I found the ideal place in which to set the novel. Aloha. A land of beauty and healing. It was the perfect place for my character, Kate Grace, to recuperate. I began another outline about a young woman who has everything going her way, until it doesn't. Kate suffers a series of concurrent events. Trials and tribulations, we all face at one time or another in our lives. The death of a loved one, the breakup of a romantic relationship, and the desire to find one's authentic place in the world. A friend, the popular TV-talk show host, Olivia Larkin, comes to her rescue, offering Kate respite as her guest in a seaside garden cottage rental in the ancient, magical paradise that is Hanalei, Kauai. As Kate welcomes the "aloha spirit" into her healing process, the angelic and otherworldly occurrences that begin to transpire during her respite are too poignant for Kate to ignore. *Lady in the Window* leads Kate towards her path of destiny: discovering true love, purpose, and the infinite bond between mother and daughter.

When I finished my book, I began the hunt for a publisher and soon discovered that to pitch traditional houses; one had to work through a literary agent. *Where do I find one?* At a business gathering, a friend shared the name of an agent she knew. She wasn't sure if they took on fiction books, but why not call?

I did. I was asked to send in my manuscript. Approximately three weeks later, the agent asked to represent me. Two months later, I had my first book deal. While I was told it usually doesn't ever happen as quickly, I felt I had been on this track for years. I was over the moon when my novel was honored, the winner in the 2017 Best Book Awards Fiction: Romance Category, the 2018 American Fiction "Visionary" Award, and nominated for a 2019 Ka Palapala Po'okela "Aloha from Across the Sea" Award by Hawaii Book Publishers Association.

In my novels, I incorporate another passion of mine, cooking and entertaining. I grew up in a big Italian-Irish family, and we partied and entertained with friends. I have such beautiful memories cooking in the kitchen with my mothers, sister, and grandmothers. My family loves to party, and we've made so many beautiful memories. These gatherings prove to be a great way to connect, enjoy, educate, and help and heal one another.

This passion and my work experience producing many cooking shows and working publicity on Food Network series led me to create, write, produce, and host my PBS-TV "How-To" healthy living/cooking series, *Simply Delicious Living with Maryann®*" (and SimplyDeliciousLiving.com blog). When a TV network inquired about locally produced programming, I offered to create a pilot for a cooking series. On a limited budget, I cast myself and my recipe creations. I was an established freelance food and lifestyle magazine and newspaper writer and editor, so it worked. Upon viewing the pilot, I scored a network deal. I'm happy to say that *"Simply Delicious Living with Maryann®" has gone on to win many awards, including a 2018 Telly Award in the "How-To/DIY" category.* I hope through further networking and hard work, I will create a national network opportunity for this series.

My love of food, cooking, and entertaining with family and friends also led me to incorporate life-experiences in writing *"The Paradise Table,"* the second book in the Kate Grace Mystery series. It's through these gatherings that a long-held secret is revealed. Through the exploration of that secret, lives are changed for the better. The Kate Grace mysteries continue in the third book in the series, *"Secrets of Grace Manor,"* slated for publication in late 2020.

Looking back, I realize there is a thread in my experience that I could never have envisioned. I followed my passion but could never have anticipated this journey. It took time to gather knowledge from my different backgrounds, each experience led me closer to the dream I've always envisioned, and where I'm most authentic. There were times when I was younger that I moaned about my salary, how hard life was, or how many hours I was working. Sometimes things didn't make sense. Now they do.

The theatre and production background have helped me with my writing and producing for television and film. My freelance writing has helped me further hone my skills. My public relations experience and creating content for multiple media platforms is useful with all I do, including knowing how the entertainment business works to promote my projects and books. I've also now formed a publishing company, SantaRosaPress.net, to help other writers achieve their book dreams.

While I have worked many years, it's only been of late that my experiences have truly made sense to me.

Also, looking back, most of my opportunities have come in the form of "asks." I also feel compelled to share, network, and refer to others when they ask me.

Some of the techniques I use or have picked up along the way to help me focus include creative visualization by assembling a vision board. I cut out photos or words from magazines and put them in a scrapbook or large piece of oak tag paper. I might have a board for places I'd like to travel to, books I'd like to write, experiences I'd like to enjoy, my relationships, a place I'd like to live, and so on. It's not only a fun and creative experience, but it also helps me to identify my desires, goals, and priorities.

At the beginning of every year, I also write my immediate goals for the year. I then put the piece of paper away. By year's end, I take that paper out, and I'm always surprised at how many items I've accomplished. Let your subconscious mind take over.

In addition to asking questions of others, it's essential to ask questions of yourself. Are you happy? Is your work fulfilling? Are you doing what you feel is your unique mission in life? Do you think you are putting your talents to best use? If not, work to make changes and start to implement them. Ask for guidance if you need it. Believe in yourself, stay positive, and have faith. Prayer works wonders, and I do it daily. Ask the Divine to show you the way. He will! Also, I've learned to be mindful of what I think. I work to filter out the negative out and contemplate the positive. It makes me feel happier, energized, and in that mindset keeps me on track. Again, feeling down or helpless? Pray. Get out in nature. Research shows that being in nature is vital to our mental and physical health.

When you're happy, you're a magnet. Your energy shines and brings about possibilities.

Passion and love always plays a significant part in living your authentic life. *How?* I believe that when you're passionate about something, you're more aware and open to opportunities. These opportunities may come from the most unlikely sources. It may happen fast, or it may take time. Your search may take you down a different road, and to something different than you anticipated. And that's okay! What's important is that you keep an open mind, discover who you are and what matters most to you. Whatever your passion is, you'll be so much happier doing what you love!

LIFE IS A DARING ADVENTURE!

Dr. Sharron Stroud

H elen Keller eloquently stated: "Life is a daring adventure, or it is nothing!" This statement has served me well throughout the years in a profound way! As we participate in the Circle of Life and join in the energy field this is where the magic happens.

I had a dream of presenting in both Oxford and Cambridge Universities in England. For me it was the next level of my unfoldment as a Speaker and International Presenter. I had no idea how this would happen, however, I knew I had a contribution to make and I felt deeply and passionately about my subject matter on World Peace. I envisioned myself traveling all over the world sharing my body of work.

I facilitated a Master Mind Group for several years and my request was to travel the world presenting on World Peace and our New Thought way of life! We know that *where thought goes energy flows*, and this made me extremely mindful of using conscious language at all times! If we Master Mind for something and then "hope" it works out, this neutralizes our request. It's rather like an unconscious compromise and has no place in an effective Master Mind Declaration. We know that "hope springs eternal in the human heart", however, when Master Minding we must use only the language that will get us where we want to go! If we don't A-S-K we won't G-E-T! Speaking our Intention into the Law of Mind is a sacred commitment and must be stated in the positive. The Universe always says "Yes!."

That's right! Speaking our Intention in the Positive tense allows the seed thought to take root and begin to grow into the perfect manifestation we have aligned upon.

Through the Passage of time I received a letter from St. Catherine's College in Oxford, England, asking me to speak on something in my chosen field for a symposium they were hosting for the International Cultural Convention. I was so deeply and profoundly struck by how quickly the Law of Attraction worked on my behalf. I placed the intention within the Law of Mind and allowed the corresponding energy to take its natural course. And as if by magic, it did and all I had to do was show up! And show up I did! My daughter asked if she could go with me and I thought it was a great idea, as she had been to Europe and I had not!

When I arrived at St. Catherine's College in Oxford, England, I was thrilled and very excited! I was to be the third speaker on the second day, in the morning session. I noticed that all of *academia* seemed to be represented in the assembly hall. University Professors, Medical Doctors, Attorneys, Scientist, Physicists, Chancellors of Universities, and other notables from the Global Community were all congregated in the assembly hall. I was tempted to feel a bit intimidated by this, however, I knew I had a contribution to make and I showed up to get the job done! When I listened to the presenters I was struck by the fact that they were reading their presentations. English was a second language for many of them and we had to listen intently and follow the Power Point presentation very closely!

When it was my turn to give my presentation I boldly made eye contact with my esteemed audience and spoke from my heart. I shared that I was originally drawn to the awesome topic of World Peace because I was raised in domestic violence, and subsequently, my sister had taken her own life. I went on to share that I felt World Peace was possible, beginning with one person at a time. My thesis is mainly centered around healing our own issues and thereby healing the world.

There is an ancient Chinese Legend entitled: I WANTED TO CHANGE THE WORLD:

"When I was a young man, I wanted to change the world.

I found it was difficult to change the world, so I tried to change my nation.

When I found I couldn't change the nation, I began to focus on my town. I couldn't change the town and as an older man, I tried to change my family.

Now, as an old man, I realize the only thing I can change is myself, and suddenly I realize that if long ago I had changed myself, I could have made an impact on my family. My family and I could have made an impact on our town. Their impact could have changed the nation and I could indeed have changed the world." *Author: Unknown Monk 1100 A.D.*

When I completed my presentation, I was stunned when the audience arose to their feet and gave me a standing ovation. I then had three representatives from various countries invite me to speak at their special conferences around the world. I said "YES!" to all three!

The Chancellor of Madonna University in Nigeria, Africa wanted me to give my presentation to 25,000 students and faculty and the time frame was a 2-month window! This seemed daunting; however, I was compelled to show up and give my gift!

When I arrived in Nigeria, Africa it was late and there was a huge line to enter the country. One of the Military personnel asked me if I was the Minister from the USA presenting for Madonna University. When I told him I was, he took me to the head of the line and we quickly passed through customs with the necessary documentation and vaccination reports for yellow fever. It was a 21-hour flight and I felt the combination of excitement, exhaustion and exhilaration simultaneously!

As I stepped out on the World Stage I saw into the soul of the beautiful expectant faces of the student body and the esteemed faculty! I had never presented to more than a couple of thousand people in an audience, prior to this moment, however, here were 25,000 students awaiting my message with joyous anticipation.

By showing up for this one singular speaking engagement, in deepest darkest Africa, an amazing and almost miraculous flow of events began to unfold. I was asked to return for the next several years and be a part of the International Foundation for World Peace and Research. When the International Foundation for World Peace and Research was founded, I was then asked to serve as the President of the organization. I declined the offer as I felt the other board members were far more qualified than I was. The former Chief of Staff of Hamburg University Hospital was creating a medical clinic on the grounds of the University and the Doctors without Boarders were represented along with Attorneys, Professors, and other esteemed professionals. The moment of reckoning for me was their response when I declined the offer, they said: "When you speak, we learn!" I was stunned and humbled by this level of vulnerability and unconditional faith in my abilities.

I said "Yes!" Out of saying "yes" I would be hosted all over the world speaking on World Peace.

The Vice President of our Board was Professor Miroslav, from Croatia who nominated the Chancellor of the University for the Nobel Peace Prize, in which I was asked to fly to Oslo, Norway and meet with the Director of the Institute and present him with the nomination papers.

After my flight tickets were in order, I received a call from Professor Miroslav in regard to the Nobel Peace Prize Institute being closed the first week of December, due to the preparations for the Peace Prize Awards the following week. I had secured a guest speaker for my Sunday Services and procured a non-refundable ticket. My treasurer of the board, Elisabeth Van Gulick, M. D. was to meet me in Oslo as well. She too felt we should cancel, however, I felt compelled to go, survey the lay of the land and get a sense of what I was dealing with. This was all uncharted territory for me, and I needed to feel more secure in the process. When I conveyed to my board members that I was going, irrespective of their decisions, they jumped on board and met me in Oslo, Norway. Out of my "showing up" they too felt compelled to show up!

Once we arrived in Oslo, we needed a game plan. I made the decision to go to the Nobel Peace Prize Institute and put forth our nomination for the Peace Prize. Dr. Miroslav and Dr. Elisabeth felt it was too aggressive, however, I did not share their sentiments. I related that I wanted to get a sense of what I was dealing with and I would ask to see the Director of the Institute, whether they were closed or not. I then shared: "If we do not A-S-K we will not G-E-T! Dr. Miroslav related that he went to the Institute the day before (he arrived a day early) and spent time in the Institute's library and he did not feel comfortable returning so soon. He suggested that he wait in the Espresso Cafe across the street from the Institute until he heard from Elisabeth and I. On one level I felt like one of the characters in an Agatha Christie novel, however, I could feel an air of excitement and expectancy building within me, as I had always dreamed of going to Oslo, Norway and experiencing the Nobel Peace Prize Institute first hand!

What unfolded next was nothing short of a miracle! I walked into the Nobel Peace Prize Institute, announced that I was Dr. Sharron Stroud from the United States of America and I would like to see the Director of the Institute. The receptionist said, "One moment please" she then picked up the phone and dialed into the Director's office announcing my arrival and request to meet with him. She then said, "You may go in now." We were almost giddy at the prospect of being in such esteemed company and knew this was a momentous occasion on so many levels.

As Mr. Dag Ulrik Kühle – Gotovac greeted us we were immediately put at ease as he asked us to please be seated. I stated our business of wanting to submit the Chancellor of Madonna University for the Nobel Peace Prize. I handed him our documents, as he perused them, he stated that everything was in order, except Professor Miroslav had not signed the formal nomination document. I could not help but laugh! I shared with Dag that

Professor Miroslav was hiding out across the street at the Espresso Cafe, as he did not want to appear too forward! We had a good chuckle and when I shared that Miroslav was Croatian, he disclosed that his wife was also! Elisabeth went to fetch Miroslav as I shared who I was and how I became involved with the Nobel Peace Prize Nomination Commission and the Foundation for World Peace and Research. When Elisabeth and Miroslav returned the formal documents were signed, sealed and delivered! Then Dag asked us if we would like a personal tour of the Institute and our elation was palpable! To walk the halls where such glorious history was made was an opportunity of a lifetime. As we experienced the energy of the elegant Assembly Room with all it's pomp and circumstance, it was like peering through a Window in Time and we were transported through the annals of wisdom where history was made. I tapped into the presence of all those who made a profound difference on a global level. I felt Mother Teresa accepting her award in her own inimitable and humble way, yet a face filled with determination and conviction for her mission to attend to the dying souls and the orphans of war-torn countries. When the Bosnian/Serbian war was being waged she called for a truce on Christmas Day, to open a way for she and her nuns to cross the terrain safely, without the fear of crossfire and grenades going off. She spoke her Word in such a way that those in command listened and called for a cease fire. Mother Teresa and her little band of nuns marched into hell for a heavenly cause! She showed up and made a difference! When she went to New York to open a Hospice Center for the AIDS patients she was met with hostility and anger as the rallies screamed at her to "go home and take the homos with you!" When a member of the press asked her how she felt about all of the opposition she responded: "They are each one my Christ in distressing disguise." She opened the Hospice Center and the AIDS patients were treated with care and respect.

As I gazed at the Nobel Peace Prize Certificates on the wall, Dag explained that two copies of the Award were always created. One award was for the recipient and the other was for the Institute, as a noble keep sake for all those who had reached the pinnacle of excellence in their chosen field. I noted the Certificate of Dr. Albert Schweitzer for his propagation for the reverence for life. The very foundations of a lasting peace between individuals, nations, and races. Dag Hammarskjold Secretary General of the U.N. awarded for strengthening the United Nations. Dr. Martin Luther King, Jr. Campaigner for civil rights, he was the first person in the Western world to have shown us that a struggle can be waged without violence. King spent his time working in various areas of the civil rights movement, from equal education to economic disenfranchisement of minorities. King also organized the March on Washington, where he gave his famous "I Have a Dream Speech". The 14th Dali Lama, for his struggle for the liberation of Tibet, as he consistently opposed the use of violence. He has instead advocated peaceful solutions based upon tolerance and mutual respect in order to preserve the historical and cultural heritage of his people. Nelson Mandela, for his work for the peaceful termination of the apartheid regime, and for laying the foundations for a new democratic South Africa. Elie Wiesel Chairman of "The President's Commission on the Holocaust". As I stood in the Center of this amazing collection of those who prepared the way for the freedoms that we enjoy today my eye fell on the 44th President of the United States of America, Barack Obama. He was acknowledged for his extraordinary efforts to strengthen international diplomacy and cooperation between peoples.

As I quietly left the room with such astounding greatness, I was very moved that I too could make a difference in my own small way by showing up, saying "Yes" to the adventure of life as it presents itself. As a seasoned woman I realize the only thing I can truly change is myself, and out of changing myself, I can make an impact on my extended family, moving out in waves of light to my town, my nation and the world.

Asking Often Spells the Difference Between Success and Failure: The One Question That Separates You and Your Business from The Rest

Deborah Thorne, The Information Diva

My mother, brother, sister, and I were riding along in the family car. My mother pulled the car to a stop in the parking lot of our neighborhood grocery store. As she prepared to get out of the car, she turned to face her three small children, who are sitting in the backseat. She prepared to give us our final instructions before entering the store… Looking directly into our waiting eyes, she said, "Ok, we are going into the store to do some shopping. Do not ask for anything. Do you understand? Do not ask for anything!"

"Yes, ma'am, we understand." We said in unison.

But the grocery store held many desirable items. There was the food, special treats and even toys. What if I wanted something? What if I needed something? The message had been very clear, do not ask for anything!

Life finds us, again, in the family car. Again, there were three small children sitting in the backseat. We were on our way to Mrs. Reed's house. Mrs. Reed was a very nice lady. She liked to bake. Her house always smelled like the confection she had just created.

As we arrived at her house, my mother pulled the car to a stop. Again, she turned and faced her children in the backseat.

"Alright, we're here. Be sure you speak to Mrs. Reed when you enter the house. Do not ask for anything. If she offers you something to eat or drink, say no thank you. Do you understand? Do not ask Mrs. Reed for anything to eat or drink and say no thank you if she offers."

"Yes, ma'am, we understand," we said.

What's up with that? Mrs. Reed was a good baker. Her house always smelled like freshly baked cookies. The cookies looked good, too. My thought must have shown on my face because again my mother asked; "Do you understand?"

"Yes, ma'am," we answered.

Message received, do not ask! Do not ask even people you know. Do not ask people who offer you things.

I have always been an avid reader. I liked reading because the stories took me to places where I've never been. Reading also introduced me to worlds that were different than mine.

I've always loved water, so when I saw an ad for swimming pools, I asked for one. You see, I was a daddy's girl, but his answer this time shocked me.

"Daddy, do we have any money?" I asked. "Yes, we have some money, why?" he replied. "I just read an ad in the paper and we could get a swimming pool. Our backyard is big enough, and they say you can get it with no money and just make payments," I replied. "Well, Chicken (his pet name for me), we have money but not for a swimming pool," he chuckled. "You always want things that are just out of the question," my mother chimed in.

I knew she would say "No," that's why I asked my daddy! But not only did he say "No," he laughed.

Message received, do not ask. Do not even ask daddy!

The things we learn as children stay with us into adulthood. The child in me didn't understand that my mother was managing a grocery budget for a family of five. And the extra things would probably wreak havoc on the family budget.

Nor did the child understand that you don't take food from everyone. Who knows what my mother's real reasons were for not letting us eat at Mrs. Reed's house?

And my father, I knew he loved me. After all, I was a daddy's girl, and he liked to make me happy. The child never considered the fact that my father was blind and no longer able to work. But to a child, he was still daddy and daddy could do anything.

The message I received loud and clear was do not ask. You can't even ask daddy!

Those stories and similar ones helped shape my opinion and attitude about asking. Do you have similar stories? What did you learn, as a child, about asking?

A-S-K

That three-letter word carries a lot of weight. Somewhere along the way many of us were taught not to ask. This can really affect our ability to do business. It particularly affects women.

Many of us have learned to do without, rather than ask.

We don't ask for help.

We don't ask for the meeting.

We don't ask for the sale

We don't ask for…

Many of us even have trouble asking for payment after we have delivered a product or service. That can really affect the bottom line.

I hear women complain that they don't feel supported by other women. They tell me they don't like working with women for that reason. Since my clientele is more than ninety percent women I really need to understand where this sentiment originates.

When I hear that, I press them further. "What did you ask the women to do that they didn't do?

The answer usually goes something like, "I attended several networking meetings, but no one bought my product or service. It was a waste of my time."

I then ask, "were these women your ideal client?"- or- "Did you ask them to buy?"

To which the response is something like, "sure, everyone needs my product or service. And I told them what I have. They still didn't buy."

This is a good time to remind them that people do business or buy from people they know, like and trust. Are you presenting yourself in a way that helps people get to know, like and trust you?

I will ask them to do coffee virtually and I schedule an appointment for us to chat for thirty minutes via phone or video conferencing. This is just a "get to know you" call, no selling.

Let's do coffee, please go to https://calendly.com/theinformationdiva/ lets-docoffeegsfebook, and schedule some time for us to chat.

Most people don't go to networking events to buy anything. They go to expand their network. I ask, "Who is your ideal client?" I then make a real attempt to introduce them to someone in my network who meets their criteria.

Telling people what you do, or sell is not the same as asking for the business. After establishing that someone is interested in what I offer, I ask if we can set a time to talk about how I might be of service. I end the conversation with, "based on what we have discussed, do you see a way we might work together?"

There are other questions I might ask,

"Do you know someone who does …?

Where else do you network? May I get an invitation?

Because I'm a speaker, I often ask, does your business or organization use speakers? Are you willing to introduce me?

These are some of the ways I get women to support me. It has paid off. I was awarded the 2019 Orange County chapter of Connected Woman of Influence Award, based on my success and Now, I ask you:

What do you need in your business?

Who can help you accomplish that?

What do you need to ask for?

Who can you ask?"

I'm an award-winning, international author, coach, trainer, and speaker.

I help motivated women, of a certain age who are ready for their next act, to reduce their learning curve. I help them to clarify, set priorities, find the tools and resources so they can transition from employee to entrepreneur. I teach them to create income generating businesses not glorified hobbies.

I always encourage them to do business like a woman, not like a man... She E.O. ...not C.E.O.™

Is there something The Information Diva can help you with? Just ask. Now to that one question that separates you from the rest? What is your ask TODAY?

It's All about Showing Up

MY HAPPIEST SELF

Angel Toussaint

August of 2016, I was working as a Marketing Consultant. My phone rang, and as always, I answered with a smile.

The caller was Angela Covany. I could not provide advertising to fit Angela's needs. However, we chatted about other advertising options through other platforms and during our conversation we discovered our similar mindsets on numerous topics. Our conversation lead to an invitation to meet in person at a function she was attending with other business owners.

When my workday finished, I was tired and did not feel like going anywhere. However, I did not have a single friend in the area. I just moved to the area April 2016. Thinking I should show up, not only to be polite since I was invited, but also it would give me a chance to meet people.

Walking into a room full of business owners, listening to their stories, ambitions, goals, and challenges, gave me a renewed strength. I met Joan Wakeland, the host. I knew a friendship was in the making. I started showing up at meetings, events, social gatherings, joint projects, and the like. I became a member of the NAFE organization (now GSFE). I met so many phenomenal people who encouraged me to follow my dream.

I also met Robbie Motter, who was the Regional Director of NAFE, and is now the Global Founder of GSFE. I was so impressed by her drive, motivation, and willingness to help everyone around her. She not only possesses wonderful qualities, she brings out the wonderful qualities in others, and she never lets anyone forget their value. I often meditate on words she shares:

- The importance of showing up, you never know who you will meet.

- "Ask", do not be afraid, ask for what you need, others may want to give you exactly what you need.

My new connections began in 2016 and continued through most of 2017. Life got busy and being a business owner was moved to the back once again. I lost touch with many of the connections I made. I also found close friendships that will last a lifetime. In mid-2019 I was back on the mission to start my own business. Eager and energetic in finding the perfect business to passion ratio. Opportunities come and go; the key is to know which opportunity to take. It was clear to me when the right educational opportunity came along. I hesitated for a moment, then jumped in with both feet. I am truly my happiest self when I help facilitate a person's education and I watch their life change when they realize the power they have over their financial destiny. I am exactly where I belong!

It's All about Showing Up

Move out of your comfort zone! Show up!

Joan Wakeland

My friend, Puchie was the first person to tell me about this beautiful City. It was located approximately sixty-five miles south of where we lived. At the time we were both looking to buy new single-story homes. She invited me to an open house in an area that she considered for her retirement years. I was interested and curious, so I showed up!

Before going to the open house, I decided to drive around the neighborhood to get acquainted with the area. The homes were nice and were enveloped by beautiful gardens. There were beautiful flowers, birds chirping, and I was enthralled with the little cottontails scurrying across the road. I was mesmerized by the sunset as were the people sitting in parked cars enjoying the beautiful view of nature at its best! It was 2001…welcome to Menifee!

We both found a home in the community just four doors apart and on the same side of the street. Our grandchildren would spend many wonderful years visiting each of our homes.

That's one of the nice things that happened to me because I showed up!

We all know that moving can be stressful, but for me it was a super size stressor! Why? Because I forgot to take travel time into consideration before deciding to buy the house. I actually added sixty-five miles a day to my drive to work and back. I also had the added responsibility of caring for an elderly parent. My mother had fallen down the stairs in our tri- level home. To avoid this happening again, and to make life easier for her, I just wanted to find an affordable one level home. After about three months of commuting from Menifee to Glendora my boss started to question me about the time I actually started working in the territory. I told her I always showed up on time because I left home early. She explained that the company's policy was that employees must live no more than ten miles outside the territory they serve, and I was well outside the limit.

I panicked when I heard that I could lose my job if I didn't find another affordable house closer to my job. I was passionate about my job and I knew that my manager was just adhering to company policy. I knew she was going to fire me but luckily, I learned that there was a vacancy on another team and the territory was close to my new home. I called my manager and asked for a transfer. My request was granted and today I thank the Lord for opening doors and windows for me!

I think of myself as a connector and have never met a stranger. One day, I was having a conversation with an older woman in Menifee and asked her, "how is the neighborhood?" She replied, "like any other neighborhood. There are good and bad people everywhere. "Where did you come from?" the nosy lady asked. I said, "Phillips Ranch" "How was it there?" she asked. I told her that I had wonderful neighbors. She looked at me and in a very comforting way she assured me that it would be the same here. Surprisingly she gave me her phone number and said, "when you want to talk, I am a phone call away." I had found a friend. Dorothy and I started taking early morning walks in our beautiful neighborhood and I learned much about life from her. She was in her late eighties and sadly, she passed away a couple of months later.

Dorothy had advised me to always keep moving…and to never stop walking. She said that if you stop, you become stiff. I know that she is right! I didn't lack friends during the work week, and I was busy. People pass you; everyone is busy or lost in their own world. I would say hello when someone came into my space. Some would answer, some grumbled and others stared at you like a deer in headlights. Probably thinking, 'I can't be bothered!'

Others may think you're after something…you know the kind of people I am talking about. The ones who ask for direction, recruit you into their cult or soliciting for your hard-earned money.

I wanted to meet people, but I didn't want to look too eager or desperate. I had to be patient and find some likeminded people. I was rejected by my neighbor when I first came to this country because I mistakenly told her that I was a "druggist". Perry heard the word drug and avoided me after that. When I met her later with a friend who knew me well, I was able to explain to her that I was a pharmacist. I learned to use clearer language when talking about my profession. I met people on the job and eventually learned to differentiate between business associates and friends.

Computer chat rooms were impersonal, so I decided to find a church group. I wanted to find Believers like myself. My first visit to a church was a nice experience. I was greeted with handshakes and smiles. But as soon as the service was over, people bolted for the door. They all had so much to do, and so little time to do it! Sunday was not only for church but a day to relax with the family, watch TV or go to the movies, the beach, etc. Next, I checked out a local restaurant. There was a big blue "A" in the Window indicating that it's been inspected and was deemed to be clean. Great, I looked forward to having a nice meal at this establishment. A friendly greeter showed me to my seat, and I ordered a nice salad. As I slowly masticated this rabbit food, I was deep in negative thought. I now decided that I had moved to the wrong place. When I finished my salad, the greeter came over and asked me if I had enjoyed my meal. I told him it was fine.

He was pleased and said he wanted me to see another side of the business. He showed me an array of ornaments and other dust collectors that I actually found interesting. Before I left the restaurant, I did make a purchase. I paid for it and got change, but when I checked my changed, I noticed that it was more than it should be. I joked with the clerk that he gave me back some of his profit. His eyes lit up and smiling, he thanked me for my honesty. I had earned his trust and respect and he became my first friend in my new neighborhood. I introduced myself and told him I was new in the area. He introduced himself as Abe and told me that he was the owner.

I visited the restaurant several times and one afternoon he invited me for the Friday night Karaoke. I SHOWED UP! Abe became my "connector". He was also the honorary Mayor of the City and knew everyone and he came over and said, "I want you to meet Robbie. Robbie knows everybody." I met Robbie Motter that night, and I met Sue Lopez, who is a realtor. I also met the DJ Nicole Farrell who was originally from Canada with a beautiful voice and sang in both French and English. I sat with a group of new friends and enjoyed the music.

I showed up to a networking luncheon meeting a month later and found it to be exactly what I was looking for. There was a dynamic inspiring speaker and great networking opportunities. I met professional women, executives and entrepreneurs just like me. They were like family. Always there to support its members. A couple of months ago, one of the members fell ill with stage four cancer. She was visited and helped out by many of the members. I was very impressed with this group of caring and compassionate women. I started to believe again that there were a lot of good people here. I became a regular at the meetings and started to build some wonderful relationships.

Technology has made it easy for people to connect, but I prefer the face to face connections that these networking meetings offer that allows us to build stronger relationships. When I showed up at the restaurant that night for Karaoke, I didn't know whom I would meet. I'm glad I showed up. Meeting Robbie has changed my life. I want to share with you about some of the experiences that happened because of her.

She invited me to become a member of the newly formed Menifee Lion's Club. I took her advice and became a Charter Member. I had been a member of the Kiwanis club before moving to Menifee, and so I understood what being of service was about. I never would have believed that I could write for the local newspapers, until Robbie encouraged me. Today, I am writing a book. She then, introduced me to the General Federation of Woman's Club in Menifee/ Sun City, in which I served as President from 2018 - 2020.

I've been challenged with carpal tunnel syndrome in both hands and have excruciating pains, especially at nighttime. Robbie introduced me to her friend who told me about a medical device that might help me. I called Hollywood and he invited me to check out the device and I showed up! Yes, I was skeptical but went anyway and within eight minutes I was relaxed. Later I called again for another try. He was very accommodating. I ended up buying the device and have been sleeping better since. I showed up and found a good night's sleep. I enjoyed its benefits but didn't tell anyone about it until my Colon Therapist at the Inner Health Care Colonics who noticed the changes in my body and asked me what I was doing differently. I told her about the medical device, and she told me that I was so much better. "I can see the difference in your body." I thanked CeCe. A few weeks later she introduced me to a Gentleman, George, who wanted to know about the device. I shared information about it when he showed up! CeCe saw the difference in both of us. Now she and her husband Bernie also own one of these medical devices. Now, her family and friends are benefiting! My neighbor, Donna, showed up and now she's also enjoying its benefits!

Look at the ripple effect of showing up to an event and meeting one person who introduces you to their large circle of influence! You never know who you will meet, you never know who will become an influencer For you, also you never know who can help catapult you to the next level!

Robbie Motter has opened so many doors for me and for many other women. We just have to walk through them. We have to recognize the opportunities. I got involved in Community Service in Riverside County. I got involved because I wanted to give back to the country that allowed me to be who I am today. I got involved to be useful to society helping where I saw a need to connect people to resources regarding Cancer. I teamed up with the Inland Empire's Susan G Komen organization.

I encourage you ladies to move out of your comfort Zone. Yes, do something different, Move Out and Show Up! Your treasure is waiting for you!

Joan is a retired Pharmacist and an Entrepreneur in the Health and Wellness industry. Prior to coming to the United States from Jamaica, she was a successful pharmaceutical businesswoman. In the United States, she worked for Big Pharma for over 30 years and retired from the corporate world in 2013 due to health challenges.

Joan is the Director of the Riverside and Hemet GSFE chapters. Her passion is volunteering. She is a Charter Member of the Menifee Lions Club and Past President of the Sun City/Menifee General Federation of Woman's Club.

In 2019, President Trump recognized Joan for her Community service. She was an honored recipient of several awards, including President Trump's Community Service recognition in 2019, The Lifetime Achievement Award from President Obama in 2016, Senator Mike Morell's Woman of Distinction Award in 2015, and President Obama's "Call to Service Award in 2014." Joan loves connecting people and she truly believes that "together" we can achieve more!

She recently wrote a #1 Best Selling book entitled "The Run for Freedom," which is about sharing successful principles for living the good life that was published October 2020.

It's All about Showing Up

SHOWING UP, IT'S YOURS FOR THE ASKING!

Violet Williams

The Bible is one of my favorite books to read. In my life, it has been a lamp to my feet and a light to my path. I have used its many principles to navigate the roads that I have traveled throughout my lifetime. In Matthew 7:7 Jesus admonishes the believer to "Ask and it will be given to you; seek and you will find; and knock and the door will be opened to you." This scripture has provided me with hope. This scripture has encouraged me to action. Show up and whatever you ask will be given to you. As a young adult I wished for various things in my life, a college education, a husband, children, a successful career as a Chaplain that included public speaking and being an author.

To wish is to express a strong desire for something that cannot or probably will not happen. As I am writing this it has dawned on me that I seldom use the word "*wish.*" I Corinthians 13:11 states "When I was a child, I talked like a child, I thought like a child, I reasoned like a child; when I became a man (woman) I put the ways of childhood behind me." I don't wish anymore; all of my hopes and dreams were attainable; I just needed to ask and show up. When I was young, but my vision was clear, I wanted to become a Chaplain and serve people as the Lord had gifted me to do.

After completing my AA degree, I realized that I had no money and no support to continue at a four-year university to complete my bachelor's degree, therefore, I needed another option. That option would come by way of the United States Navy. My plan was to join the Navy as an officer. Since I had previously obtained my AA degree, I understood that the Navy tuition assistance program would pay for my bachelor's degree and therefore I could serve as a chaplain in the United States Navy. All I needed was to take the entry exam, which would prove more difficult than I had anticipated.

I took the exam two times in two days. Yet, both days I was told there was a discrepancy in the math portion of the exam and that I would have to try a third time, however I would have to wait six months for that third try. I was not destroyed, and this set back did not deter me. I was willing to take the test a third time. I had also decided I would use the next six months to seek and to find as the scripture advises. I believed that there had to be another path to completing my bachelor's degree and I was seeking, so I could find the way.

I was familiar with Biola University's faith-based programs; therefore, I chose Biola as the school I would apply to. I submitted my application and to my disappointment I was denied, but I was not deterred, I appealed the decision, once again I was on hold. Always reminding myself that if I ask it will be given, if I seek, I will find, and if I knock the door will be opened. My faith would not let me quit. I was living in West Covina, but I had family in San Diego. While visiting with them one weekend, I went on tour to San Diego State University and fell in love with the campus. I concluded that the city of San Diego would be my next move. My ultimate goal was to attend San Diego State University. Although I had an AA degree, I did not have all the credits I needed to transfer to the University. Hence, I decided to make a trip from West Covina to San Diego to register at San Diego City Community college.

My thought was that as I waited for an appeal which would take six months, I would continue to *ask, seek and knock*. Weeks would pass and still I had not heard from Biola University. Classes were soon to start at San Diego City College, so I made a decision to move on; I gave my employer a two-week notice and prepared myself for a new journey. Two days before I was to leave, a letter arrived from Biola University; my appeal was approved, and I was admitted to Biola University (the faith-based University I had originally hoped for). I held the letter in disbelief and yet I knew this was my opportunity to fulfill my goal of becoming a faith-based psychologist.

Although I was excited, elated and relieved, the reality was still the same. I did not have the financial resources to attend Biola. And, moreover, I could not explain that I was still drawn to San Diego. I was still four months away from being able to take the exam. So, with much prayer I decided to move. I would go to San Diego. The memory of that day is still vivid, my car was packed; I said my goodbyes; popped my Vanessa Bell Armstrong cassette in the player and made the two-and-a-half-hour drive south alone with my thoughts and my emotions all over the place. Regardless of what was ahead of me, I had made my decision. In spite of the anxiety, fear and doubt, I knew that once I laid my head down and rested, the morning would provide me with new mercies. I decided that whatever I faced, fear, weaknesses, doubt, being strong, courageous or bold, I would just ask and show up!

This was more than twenty years ago. My life has turned out better than I could have imagined. I graduated from San Diego State with a BA degree in psychology and met the love of my life through a mutual friend at this college. If I had not showed up, made the decision to choose this college, I would not have met him. I met my husband because I showed up. It was during the finals in my junior year, and I decided to do nothing other than study. I ignored everything else. No entertainment, and definitely not going out with friends. A friend invited me to a venue where her boyfriend's reggae band was performing. He was the drummer and I really wanted to support him and my friend. I spent the entire day studying and by the evening I knew that it would be good for me to take a much-deserved break, so I decided to go with her.

After the show a friend of theirs came over and after a few minutes he introduced himself to me and asked why he hadn't met me before after both of us having been their friends for many years. On this night, his brother had asked him to come to this venue...so it was because we were both asked, and we showed up that we met. We were married two years later and four years after we were blessed with two beautiful children. It's been a great ride. We had our ups and downs and we grew closer.

Then ten years ago my life hit a wall and knocked the wind out of me. I was in a car accident and sustained multiple injuries. I started to feel as if my whole life had become an accident. I started to question everything I believed to be true. I started to question my purpose and that question became a matter of life and death. I needed to be present with all my being…mind and body. I needed to embrace my life and live intentionally. A physical injury has a tremendous impact on your emotions. After two surgeries and multitude treatments for a head injury, I'm just now beginning to heal physically. My spiritual healing is taking longer. The healing process required a great deal of soul searching. I made a pact with God. I said, "if you heal my brain, I will do your bidding." I asked for guidance and promised to *show up and serve*.

I had a wonderful career as a teacher and behavior counselor before the accident. After the accident I had to make some changes in what I did and how I did it. A friend pointed out that my real gift was to offer spiritual guidance, so I took courses to become qualified as a certified temperament counselor, yet I continued to aspire to become a Chaplain. For years I had believed that the only way to get there was through the military, so I put the possibility out of my mind. I was still very motivated and continued to learn. I already had one master's degree and wanted to work on another, or perhaps start a doctorate in ministry. During my research for the appropriate program, I spoke with a faith-based university, and during a very inspiring conversation, I mentioned that what I really wanted was to be a Chaplain. He told me about their program and assured me that I had all the qualifications for it. Before he even finished the sentence, I knew that I had found the perfect program and school. There had been so many obstacles and difficulties over the years. I recognize in retrospect that I had to overcome these in order for this door to open and my plans were now coming to fruition.

I enjoy public speaking and connecting with an audience. I studied speech and psychology, both requiring using my voice and understanding people. I enjoy preparing for a talk and look forward to seeing the beautiful faces of students in a classroom or an audience of my peers and engaging them both with the sound of my voice and the content of my talk. I had some excellent teachers who motivated and appreciated me. I studied with some inspiring speech professors and after college, I continued to seek out opportunities to speak at my church and host various events, which led to me becoming a transformational personal growth speaker.

In all I have dreamed about, accomplished and desired, I have used my voice to *ask, seek, knock and show up*. I have encouraged many individuals to do the same. The Bible says, "ask and you shall receive," but after you ask, make sure that you "ACT on it and CONTINUE TO SHOW UP."

Violet Williams,
Temperament Coach, Speaker, Author, Chaplain

All in A Day

Dorothy Wolons

Never ever did I imagine the new world I would be waking up to, where showing up meant something so new and the feelings associated with it so strange. Yes, we were now confined but our lives didn't have to stop. We were now showing up in a different way.

Nothing was normal. Nothing was what we expected. Normal no longer existed.

The global pandemic reached the United States in January 2020. The first confirmed case of local transmission was recorded in January and the first known death occurred in February. By the end of March, it was in every 50 states, except in American Samoa. As of May 27, the U.S. had about the 6th most confirmed active cases and deaths in the world, with a death rate of 311 per million people. We couldn't leave our homes for weeks, and on this day, I realized that nothing was normal anymore. Normal, no longer exist. But until this extraordinary day I didn't realize how much our lives have changed and what our future might look like.

With that back story, let me walk you through a day in May 2020.

Like so many days in beautiful California, it was a sunny day. The country is in LOCK-DOWN and we cannot go anywhere. But I wake up thinking that can't be, I have so much to do. I took out my list and got busy. I had groceries to order. My friends were already using the online app Instacart, so I decided to do the same. I downloaded it to my cell phone and placed my order. I didn't have to leave the house, shower, get dressed, fight for a parking spot, put on a mask, wait in line, use gas, cut coupons or buy unnecessary items. My groceries were delivered to my door by noon. The first item on my to-do list was checked off. Done.

1. Grocery shopping - Instacart—CHECK!

As my groceries were on their way to me, I was on a call with my doctor. I still had not left the house. I had a prearranged appointment on another internet platform called Teladoc Health, which uses telephone, videoconferencing, a mobile app, and provides on-demand remote medical support. She and I had a video conference, discussed my current health issues and decided on a plan of action. I didn't have to leave the house and be exposed to sick people in the waiting room, especially during the Covid-19 virus which is extremely contagious. It was so much more comfortable and produced less anxiety than I usually feel before a doctor's appointment. No waiting times. We logged on at a specified time, discussed my health, and we were done in 10 minutes!

2. Doctors appointment via Teladoc Health -- CHECK!

Then came a sad moment, I had a family funeral for a young cousin in Texas and couldn't attend in person. But no problems, the funeral was held virtually on the meeting platform, Zoom. The minister gave a heart-warming tribute to her. More than 50 people were together on Zoom and afterwards the family created a beautiful montage of pictures. This was a new experience for me as it was for all of us. The feelings were difficult to sort, but I'm glad that I could still be there to comfort the family in some live form. We could still see and talk to each other. We could still grieve together and smile when we tried a virtual hug. If we have to adopt some new behaviors for a while, and even if we can't hug each other for a while, we can still pay our respects and be there for our family and loved ones. People don't travel to funerals because of the cost, and now they will not have to miss them.

3. Funeral via Zoom -- SAD!

The next item on my to-do list lifted my spirits. I attended a virtual baby shower on Facebook Live. One of our employees is having a baby. I logged on to Facebook, found the family's site and saw them in their house as if they were with me; he and his wife, their two kids, and grandma. They talked about the new baby who was due in a week, opened a load of great presents, and thanked everyone for their generosity. It was so well organized. I received the invitation via Facebook events, and I could buy and send a gift through Amazon gifts registry. I ordered the present a week earlier on my Amazon Prime account and delivery was free, a gift card was included, and it was delivered to their home. The world is changing, and this will likely become the norm. While many events will be brought to us through one of the many online platforms, more people might attend where they couldn't before. I do miss the hugs, the food, the games and the excitement of being with people I care about.

4. Baby Shower via Facebook Live — CHECK!

After the baby shower, my dad called and needed my help to pay some bills. He's in Florida and I'm in California. I called him on FaceTime and asked him to log on to his computer and together we set up an online banking account. All done. Less stress for all of us. So many of us have to help our parents often and from a distance, and now it's so much easier and efficient. I remember many years ago when my parents had to drive over to my grandparents to help them with one thing or another.

5. Help my parents, who are in lockdown in Florida, pay their bills — CHECK!

By now I was thinking that I needed some sunshine, so I walked out to the mailbox. The highlight of my day was going out to the mailbox, bringing in and opening the mail. I don't even have much of that to do these days. Mostly I have direct deposit to my bank account. However, today I had a refund check. So, I took a picture with my iPhone, scanned it into my bank app and deposited it into my back account.

So far, I haven't needed to get into my car and drive anywhere today.

6. Made a bank deposit -- CHECK!

Since I've been in this lockdown, I've been trying to work on myself. I've been eating better, exercising, and taking classes online. I've been taking a class on trading on the stock market, live on YouTube. YouTube is an American online video-sharing platform headquartered in San Bruno, California. So, I would log on and watch a 30-minute class. You can learn everything from changing the oil in your car to great recipes. Many classes are live and allow you to actually interact with the teacher.

7. Took a class online — CHECK!

Then I went on the internet and traded a few stocks. I bring this up, because not too long ago you would have to call your financial advisor, explain what you were thinking and pay them to transfer funds for you. Sometimes, your advisor was busy and would have to call you back when THEY had time. Today within minutes I logged onto my own account, made my own decisions and boom it's done.

8. Traded the Stock Market on the internet- CHECK!

So, with all that I was doing I forgot to start dinner and now it's almost 5 pm. So, the tri-tip that I was planning to put on the grill an hour ago, had to be cooked faster. I "GOOGLED" (*verb*/past tense: **googled**; past participle: **googled,** to search for information about someone or something on the Internet using the search engine Google) how to make a tri-tip in the Instant-Pot? Found a recipe, dropped everything into the pot and like magic, dinner was ready.

9. Made a tri-tip for dinner in 25 minutes in the Instant Pot. — CHECK!

Instant Pot is a Canadian brand of multi-cookers. The multi-cookers are electronically controlled, combination pressure cooker and slow cooker. The original cookers are a 6-in-1 appliance that can consolidate the cooking and preparing of food to one device.

Wow, I'm beat. I cleaned up, put the dishes into the dishwasher and hit the button. Time to relax.

Here's a bit of trivia. Did you know that a woman invented the **Dishwasher?** Josephine Garis Cochran invented the first working **dishwasher** in Shelbyville, Ill., and patented it on December 28, 1886. Cochran was a wealthy woman who entertained often and wanted to clean up faster without breaking the dishes.

Well, my day is almost over. We all jumped on the couch, got the "clicker" (remote control) and turned on Netflix and watched a movie on our 80-inch television. We were joking that we don't have to go out to the movie theater and could just relax at home, when it hit me.

Streamed a movie, what does that mean? **Netflix** is a media-service provider. It's primary business is a subscription-based streaming service of a library of films and television programs, including those produced in-house. Netflix's initial business model included DVD sales and rentals by mail. Do you remember when you had to wait to get a movie in the mail, or when you had to go to a store like Blockbusters to rent a movie and then take it back a couple of days later? Just ask a teenager if they know what a Blockbuster store is? Times are changing fast.

While relaxing and sharing my day with my fiancé, I told him everything I did today and never left the house. I SHOWED UP at two different events where I wouldn't have had that option. I got so much done helped my parents, went grocery shopping, did banking, made dinner, had a doctor's appointment and took an educational class.

SHOWING UP today has taken on an entire new meaning for me. I no longer have to say NO, because of a busy schedule, distance and/or the cost of doing something. Because of technology I am able to attend more, I am given more opportunities and I have more control over my own financial decisions. I also found it CRAZY, the vocabulary we use today to describe OUR day. My parents would not have understood even half the stuff I just said or how I got it done without leaving the house.

I believe that anyone reading this book in 5 years or maybe less, will be able to say they did all that in half the time, and will use an entirely new vocabulary to explain it.

Though SHOWING UP is taking on a new approach for me, I am so grateful that I was able to attend both events today. I'll remember this day in 2020 as one that changed my life. I learned so much about myself and that I can handle everything...all in a day's work.

You can't stop us women now, Just SHOW UP, however you can and whatever it takes. GO!

Thank you for spending a day with me!

MOM
Grandma
New Hub Auto Service
Advanced Emission Specialist
GSFE-Globalsocietyforfemaleentrepreneurs.org
NAFE-National Association for Female Executives
GFWC Menifee/Sun City Woman's Club
WOTM-Women of the Moose
"Fabulous" DIVA
DESCRIPTION TAKEN FROM WIKIPEDIA

It's All
about
Showing
Up

Directory of Resources

Authors

Mirjana Anastasijevic

Email: mirjana.musicpro@gmail.com
www.mirjanamusic.com

Kimberly Anderson

Intuitive Transformational Coach & Business Creative
Aphrodite Enterprises Inc.
KimberlyACoaching.com
Support@kimberlyAcoaching.com

Angeline Benjamin

Email: albenjamin.bb27@gmail.com
www.angelinebenjamin.com

Barbara Berg

Email: babsberg@earthlink.net
Phone: (909) 786-7201
www.barbaraberg.com
Barbara@ringshui.com

Kelly Breaux

Founder / Hoopitup Worldwide
www.hoopitupworldwide.com
Phone: (323) 449-0938
Email: kellybreauxfitness@gmail.com

Angela Covany

Founder/CEO, Havana Book Group LLC
Phone: (951) 249-6831
www.havanabookgroup.com
Email: havanabookgroup@mail.com
Email: hbgpublishing@gmail.com
G.S.F.E: Director for Ventura; Central Coast
NAFEdirector@GMX.com
Women Empowering Other Women/ Meetup.com

Caprice Crebar

Phone: (949) 922-8072
Email: ForHealthyConnections@gmail.com
www.eatgreen.juiceplus.com
https://www.meetup.com/The-Heart-Link-Womens-Networking-Group-SoCalandVirtual
www.eatgreen.towergarden.com
https://www.facebook.com/groups/theheartlinknetworksocalandvirtually

Marcy Decato

Creative Solutions Marketing & Printing, Inc.
Email: Marcy@creativesolutionsmktg.com
Phone: (951) 707-6338
marcy@creativesolutionsmktg.com
www.creativesolutionsmktg.com

www.facebook.com/CreativeSolutionsMktg
www.instagram.com/creativesolutionsmktg

Darla Delayne

Email: darla@darladelayne.com

Virginia Earl

www.sevenmysticrings.com
www.virginiaearl.com
Text or Call: (951) 551-4566.

Sandie Fuenty

Email: sandiesldy@aol.com

Raven Hilden

Founder/CEO, Valley Resource Center
ceo@valleyresourcecenter.org

Nanciann Horvath

WWW.ImprovForHealth.com
ImprovForHealth@gmail.com
Phone: (714) 394-4989
Twitter: @NanciannHorvath
Instagram: HorvathNanciann
Facebook: ImprovForHealth

Lauryn Hunter

Huntertherapeutic.com
Hunterarttherapy@gmail.com
Phone: (310) 740-7521

Deborah Irish

www.ArtUncorkedPainting.com
www.facebook.com/ArtUncorkedPaintingParties
www.instagram.com/artuncorkedpainting/
www.DeborahIrish.com
www.facebook.com/deborahirishfineart
Phone: (951) 536-3580

Rosalyn Kahn

Email: Kahn.rosalyn@gmail.com
www.rosaynkahn.com
Prof. Rosalyn Kahn
Phone: (818) 583-7328
"Master the Message with Passion & Purpose."
Breaking Cultural Barriers
TedX Walnut
https://youtu.be/rwow_3uKM0o
Rosalyn's newest book, Dogs and Roses
https://www.amazon.com/Dogs-Roses-Reducing-Anxiety-Troubled-ebook/dp/B0721ZTPSK
Follow me on LinkedIn
www.linkedin.com/in/rosalyn-kahn

Aggie Kobrin

Aggie@CECGlobalEvents.com
Aggie@e360tv.com
Aggie.Kobrin@NSS.org

Wendy LaDuke

wendy@verdaniafields.com

Gillian Larson

www.gillianlarson.com
www.realityrally.com
www.gillianlarson.com
www.facebook.com/realityrally
www.facebook.com/gillianlarson
Instagram: @realityrally
Twitter: @realityrally
www.michelleplace.org

Florence LaRue

PO BOX 10306, BEVERLY HILLS, CA. 90213
churldy@aol.com
Phone: (818) 594-2314

Dr. Cherilyn Lee

Seen on YouTube:
NuWellness TV/Radio with Dr. Cherilyn Lee
For more information, please go to:
https://www.justbreatheez.com
http://www.nuwellnesshealthcare.com/
Phone: (310) 419-4300

Jeannette LeHoullier

DJ's VIRTUAL MANAGEMENT/SENIOR TECH TUTOR.
P.O. Box 2138, Temecula, CA 92593-2138.
www.djsvirtualmanagement.com
Business Cell: (951) 595-7248
Office: (951) 458-9301
jeannette.lehoullier@gmail.com.
Facebook: @djsvirtualmanagement.

Diana Londyn

Email: TinselTownGSFE@gmail.com

Sue Lopez

Email: suelopez@verizon.net
Phone: (951) 282-6547

Debbie Love

Phone: (760) 455-8562
Founder | Heads Up Self-Defense for Women
www.headsupselfdefense.com

Marlena Martin

Marlena@womanofachievement.com
Phone: (800) 878-0776

LuAn Mitchell

An Empowered Woman Extraordinaire.
President Big Media USA
BMBC.TV
LuAn@BigMediaUSA.com
Author of International Best Seller:
Paper Doll
A Revelations Time Machine
The truth about your past
A Leading Woman Entrepreneur of the World. President and Co-Owner
of Big Media USA - Host of
Paper Doll Internet Podcasts, Life Coach and Corporate
Motivational Speaker

Pamela Moffat

Pamelamoffat@verdaniafields.com

Robbie Motter

I invite you to be a guest on my radio show and welcome you to connect with me.
Founder/ CEO, (G.S.F.E)
globalsocietyforfemaleentrepreneurs.org
robbiemotter.com
Email: rmotter@aol.com
Phone: (951) 255-9200
I am on Facebook and LinkedIn as Robbie Motter
& Twitter as Networking queen
connectedwomenofinfluence.com
divaregistry.org

Mercedita Noland

Founder/CEO, VeriDiva Women's business networking group
Email: mercynoland777@gmail.com
Contact Page of veridiva.com.

Katherine Orho

katherineorho@digitalroundtable.tech

Kisa Puckett

Interested in connecting?
Email: kisak@getpinkicing.com with the subject line,
"I'm Showing Up".

Lori Raupe

If you want to learn more about my work or get involved in my projects,
I would love to hear from you.
LoriRaupeCoach@outlook.com or find me on Facebook

Reanna Ritter, MBA

President/ Ritter Accounting&Consulting, Inc.
www.ritterac.com/contact
RRitter@RitterAC.com
Office: (855) 459-4900

Dr. Iris Rosenfeld

To find out more about our Wellness Center,
Phone: (949)380-7215
driris@driris.com
www.driris.com

Shelly Rufin

Contact Information: Shelly Rufin, MSHS
College Planning Expert
EDFIN College Planning
27420 Jefferson, Suite 104E
Temecula, CA 92590
Phone: (951) 261-9799
Cell: (951) 375-6125
Fax: (888) 681-3253
shelly@edfincollegeplanningexperts.com
info@edfincollegeplanningexperts.com
www.edfincollegeplanningexperts.com
College Planning Consultant
PhD Psychology Industrial Organization (2021)
Harvard University Business School

Published Author/Speaker
9 Key Decisions for Better College Planning Better Life: Making College
DREAMS a Reality
Co-Director of Temecula Global Society for Female Entrepreneurs (GSFE)

Dawn Schultz

If you would like to know more and help more, please contact me.
23905 Clinton Keith Rd. 114-299 Wildomar, CA 92595 P
Phone: (951) 457-1363
Email: dawnkellyschultz@yahoo.com

Rhonda Sher

LinkedIn.com/in/RhondaLSher
RhondaSher.com

Kelly Smith

Kelly D Smith
Warriorprincess4god.com
Inthelightcopywriter.com

Maryann Ridini Spencer

MaryannRidiniSpencer.com
AlohaWriter.com

Dr. Sharron Stroud

www.innerfaithworldwide.com
Email: dr.sharron@gmail.com
Phone: (760) 902-3408

Deborah Thorne

The Information Diva
TheInformationDivaOnline.com
TID@TheInformationDivaOnline.com

Angel Toussaint

Forex Educator
Phone: (951) 397-9739
angel@thetradertreasury.com

Joan Wakeland

Email: joanewakeland@gmail.com

Violet Williams

Should you wish to get in touch with
me to share your dreams and vision,
I can be reached at yourbestspirit@gmail.com

Dorothy Wolons

Phone: (951) 240-0219
Dorothy.Wolons@yahoo.com
29484 Camino Cristal, Menifee, CA 92584

Contributors.

Michelle Bergquist

CEO/ Co-Founder of Connected Women of Influence
www.connectedwomenofinfluence.com
Direct: (760) 420-3785
Main: (800) 591-1673

AnGele Cade

Speaker, Author & Coach
President and CEO-Executive On the Go
www.executiveonthego.com
Chairman of the board and Co-founder
-Cale Now! Inc.
www.calenow.org

Chebra Dorsey "OCHEA" Celebrity Designer

Email: ocheafashions1@gmail.com

Ardice Farrow

Founder, Director Net Effects Traders
Co- Publisher. "Wake Up Women"
Email: neteffectstradersco@gmail.com

Pink Lady Jackie Goldberg

Founder/ Senior Star Power Productions
PinkLadyPresents.com
Author: "Get Up, Get Out, & Get A Life!"
Email: pinklady7@earthlink.net
Phone: (818) 606-6679

Tammra Graves

Sales Vice President/ Park Lane Jewelry
https://parklanejewelry.com/rep/tammragraves
tammragraves@gmail.com
Phone: (760) 434-6500

Lisa Gritzner

Founder/CEO, LG Strategies
Email: lisa@lgstrategies.net

Melissa Hull

www.MelissaHull.com
Email: melissa@melissahull.com

Dame Shellie Hunt

Founder/CEO, the Women of Global Change
Founder/CEO, Success by Design
shelliehuntt@thewomenofglobalchange.com

Felisha Kay

Founder/CEO, FeliKay LLC
Phone: (303) 884-9135

William Kidston

www.williamkidstoneventphotos.com
Email: williamkidston7730@gmail.com
Phone: (310) 739-6904

Jean Olexa

Owner: "O" To be Organized
Email: gigi8247@gmail.com

Robert "Hollywood" Moreno

Wealth Academy Keynote Presenter/Advisor
Phone: (949) 698-2975

Joel Reese

Entertainer
Sales Manager
Hampton Inn & Suites; Murrieta, Ca.
Phone: (951) 490-2387

Heather Schneider

Email: Schneiderheather7@gmail.com

Rayona Sharpnack

Founder/CEO, Institute for Women's Leadership
Founder/CEO, Institute for Gender Partnership
http://www.genderpartnership.com
http://www.womensleadership.com
Phone: (415) 331-3222
Author: "Trade-Up: 5 Steps for Redesigning Your Leadership & Life from the Inside Out"
Co-Author: "Goddess Shift: Women Leading for a Change" and "Enlightened Power: How
Women Are Transforming the Practice of Leadership"

Lori Soltas

Account Manager/ First Heritage Mortgage
Email: lsoltas@fhmtg.co

Carl Wilson

Founder/CEO, CD Wilson Events
All Women Rock- Creator
Email: cdwilson0115@gmail.com

Additional Resources

I AM Enough Movement/ Freedom Haven
http://iamenoughmovement.info
http://thefreedomhaven.com/
Dresses and Dreams Project
https://thedressesanddreamsproject.org/
Leave No Woman Behind
http://leavenowomanbehind.org/
Michelle's Place Cancer Resource Center
41669 Winchester Rd. #101
Temecula, Ca. 92590
www.michellesplace.org

Acknowledgment

I spent 25 years in the corporate world and wondered why women were not getting the support and encouragement that was afforded to men. I wanted to reach out to every one of them and tell them that they weren't alone…anymore. But how?

This incredible journey began for me the day I 'showed up' and vowed that I would spend my life being a mentor and a cheerleader to make their journey easier. That was the day my life changed, and I have been doing just that. I wanted to tell some of the success stories, but more importantly, I wanted some of these incredible women to tell their stories in their own words. Once again, I SHOWED UP and ASKED. I asked for the stories and I asked for help to get this book published. And you came through!

I'm 84 years old and this beautiful journey will continue until I say, "This meeting is over, but keep SHOWING UP and ASKING."

This book is a gift to the many people who have joined me on this journey called life. You have been my joy:

My daughters Lori Soltas, Lisa Gritzner and my son Ed Burtnette, My son in law, Glenn Gritzner and daughter-in-law Jeni Burtnette, and my precious and treasured grandchildren, Joe and Jessie Soltas, Heather and Amber Burtnette.

My GSFE Board of Directors: Lori Soltas, Pamela Moffat, AnGele Cade, and Johnathan Carlson

My GSFE Advisory Board: Cecelia Burch, Robert Hollywood Moreno, Jean Olexa, Joan Wakeland, and Dorothy Wolons.

My California GSFE Network Directors: Angeline Benjamin, South Orange County, AnGele Cade- San Fernando Valley, Angela Covany- Ventura, Sharon Doyle-Beverly Hills, Sandie Fuenty-Lake Elsinore/ Murrieta, Tammra Graves- Oceanside, Terry Lea Hoard- Victorville, Diana Londyn- Long Beach and West Hollywood, and Joan E Wakeland- Hemet & Riverside.

My GSFE California Network Co-Directors: Angeline Benjamin- Menifee, NanciAnn Horvath- South Orange County, Debbie Love- Oceanside, Lori Raupe- Hemet, and Shelly Rufin- Temecula.

The 45 Co-Authors, who shared their beautiful and heartfelt stories: Mirjana Anastasijevic, Kimberly Anderson, Angeline Benjamin, Barbara Berg, Kelly Breaux, Angela Covany, Caprice Crebar, Marcy Decato, Darla Dalayne, Virginia Earl, Sandie Fuenty, Raven Hilden, Nanciann Horvath, Lauryn J Hunter, Deborah Irish, Rosalyn Kahn, Aggie Kobrin, Wendy LaDuke, Gillian Larson, Florence LaRue, Dr. Cherilyn Lee, Jeannette LeHoullier, Diana Londyn, Sue Lopez, Debbie Love, Marlena Martin, LuAn Mitchell, Pamela Moffat, Mercy Noland, Katherine Orho, Kisa Puckett, Lori Raupe, Reanna Ritter, Dr. Iris Rosenfeld, Shelly Rufin, Dawn Schultz, Rhonda Sher, Kelly Smith, Maryann Ridini Spencer, Dr. Sharron Stroud, Deborah Thorne, Angel Toussaint, Joan E Wakeland, Violet Williams, and Dorothy Wolons.

I'm so grateful to:

The many who endorsed my book for their support and kindness.

My dynamic marketing research team: Angela Covany, Jean Olexa, Angel Toussaint, Heather Schneider, Madison Warren, Judy Winestone and Joan Wakeland. They enthusiastically read through every story and helped me ready the book for publication.

To Angela Covany, for the beautiful cover design and her company Havana Book Group LLC for publishing the book, and making a dream come true.

You have all been like family and I am so grateful to have you in my life.

I also want to dedicate the book to you our readers who, I hope, will continue to apply and share this little-known secret to success…Just Show Up and Ask. You will be rewarded with friendships and opportunities that you wouldn't otherwise have known.

With love and appreciation,

Robbie Motter

CPSIA information can be obtained
at www.ICGtesting.com
Printed in the USA
FSHW020005080421
80271FS